BERLUSCONI

BERLUSCONI

The Epic Story of the Billionaire
Who Took Over Italy

ALAN FRIEDMAN

hachette
BOOKS

NEW YORK • BOSTON

Hachette Books
Hachette Book Group
1290 Avenue of the Americas
New York, NY 10104

www.HachetteBookGroup.com

Printed in the United States of America

RRD-C

First Edition: October 2015

10 9 8 7 6 5 4 3 2 1

Hachette Books is a division of Hachette Book Group, Inc.
The Hachette Books name and logo are trademarks of Hachette Book Group, Inc.

The Hachette Speakers Bureau provides a wide range of authors for speaking events. To find out more, go to www.HachetteSpeakersBureau.com or call (866) 376-6591.

The publisher is not responsible for websites (or their content) that are not owned by the publisher.

Library of Congress Control Number: 2015947610

ISBN 978-0-316-30199-2

For Gabriella

CONTENTS

AUTHOR'S NOTE

As an American journalist who grew up in the 1970s, I have always been fascinated by the Frost-Nixon interviews, that famous series of face-to-face television interviews which British journalist David Frost conducted with President Richard Nixon in the spring of 1977, more than two years after Nixon's dramatic resignation.

I was obsessed by Watergate, even as a teenager, the way kids today are obsessed by video games and Facebook. The drama. The intrigue. The White House tapes. The cover-up. The *Washington Post* scoops by reporters Bob Woodward and Carl Bernstein. The humbling of the president of the United States of America! The famous statement by Nixon that "people have got to know whether or not their president is a crook. Well, I am not a crook."

I couldn't get enough of it. I craved the next installment in the Watergate saga. I consumed it like candy.

In the summer of 1974, at our summer house on a lake in upstate New York, I forced my thirteen-year-old sister to join me in watching the daily TV coverage of the impeachment hearings, which culminated in August in the dramatic resignation of President Richard Nixon. We watched him resign and then we watched him say good-bye to the White House staff, with that bizarre salute, that wave of despair he offered to the American people before boarding his helicopter on the White House lawn in order to fly to Andrews Air Force Base and then begin the long flight back to California, in disgrace.

All of these memories came flooding back in early 2014 when my Italian publisher at Rizzoli in Milan first suggested I try to get Silvio Berlusconi, the most colorful and controversial leader in modern Italian political history, to agree to tell me his life story. I had known Berlusconi for thirty years, from my early days as a foreign correspondent in Milan for the *Financial Times* of London in the 1980s. At times I had been a fierce critic of Berlusconi, then later I became intrigued by his personal story. This was not only because of his alleged "bunga-bunga" parties and the corruption trials but because of the extraordinary, epic-like story of his life. I followed closely the events surrounding his political downfall in 2011, his conviction in 2013 on tax fraud by Italy's Supreme Court, and his eviction from the Italian senate later that year. Yet even today Berlusconi still casts a long shadow in Italy, so I remained curious about the story.

When I first went to ask him if he was interested in cooperating on this book, I had low expectations. It was late on the morning of March 12, 2014. I went to see him at his ornate residence in Rome, the second floor of a seventeenth-century palazzo, resplendent with frescoed ceilings and gold tapestry-covered walls. Berlusconi, now seventy-seven years old, seemed to like me, mainly because I was an American (and therefore not an Italian journalist with preconceived notions) but also because he felt vindicated by another book I had written about Italian politics, a result that had not been my aim in life.

I informed Berlusconi that I had decided to write a book about his life story and I proposed that he provide me with full cooperation and unfettered access to archives, family members, friends, business partners, and political allies. He first gave me a long stare in the eye, then told me that over the past decade he had refused at least fifteen similar requests. I told him this would not just be a book but also a series of ten or fifteen television interviews, modeled on the famous Frost-Nixon interviews of 1977. He kept staring at me, muttered something about understanding that today "everything needs to be multimedia," and then suddenly he proffered his hand. We shook hands, and he was very clear in what he then said: "I trust you to tell my story in a fair and honest way." I thanked him for his confidence and informed him directly: "This will not be hagiography. I will not write the story of a saint, or of a victim, I will not be hostile but I will not do you any favors. I will write in a fair and balanced way the story of an extraordinary life, as I see it, but with you answering my questions about each chapter of your life, and all of it taped on video."

Silvio Berlusconi agreed to my terms. Later that day one of his advisers shared his opinion as to why Berlusconi had said yes: "His world is collapsing around him, and while he dreams of making another political comeback, he sees this as his legacy, with you as his witness, as the first and last journalist with whom he will share his life story, in his own words."

In the seventeen months that followed, from the tumultuous spring of 2014 until the end of the summer of 2015, I observed Berlusconi up close, mainly at home. We had numerous conversations and interviews during a period full of emotion for Berlusconi, a period marked by a fair amount of bitterness and defeat and at the same time a period of constant planning for a political comeback. In some ways I watched a real-life psychodrama playing out before my eyes. I was also privileged by the unusually free access, which allowed me to really get to know the man, and his default mechanisms, his thought patterns, his pet peeves, even his favorite anecdotes and jokes.

For a while, each time I went to interview him, whether at the palazzo in Rome or in the garden of his spectacular villa in the village of Arcore, on the outskirts of Milan, something bad was happening. He was emotional at times, usually in the run-up to another court ruling in one of his many cases. Often, after the interviews, he would ask me to speak in private, and he would pour out his heart, speak of his enemies, or confide in me his concerns, his hopes, his ambitions.

I always told Berlusconi that my model was the Frost-Nixon interviews. I said it on many occasions. I said it when he signed the release forms for this book and for the TV series in front of me and three other witnesses, including his girlfriend, Francesca Pascale, and his spokesperson, Deborah Bergamini.

When he signed the legal authorization documents, the release forms that were needed to proceed with the project, for some reason I was reminded of the most famous words uttered by President Nixon to David Frost in those legendary interviews: "I brought myself down. I gave them the sword and they stuck it in, and they twisted it with relish..."

I wondered what Silvio Berlusconi would say about his own part in his incredible and epic journey. As the weeks and months progressed, I would not be disappointed.

Lucca, Tuscany
August 26, 2015

BERLUSCONI

PROLOGUE

Silvio Berlusconi is at home alone. He is strolling through a garden in the middle of his 180-acre property, not far from the stables and the helipad.

It is high summer and he is proceeding, hands in his pockets, along a tree-lined path that leads to his eighteenth-century seventy-room villa. As we approach the huge mansion, the borders of the walkway are lined with closely cropped hedges and terracotta pots full of geraniums. The grassy avenue passes beneath a stone arch and then gives way to sprawling gardens, manicured lawns, beds of red azaleas, lemon trees, and hedges, all immaculate.

Not far from his house, the seventy-eight-year-old billionaire pauses. He smiles, almost a trifle sheepishly, with the self-deprecating charm and courtesy that tends to disarm his guests, especially those expecting to meet a flamboyant playboy. He smiles broadly, with the empathy that helped him to rise to power, and which over the past twenty-five years allowed him to transform himself from a media mogul into one of the world's richest men into the longest-serving and undoubtedly the most controversial prime minister of Italy.

"This," says Berlusconi, "is the main home in my life."

Despite the warm weather, Berlusconi is wearing a light black sweater, a navy blue blazer, and cotton tracksuit trousers. The gravel crunches under his black Hogan sneaker-boots as he marches forward, talking about the importance of this property to him, describing it as the place where he has made all of the momentous decisions in his life. Neoclassical statues on marble pedestals are visible as far as the eye can see, and they seem to stare across the walls of the gardens, which are almost too perfect. The big old villa is located in the Milanese countryside in a Lombardy village called Arcore. It is called the Villa San Martino and it was built in the early 1700s on the foundation of what had been, from the twelfth century onward, a Benedictine monastery. Berlusconi bought it in the 1970s and refurbished it in grand style. He kitted it out with more gadgets than a James Bond movie, plus a stable packed with racehorses, a helipad for his chopper, and even a private soccer field. The house is tastefully appointed, if a bit long on tapestries and Old Masters. Every corner is a potpourri of old and new, with a 1980s aesthetic that at the time allowed Italy's rising class of nouveau billionaires to juxtapose even Renaissance paintings with Late Modern. As a result, in the 1980s many architects and interior decorators in the Milan area became quite rich, quite quickly.

Berlusconi is strolling toward the big house now, relaxed and proud, believing that the finest appreciation of a great Italian villa often begins outside, with its landscape.

"This is the main home in my life," he repeats. And life, for Berlusconi, always means both the public and the private, and often the two flow into each other, overlapping in a manner that sometimes causes scandals, but which somehow always involves a return to this villa.

Now Berlusconi is speaking of the first visit here by Mikhail Gorbachev in 1993, and of the long afternoon and evening they spent together. "It was a very enjoyable, stimulating day together," Berlusconi recalls. "Mikhail Gorbachev came with his wife, Raisa, and she spent time with my wife, Veronica. He wanted to meet with an Italian business leader and talk about the economy. He asked me many questions, about the economy and about financial markets. At five in the afternoon we sat down for some tea, and then he was scheduled to leave. As we were walking to the door to say good-bye, he said to me, 'But, Silvio, there is one thing I did not understand. Which is the ministry or the institution which fixes the prices for the products that are sold?'

"I asked him to repeat the question. He did. 'Which institution determines prices?' And I said, 'Mikhail, please don't go. Stay for dinner. We need to talk more.' We talked and talked, with the help of a few glasses of really good Rosso di Montepulciano. I explained how in the West it is the market which determines prices, and not a government agency. It is market competition. It was incredibly gratifying to explain the workings of market capitalism to Mikhail Gorbachev. At least he seemed to appreciate the time we spent together."

Now Berlusconi is describing the visits to Arcore by his friend Vladimir Putin, pointing out the room that Putin slept in when he last came to stay.

Arcore. In the life of Silvio Berlusconi this Italian villa is far more than just the site of visits by Mikhail Gorbachev and Vladimir Putin. It is his residence, his refuge, his command center, his general headquarters. It was here that he planned and built his real estate empire, the satellite cities that helped make him a billionaire. It was here that he made decisions that would see him morph into a media mogul, with a television empire spanning half of Europe. It was here that he invented commercial television in Italy and became a first mover across the European stage in the 1980s. It was here, in these dainty and somehow overly pristine drawing rooms, dining rooms, and baroque salons that Berlusconi decided to buy the AC Milan soccer team. It was here that he first decided to go into politics, to invent and launch a new national party, and to go from being a rich businessman to gaining the prime minister's office in less than ninety days in early 1994.

Arcore became an Italian version of Camp David. In later years, it also became a bunker, where Berlusconi would hold endless late-night sessions with defense lawyers, batteries of attorneys and investigators, and armies of advisers who helped him face a storm of more than sixty separate indictments and trials on corruption, bribery, tax fraud, and even underage prostitution charges.

Arcore was Berlusconi's Rosebud, his compass, his touchstone. In life, in business, in politics, and in questions of love and family. It was here in Arcore that Berlusconi's first marriage ended, it was here that the alleged bunga-bunga parties took place, it was here that he lived for a year in a semi-curfew and semi-imprisonment, his passport confiscated by the courts, doing community service in a home for elderly Alzheimer's patients after being convicted of tax fraud. And it was here that he plotted his latest political comeback in 2015. It was here in the family chapel that he interred the ashes of his parents and of his sister. It was here that his son and daughter-in-law and grandchildren still lived. It was here that at the age of seventy-six he took a new girlfriend, some fifty years his junior. It all happened here. At Arcore.

I am reminded of the very first time I went to see Berlusconi at Arcore, back in the 1980s when Tina Brown asked me to write a piece for *Vanity Fair* about the "New Princes" of Italian capitalism who were challenging the "Uncrowned King of Italy," Gianni Agnelli. It was the wild and crazy 1980s, with half of the world drunk on a golden age of newfound prosperity, from the yuppie classes of Wall Street to the money men of the City of London in constant celebration mode, with booming economies and a rising middle class. Ronald Reagan and Margaret Thatcher ruled America and Britain. In Italy in the 1980s, Berlusconi was a self-made man, an outsider, a fast-rising tycoon, an entertainment industry and TV mogul, a newly minted billionaire, on his way to becoming one of the world's richest men. Back then Berlusconi caused a particular discomfort among the financial elites of Italy because his folksy style of salesmanship had made him incredibly popular, and his TV fortune had made him richer than even the Old Money heir to the Fiat fortune, the urbane and cosmopolitan playboy-turned-industrialist, Gianni Agnelli.

Meeting Silvio Berlusconi at Arcore was like a trip to a rich man's Disneyland. It was push-button everything. Everything was about beauty, perfection, order, and, yes, hedonism.

"This is my indoor swimming pool," Berlusconi said in 1989,

as he toured the villa with a guest. He was trim and fit in his trademark double-breasted Brioni suit, with a year-round tan and a boyish energy and enthusiasm that was contagious. He pointed out a six-foot-wide wall screen suspended high above the swimming pool. Why was it there? "That way," he said, "I can be in the pool and watch my own television channels while swimming, even while doing the backstroke."

He beamed as he showed off a "fitness and rest area" near the pool that featured a sauna, a Jacuzzi, a steam bath, a gym, and the pièce de résistance, a corner den area in bright Scandinavian pine, full of plush couches and with a wall covered by no fewer than nine television sets in a tic-tac-toe formation, each of them broadcasting live one of Berlusconi's three main TV channels. My host then pointed to a roll-out drawer that had buttons to control the music, the special mood lighting, or to summon the butler. Even the bathroom held a surprise. Embedded on either side of the mirror were two-inch TV screens, quite a technical achievement for the 1980s, in the days before Wi-Fi and LED. Berlusconi happily explained, "I can watch my TV channels while I shave in the morning, without cutting myself."

Today, not very much has changed at Arcore, except for the owner, who is nearly eighty. He has lived what can only be described as a larger-than-life trajectory, and today, in his native Italy, he is both hated and loved by millions of his countrymen.

"This has been my principal residence for more than thirty years," he notes, wandering across the pale gray stone-floor of the loggia out front, and pausing near the gated entrance. There we find a sculpted medallion mounted on the wall. It resembles a family coat of arms but it bears the likeness of St. Martin, the fourth-century bishop of Tours, whose shrine in France became a famous stopping point for pilgrims on the road to Santiago de Compostela in Spain. The early Benedictine monks who came to Arcore and founded their first monastery here nearly a thousand years ago named it after the Christian saint. The Berlusconi family chapel remains the only surviving twelfth-century structure built by the Benedictine order.

The stone-engraved bas relief that Berlusconi is now describing has the bishop seated upon a horse, and he is using his sword to cut his cloak in two, giving half of it to a beggar clad only in rags in the depth of winter. Indeed, according to the legend, when he was conscripted into the Roman army St. Martin found the duty incompatible with the Christian faith he had adopted, and he became one of the world's first conscientious objectors.

Berlusconi smiles a billionaire's smile as he recounts the story of St. Martin. The summer's light is now fading across the graveled courtyard in front of the Villa San Martino. But Silvio Berlusconi is ebullient, warm, indefatigable. He enters one of an endless series of storage rooms to rummage through piles of memorabilia. He fingers little bobble-headed plastic figurines of himself, pointing out shelves that are stacked high with photographs of himself with any number of family members and heads of state: his mother, Rosa, Barack Obama, George H. W. Bush, George W. Bush, Tony Blair, Bill Clinton, Hillary Clinton, Queen Elizabeth, and Pope Benedict XVI.

Pitched across one wall of shelves is a photograph from another time, faded, yellowed, of a young Berlusconi attired as a cruise ship crooner, a handsome young man wearing a natty jacket, tie, and a straw boater hat, singing his heart out into a 1950s-style nightclub microphone.

"That's me!" says the irrepressible Berlusconi. "That's a picture of me singing when I was sixteen. Like my mama used to say, I was always the most handsome boy on the beach." And with that he moves quickly on to another room stuffed with relics and trophies from his past.

Suddenly the air is thick with nostalgia here at the Villa San Martino. Berlusconi is ever the amiable tour guide, ever keen to please. He desperately wants to put on a good show. He is a relentless entertainer, an unabashed salesman, a seller of dreams. Over the years he has been an Italian Ronald Reagan, with his jelly beans and bonhomie, and also a folksy Bill Clinton, scarfing down the Italian equivalent of a Big Mac, schmoozing voters with charisma and charm, promising lower taxes, promising the world, clapping on backs and hoisting babies, throughout his life and political career ever the populist. "We aim to make our customers happy!" seems to be his slogan. Over the years he has also been the longest serving European leader and a man who has borne witness to a string of cataclysmic global events, from the end of the Cold War to the hot war against Saddam Hussein, from the Arab Spring and the destruction of Muammar Gaddafi to the financial crisis that rocked Europe in 2011 and nearly sank his native Italy.

How did he do it? How did this self-made man from a working-class neighborhood in Milan become a European billionaire and media tycoon who got himself elected three times as prime minister? How did this one-time crooner come to dominate the destiny of his nation for more than twenty years?

Berlusconi has no trouble explaining the secret of his success. None at all.

"I am," he says with a wink, and with one of those trademark Hollywood smiles, "a natural-born seducer."

CHAPTER ONE

The Natural-Born Seducer

I am a natural-born seducer!"

Silvio Berlusconi is grinning again. Seated in his favorite living room, with a white marble fountain at his back just outside the open bay window, he is explaining his life strategy for getting what he wants.

"When my enemies accuse me of being a natural-born seducer they think it is a criticism," he begins. "But I am always open to others. I have a great respect for others, and I always try to imagine myself in the shoes of the other person. So when somebody is convex I become concave, and if somebody is concave, then I make myself convex. In this way I always succeed in establishing a personal rapport, a feeling, a chemistry with the person I am dealing with. They call it empathy, but often it is an empathy that is a necessary tool that I use to achieve my goals, to achieve a cordial and friendly form of collaboration."

This desire to please, and the ego-reassuring pleasure that comes from making others smile, seems deeply rooted in Berlusconi's psyche. What kind of childhood produced this pleasure-seeking young charmer? Berlusconi came up in the world the old-fashioned way, from a lower middle-class family that in his early years lived amid the deprivation of wartime Italy.

He was born on September 29, 1936, to a bank clerk named Luigi who would eventually rise to the ranks of management, and to a housewife named Rosa who would later work as a secretary at the Pirelli tire company in Milan. The Berlusconi family lived in a small apartment in a none too salubrious neighborhood of Milan that was nicknamed "The Island," a kind of no-man's-land situated near a pedestrian bridge over the railroad tracks and sandwiched between the grunge of the city's two biggest train stations, one of them Porta Garibaldi and the other Milan's Stazione Centrale, the equivalent of Grand Central Station. His sister, Antonietta, was born in 1943 and his younger brother, Paolo, after the end of the Second World War, in 1949.

"The neighborhood was very lively, a bit working class, a bit lower middle class, a bit rough," recalls one of Berlusconi's boyhood friends, Fedele Confalonieri. "It was not exactly a neighborhood with organized crime but there were plenty of troublemakers around. It was a tough neighborhood. I remember it well because I was born on the same street as Berlusconi, in the Via Volturno. Funnily enough, I remember that Berlusconi's apartment was in a building located right across from the local Communist Party offices."

Confalonieri remembers "a kind of generalized poverty at the time," especially after 1940, when Mussolini declared war on France and Britain and entered the Second World War as a staunch ally of Adolf Hitler's Germany. Both Confalonieri and Berlusconi remember the carpet bombings of Milan, the Allied bombings of factories, churches, schools, offices, and apartment buildings that led numerous families to flee the city and to seek refuge in the nearby countryside.

"I will never forget," says Berlusconi, "the Allied bombings of Milan back in 1943. I was six and a half years old at the time, and I remember that one day the bombs fell on the very street where we lived, the Via Volturno. After that my father and mother decided to leave Milan and live in a small village in the countryside, a village of less than a thousand people. It was about an hour north of the city, not far from Lake Como, on the way to Varese. It was safe there because it was a farmland area where there were never any bombings. My mother had some relatives there, and they took us in and gave us two rooms to sleep in."

Shortly after the Berlusconi family was evacuated from Milan in the spring of 1943, Mussolini was overthrown, the Americans arrived in Sicily, and Italy signed a secret armistice deal with the Allies under which it changed sides and abandoned Hitler. The Germans, in response, invaded, occupied, and quickly subdued Italy. The Allied bombings of German-controlled Milan continued.

"This all happened very quickly in 1943," says Berlusconi, "and since my father was anti-fascist he was advised by friends to get out of Italy and to escape to Switzerland. So he went over the border to Switzerland and so there we were in this tiny village, all alone in the middle of nowhere, and without my father. Suddenly everything fell on my mother's shoulders. My mother at that point was commuting every day into Milan to work as the secretary of the director-general of Pirelli. It was dangerous to be in Milan because of the bombings and I remember it like it was yesterday. She would get up at five o'clock every morning, she would walk three kilometers to the bus stop, and from there she would take a bus to a train station and then she went by train to Milan, and then she took a tram to get to work. At five p.m. every afternoon she would finish work and return to the countryside. I used to go each day to wait for her at the bus stop. I was really sad every morning when she had to leave again, and I remember she always gave me a kiss before leaving."

Berlusconi recalls that he did not live alone with his mother during the war, when they stayed in the Lombardy village of Oltrona San Mamette, about twenty-two miles northwest of the city. "There were also two of my grandparents, my mother's father and my father's mother. So basically my mother ended up supporting five people, and there was not much food around."

It is clear that living for three years in makeshift housing while bombs were falling on nearby Milan was a formative experience for Berlusconi. He was not yet seven years old when the evacuation took place. Money was scarce. His father had gone over the nearby border to Switzerland. So it was his mother, who had just given birth to his sister, Antonietta, who became not only the bread-winner but the only constant for the young Silvio in an otherwise uncertain existence.

Like many children living in war-torn Italy, young Silvio would lend a hand to the family, picking potatoes for a few pennies after school and doing other odd jobs. He would also sometimes earn his family's dinner, which in this dairy-farming region of Italy often consisted of yogurt or milk that was mixed together with polenta (cornmeal) or with hunks of bread.

"At the time," recalls Berlusconi, "I would go and help milk the cows each evening at a nearby farmhouse. I would do this for an hour and a half, maybe two hours, and as pay they would give me a little metal bucket of what they called *cajada*, which was a kind of thick yogurtlike substance. As I walked home each night I would swing the bucket around in a kind of three-hundred-sixty-degree circle for fun, and because of the force of gravity the yogurt would not leak out. But I remember that on one occasion I met some friends on the way home and I wanted to show off with the bucket, and show them how I could spin it around without anything leaking. But somebody grabbed my elbow and everything spilled to the ground. That night, when I got home, I was in big trouble with my mother because we had nothing else to eat for dinner."

At night, even though the village was more than twenty miles from Milan, from across the fields and valleys Berlusconi could see the far-off city in flames, entire sections ablaze after a bombing raid, all of it clearly visible from the countryside.

This very real physical danger explains why everyone in the Berlusconi family was nervous about Rosa Berlusconi's daily commute to work. But Rosa Berlusconi, by all accounts, was a woman with a decidedly strong character, as stubborn as her son would later prove, and at times even courageous. In fact, one particular episode was recounted in the Knesset by Israeli Prime Minister Benjamin Netanyahu during Berlusconi's state visit to Israel in 2010.

During the last two years of the war, with Mussolini's notorious 1938 Racial Laws still in place, and the Nazis now in control of much of Italy, thousands of Jews were rounded up and shipped off to concentration camps in Germany.

"My mother took the same train every morning, along with the other commuters, and so the passengers pretty much knew each other's faces," recalls Berlusconi. "At a certain stop a fascist policeman with a gun boarded the train, saw this young girl, and said, 'Ah, there you are! I have been looking for you for some time. Come with me.' It was clear that the girl was Jewish and that going with the policeman would have almost certainly meant being sent to a concentration camp. My mother stood up to the policeman and said, 'No, you should leave her alone and just make believe you never saw her.' The policeman told my mother to shut up. 'Now sit back down or I will shoot you,' he told her. But my mom remained standing and said, 'Okay, you go ahead and kill me, but just look around you, at the faces of the people on this train. You can kill me, but I promise that you will never leave this train alive.' All the other passengers stood up and surrounded the policeman. He looked around, and understood that even if he were to shoot my mother, he would be outnumbered and crushed by the crowd. So he got off the train and this young girl was saved."

In the Israeli parliament, Netanyahu recounted the tale and added: "With this firm statement the Italian woman saved the Jewish girl, and if only for a moment she lit a ray of humanistic light and bravery in the great darkness that pervaded all of Europe. That brave woman was named Rosa, and one of her sons is called Silvio Berlusconi."

After telling this story Berlusconi takes a deep breath and pauses. He seems somehow comforted by these memories of his childhood in wartime Italy, and he is speaking now with a certain passion.

"My mother was an inspiration for me, but I really missed my father," he says. "We all felt his absence during the war. He was gone during the entire three years that we lived in this village. I remember in particular being taken every Sunday morning by my grandmother to a little country church for mass. And on one occasion I saw a man seated a couple of pews in front of me, a man whose neck and shirt collar, at least from behind, looked just like my father. For the next month or so I remember sitting every Sunday with my grandmother just behind this man, and every time I saw him I started weeping silently, really missing my father. After the end of the war many Italians who had fled over the border to Switzerland began returning home. But my father was among the last to return. I remember trudging every evening at around six o'clock to the nearest bus stop and watching people get off the bus. But my father never seemed to be among the passengers, and so I would go home each night, crying. This went on for weeks and weeks, and then one night he finally arrived. He got off the bus and we embraced, and then we had a wonderful family celebration. My father had returned home, finally! For a kid who was barely ten years old at the time, you can imagine what it meant to have been deprived of his father for three years, during years of war."

By now it was 1946, the war was over, and so were the years of makeshift existence in the countryside, of scavenging for food, and of waiting for his family to be reunited. But the experience clearly instilled a strong survival instinct in the young boy, and it also gave him a certain temperament.

"To be honest," recalls Berlusconi, "I was not very well liked at the little school in the countryside. The local kids resented having us—the evacuated Milanese children—there with them, taking up space in the school, always looking for food and such. There was a fairly vulgar saying in dialect that they used at the time, *'Milanesi mangia fistun va fora di cujun'* which translated loosely meant 'Milanesi, get lost!' There was one particular school bully who was constantly on my case. Once he threw me into the snow, another time he set a dog on me, stuff like that. I am talking about when I was in second grade at elementary school. One day in June there was a heavy summer thunderstorm, and it poured and poured. We were in the village, which was located at the foot of a hill. The school was up the hill and the church was down below. There were just two little cobblestoned streets that ran down the hill. There was no sewage system, no drainage. So when it rained hard the water came down like a torrent. So there was a flooded area down below in the piazza. On this day, as usual, he was calling me names and being very nasty. I will never forget that day because for the first time I decided to fight back, and half the school was soon gathered around us. It was a kind of a showdown at the OK Corral. We fought and struggled, and the other schoolchildren egged us on, and finally I managed to grapple him and force his head under the water. I shouted at him, 'Don't you dare ever again tell me to piss off! Don't you dare say it again! Understand? Now say uncle!' And he cried 'uncle' and he admitted defeat, and I let him go."

Berlusconi is now gesticulating like a mime artist, acting out the scene as if he were still holding the bully's head under the water. For the first time in this recollection of his childhood, his face lights up with that trademark thousand-watt smile of his as he proclaims his victory. "From that moment onward, and for the rest of my life, I was marked out as a leader."

When Berlusconi's family finally returned to Milan after the end of the war, his parents decided to send him to a nearby Catholic school, in this case a Salesian college. For many families in postwar Italy, it was not unusual to give the schooling of one's child over to the Salesian priests at the age of eleven or twelve. Wealthier, aristocratic families might send their children to be schooled by the Jesuits, but if you did not have that kind of social standing or if you lived on the wrong side of the tracks, it was the Salesians.

From the age of eleven until he was eighteen years old, Silvio Berlusconi was schooled at the Salesian College of Don Bosco, which was located less than half a mile from Berlusconi's home in the Via Volturno.

Giovanni Melchiorre Bosco was a nineteenth-century Roman

Catholic priest, popularly known as Don Bosco. He was primarily an educator and writer who spent much of his life in the industrial city of Turin, where he dedicated his life to the education of street children and juvenile delinquents and other disadvantaged youth. His teaching methods were based on strict discipline and a classical education, full of Latin, team sports, and prayers.

Don Bosco was a follower of St. Francis de Sales, a sixteenth-century nobleman who had been educated by the Jesuits, and who was known as "the gentleman saint." Don Bosco founded the Salesian Society in the 1859 in order to help the young and poor children of the Industrial Revolution. The charter of the Salesians describes the society's mission as "the Christian perfection of its associates, obtained by the exercise of spiritual and material works of charity toward the young, especially the poor, and the education of boys to the priesthood."

During the twentieth century some of the more notable boarding students at Salesian schools were film director Alfred Hitchcock, Benito Mussolini, and Pope Francis.

For those attending the Salesian schools, at least in the early days, there was discipline, rigor, and a fair amount of corporal punishment.

At the age of nine Hitchcock lasted only a week at the Salesian College of Battersea in South London. In 1908, when Hitchcock's father went to visit his son and discovered that the strict Salesian fathers believed in purging the children of all their physical or moral ailments by lacing their dinner with a strong dose of laxatives, he immediately withdrew young Alfred from the school.

For Mussolini, the harsh treatment meted out by the priests at his Salesian college in Faenza seemed to have been a formative experience indeed. Recalcitrant and rebellious, he felt victimized and persecuted at the school, where the fathers placed him in the lowest ranks and humiliated him during lessons, at mealtimes, and even in terms of sleeping arrangements. After less than two years with the Salesians, and not yet eleven years of age, Mussolini got into a vicious fight with a fellow student, pulled a knife, and stabbed him in the hand. Deemed violent and uncontrollable, Mussolini was shortly thereafter expelled from the school.

By contrast, in 1949, there was a much happier experience for another Salesian student, a young boy in Argentina named Jorge Mario Bergoglio, who sixty-four years later would become Pope Francis. As a sixth-grade pupil Bergoglio attended a school of Don Bosco's, the Wilfrid Barón Salesian College in Ramos Mejía, on the western edge of Buenos Aires. Unusually, nearly a decade later, he entered a Jesuit seminary, thus becoming a rare example of a student schooled by both the Salesians and the Jesuits; normally a family would choose one or the other.

Pope Francis would later recall that his time at the Salesian college "was everything to me, and we were immersed in a preparation for life. The days would speed by and we never had time to be idle." The pope recounted long days that began with morning mass, followed by classes, a brief lunch, more studies, after-school recreation with the priests, homework, and then the ritual "good night" for the boarding students of the school's most senior priest, and then lights out. The pope remembered in particular being inculcated with "the social values of living together."

Berlusconi felt similarly, noting that "from Don Bosco's Salesians I learned the value in life of being able to interact and to get on well with everybody."

Their characters, their lives and careers could not have been more different, but Berlusconi is almost exactly the same age as Pope Francis; both men were born toward the end of 1936, and both attended, at the age of twelve, a Salesian college.

"It was the most important formative experience of my life, those eight years at the Salesian college," says Berlusconi. "The discipline was very tough. We would be at school from eight-thirty each morning until five in the afternoon. We attended mass every morning. I was an altar boy, and then we had our classes, Latin, ancient Greek, math or literature, and then a one-hour lunch break at noon. When we finally went home at five or five-thirty in the afternoon we always had a heavy workload of homework to do. It was not easy even for a guy like me. So I had to study each night until about nine in the evening, when my father would return home from work after putting in long hours. Having lost him for three years during the war I always awaited him very eagerly. I have a wonderful memory of this because when he came home each evening I remember that, regardless of whether he had had a hard day at the office or not, whether he was worried or sad, when the door to our apartment opened it was a joyous experience. He always made us feel good. I used to say that my father walked around with pure sunshine in his pocket."

Berlusconi the student is remembered by some of his classmates as a quick study, even then a fellow with a highly entrepreneurial spirit, a teenager who would finish his homework quickly and then often help out fellow students, in exchange for candies or pocket change.

It was at the Salesian high school that he first met, at the age of thirteen, his childhood friend Fedele Confalonieri. The two spent seven years together at the school and they were destined to become lifelong best friends. Confalonieri, a year younger than Berlusconi, would become his alter ego, his chief adviser, and ultimately the head of his commercial television empire and the chairman of his holding company, Fininvest.

In the late 1940s they used to walk home from school together every day; after all, they lived just a few doors away from each other on the same street.

Berlusconi recalls first meeting Confalonieri during mass one day at the school. "It was eight-thirty in the morning," he says, "and I was already playing the organ at mass and leading the kids in the choir in a song. Well, one day Fedele walked in, and it was clear from the start that he was much better at playing the organ than me. He was taking lessons at the conservatory. So I left that to him."

For his part, Confalonieri remembers his friend as a born entertainer. "He was always entertaining the rest of us, he was a real charmer, an actor in school plays, he would write for the school newspaper, and of course at the Salesian high school there was mass every day. Each morning we went to mass, which to be frank for kids in their teens was a bit much. But I guess it was music that first brought us together. We used to have jam sessions. I played the organ or the piano and he would sing, usually American songs. You could see he always wanted to please others, he always wanted to entertain."

Reminded of this, Berlusconi now stares off into the distance; he seems momentarily lost in his memories. "Yup," he says finally, "Fedele was on the keyboards, that was his job. I, instead, began to specialize in making welcoming speeches for important guests who came to visit the school, a bishop one time, a cardinal another time. I became the emcee, the master of ceremonies, the official speech-giver among the students. My teachers were very happy with my performances, and sometimes I even gave the welcoming speech totally in Latin. After all, we studied Latin for eight years, and ancient Greek for five years. It was quite a school, and if you didn't get it right, they would throw you out. So we had to study a lot."

Now Berlusconi is grinning again.

"I did have a rather large extended family," he says, "and among all of my aunts and cousins we had a total of eight nuns in the family. Eight nuns! And some of them lived in a convent not far from the Salesian high school. So when a cardinal or a bishop would visit the school, and I was doing the introductions, they would often come and sit in the audience. One of them took me aside afterwards and said something to me that she would repeat for many years. 'What a handsome cardinal you would make!' she exclaimed to me."

He laughs out loud at the anecdote. "My last surviving aunt, like the others also a nun, once came up to me after a public speech I had made, many years later. 'What a great pope you would have made!' she told me. And I have to say that the current pope is doing the job exactly the way I would do it. But you have to admit that, although we are almost exactly the same age, I think I still look younger than him."

Before he and Confalonieri had graduated from the Salesian high school they were already in the entertainment business; they had already formed a five-piece band in their last year of school. "He was the maestro, and he played the piano, and I was the lead singer and I used to play the upright bass and the guitar," recalls Berlusconi. "We would get gigs mainly on Saturday nights and on Sunday afternoons, really good gigs, and we would make good money. We were really quite good."

The newly formed band, starring Silvio on bass and Fedele at the keyboards, seemed a natural calling for these two Salesian schmoozers. And Silvio's old boyhood friend Fedele Confalonieri confirms that young Silvio was indeed a decent singer.

"Yeah, Berlusconi had a good voice. He was quite the crooner, and at an early age," says Confalonieri. "We did all the romantic Italian melodies, and he used to write love songs. But he really sang well in French, and even in English, he was pretty modern for the 1950s, pretty up-to-date. We used to play in dance halls in those days, they were the equivalent back then of discotheques today, except in those days we went to bed by midnight, while today people don't even arrive at a disco until midnight.

"After playing in the dance halls we moved on to playing in nightclubs in Milan, and also at special occasions like parties and weddings. And yes, we did earn good money at the time. Berlusconi did a great rendition of 'My Funny Valentine,' he did a lot of Gershwin like 'Embraceable You' and 'Lady, Be Good' and 'I Got Rhythm' and 'The Man I Love,' and then he had a whole repertoire of Frank Sinatra hits he would do, and then he would do songs by Jerome Kern and by Rodgers and Hammerstein, all the great hits from Broadway musicals. By the time we were eighteen or nineteen years old, we could afford to buy lots of records with our earnings."

When the two friends finally graduated, both of them went on to study law at the University of Milan. But both continued as part-time entertainers until they were nearly twenty-one.

Confalonieri, contrary to popular myth in Italy, never went

along on cruise ships to perform with Berlusconi "because I suffer from seasickness." But if the two of them were to be musically separated after a couple of years of university, it was not just because of the cruise ships.

"We have always remained friends," says Berlusconi, "but he is a pretty judgmental guy, he can be a harsh critic at times, and so we have always argued. We have argued about soccer, about music, about a lot of things. In fact when we were about twenty years old, and we were already at university, and he was in charge of our little orchestra, he fired me."

The explanation Berlusconi now proffers speaks volumes about the marketing chromosomes in his blood from an early age.

"He fired me because he said I was spending too much time with the audience, with the people who were on the dance floor, and not enough time playing. I tried to tell him that what I was doing was pure marketing and important and useful public relations, that I was making sure the people came to hear our orchestra and didn't go elsewhere. But he wanted me to play the upright bass, because he loved the way I played the bass, and by the way I also sometimes played the drums and sometimes I played the guitar and once in a while the piano. But he said, 'Silvio! I need you on bass.' So one day we argued big-time and he accused me of spending too much time on public relations and not enough time playing the bass. So he fired me. Just like that! Of course, I went off to perform elsewhere and within three weeks everybody was coming to see me play, and he ended up going off to Beirut to perform, to Lebanon!"

It was after being sacked by his friend that Berlusconi started working in the summertime for Costa Cruise Lines, first as a crooner and then as a jack-of-all-trades. He had already been a part-time wedding photographer and a part-time vacuum cleaner salesman. But the man who calls himself "a natural-born seducer" seriously honed his schmoozing skills as a kitschy crooner, entertaining the passengers aboard the great ocean liners that plied the seas, stuffed with deckloads of blue-rinsed grannies and honeymooning newlyweds.

"At first I played the bass in an orchestra called the Lambro Jazz Band, which was named after the river Lambro, which flows through Milan. There were five musicians and I ended up as the lead singer. But at midnight each night, on the ship's main deck there was an event that in the ship's entertainment program was titled in French *Une Voix et Une Guitare* [One Voice and One Guitar]. That was me! I was a real entertainer. I had a repertoire of a hundred fifty different songs and I took requests from the audience. I even invented songs out of nothing, for some nice lady perhaps as a way of being nice. I was always good at writing lyrics and I was good at rhyming. I had a hell of a lot of fun.

"I also worked pretty hard on those cruise ships because I used to start in the morning on the games deck, and I was organizing all the games. Then in the afternoons, when the ship docked in a port and people would disembark and tour the city, I would transform myself into a tour guide, even though in most cases I had never even visited the place. But I would read up on the places and then I would become a tour guide. In the evening it was back to the orchestra, and we played from nine p.m. until midnight and the passengers danced, and then from midnight until three in the morning I was the soloist again as *Une Voix e Une Guitare*. So I was a pretty busy guy."

Berlusconi says he used to do a fair number of Frank Sinatra songs, but his true passion was French love songs.

"I specialized in Italian songs at first, and I would write the lyrics while Fedele wrote the music. But I loved the French repertoire. I loved the French love songs. I guess that is because I went to Paris for a while. This was before I had finished studying law in Milan, before I got my degree. I took a course at the Sorbonne on comparing Italian and French law. While I was in Paris I worked part-time as a singer in a cabaret. It was great. I loved it. But my father was not pleased that I had not returned home to Milan after finishing my course. He kept asking me to quit Paris and come home."

Now Berlusconi leans forward.

"One night when I was singing at the cabaret, he just showed up, silently. He stood there, staring at me from the rear of the room while I was onstage. When I finished my performance, and the curtain went down and I went back to my dressing room, he appeared at the door and said, 'So are you planning to be a cabaret singer for the rest of your life?' I knew that I had to give up. We hugged. And the next morning we left Paris. I returned to complete my law degree in Milan, and my career as a singer was finished."

Then what Berlusconi's father may have counted on happening by bringing the boy back to his studies actually happened. As soon as he graduated at the age of twenty-five from the University of Milan, Silvio Berlusconi began to display a natural flair for business. He made the leap from entertainer to fledgling entrepreneur. His showmanship became his salesmanship. He became a twenty-something deal maker. And being Berlusconi, he was thinking anything but small.

The cruise ship crooner was about to become the Boy Mogul of Milan.

CHAPTER TWO

———

The Deal Maker

Berlusconi cut his first real estate deal at the age of twenty-five. He had just graduated from the University of Milan with a degree in commercial law. It was 1961. The cruise ship crooner had morphed into an office boy and into a jack-of-all-trades, and he was now working part-time for a small Milanese construction firm.

Construction was a booming industry in Milan, which had become the financial capital of a new Italy. The early 1960s were years of amazing growth and postwar prosperity. Smokestacks were going up, the Italians were getting rich, and a new consumer class was emerging. They called this postwar economic boom "the Italian miracle." With all the new industrialization and urbanization, and with migrant workers coming to Milan from the poor and agrarian South, there were plenty of jobs and not enough housing. The spreading affluence meant that a new middle class could now afford to buy their first little Fiat 500, or a modest new house or apartment in the city.

To the young Silvio, the surging economy of 1961 meant only one thing: opportunity. He always had his eye out for a deal. He was always looking for an angle. From an early age Berlusconi had deal-making chromosomes deeply embedded in his DNA. He was a natural salesman. It was no coincidence that his dissertation was about marketing. At the age of twenty-five Berlusconi had earned top grades with his thesis, he graduated with an honors degree, and he even won a 500,000-lire prize from a local Milanese advertising agency that was scouting for talent.

Upon graduation Berlusconi turned down his first job offer. It came from Carlo Rasini, the owner of the Banca Rasini, the little Milanese bank where his father, Luigi, had served faithfully for many years, working his way up from the bottom. Luigi Berlusconi was by that time a senior manager there.

Rasini had offered young Silvio the position of bank teller, an entry-level job. But Berlusconi declined. He had bigger things on his mind. He was dreaming about his first deal. He had spotted an appetizing plot of land in an up-and-coming neighborhood just west of the city's center, on a street called the Via Alciati. He thought it had potential.

His initial business plan was devilishly simple. Mr. Rasini had introduced him to a client of the bank named Pietro Canali. Canali was a small-time builder and not really an entrepreneur. He only did contract work for others, and had never actually developed his own real estate project. Enter Silvio Berlusconi.

Berlusconi offered to form a new property partnership with Canali, a special-purpose vehicle that would buy the land on the Via Alciati, almost a city block, and then get bank loans to finance Canali's building of four residential properties. Berlusconi was not bashful. He wanted to be an equal shareholder alongside his boss. As a client of the Banca Rasini, where Berlusconi's father worked, Canali could use his influence. And Rasini had already shown that he was fond of young Berlusconi by offering him a job as a teller. So Berlusconi's brain was on overdrive as he plotted how best to marry his business strategy and his little pool of contacts.

"I talked with my father and then I went to Canali and I proposed that we start a company together. The name that I suggested was very pretty: United Builders of Milan," recalls Berlusconi.

"He offered me five percent," says Berlusconi, "I told him I preferred to have a zero attached to that five, meaning fifty percent. I wanted to be a fifty-fifty partner. He said I was crazy, that I was just a kid. He asked me how I thought I could make enough money to make this work. I told him that I would find the land and negotiate the purchase, that he would be the builder and that I would then do the real estate development, using friends of mine who were young architects, and then I would manage the sales. I also told him that we would not need a big amount of investment capital if we could get the construction financed by the banks and with deposits from buyers. In the end he agreed. He said that he was crazy but that if I had the courage to ask him to be a fifty-fifty partner, then I was even crazier than he was, and maybe two crazy people could achieve something together.

"We had a meeting at the bank, and the key problem was that Mr. Canali had never done anything like this before. But I had already checked everything out, from the market conditions to the selling price of the land, and I had even contacted the seller, who apparently needed money badly. So I did the calculations and then I went to the Banca Nazionale del Lavoro to ask for a loan. I asked for five hundred million lire. The bank offered me a loan with very high interest rates, and the bank director looked at me and said, 'Why don't you go home and speak with your papa, and let me know tomorrow if you accept our conditions or not.' I couldn't do that. My father would have fainted if he had heard I had gone out seeking a five-hundred-million-lire bank loan."

Berlusconi's father did help out in the end. "My father gave me thirty million lire when he cashed in his accumulated pension. The initial capital of the company we formed, United Builders of Milan, was for fifty million lire. Half came from me, thanks to my father, and half came from Mr. Canali."

Rasini also helped, providing the first mortgage loans and guarantees for 190 million lire of the investment, the portion needed to finance the land purchase.

Fortunately for young Berlusconi, for his new partner Pietro

Canali, and for his father, Luigi Berlusconi, at the Banca Rasini, the economy was strong and so was spending on construction and new housing developments. Timing was everything. Milan was the booming capital of a flourishing Italy. President John F. Kennedy was in the White House, the Berlin Wall was going up in Germany, Sophia Loren was the prima donna of the Italian cinema, Fellini was the top director, earnings were rising, and life was generally plentiful.

Once he secured the initial financing from the Banca Rasini, Berlusconi set about launching the residential project at Via Alciati. He had a razor-thin budget, and he tended to involve mainly close friends and family members in his business, not just his father but an uncle on his mother's side, a cousin, and a handful of his friends from college. Later on, in the early 1970s, he would convince his childhood friend Fedele Confalonieri to come and work for him.

Berlusconi was always a charmer and a schmoozer, but he was also a workaholic. From the beginning he played multiple roles in all of his business ventures: entrepreneur, deal maker, architect, decorator, finance director, construction foreman, gardener, head of sales, chief salesman, and promoter. Above all, Silvio Berlusconi enjoyed playing the role of the Salesman. This was to be his starring role in life.

"We had a lot of adventures back then," recalls Berlusconi, and he breaks out in a broad grin. On a hot summer day in July 1961, when he was twenty-five years old, he was stripped down to his waist and on a ladder outside the sales office, with a paintbrush in his hand.

"So there I was, at the project in Via Alciati. We had to build a showroom, a kind of sales office on the site and near the street so that people would visit. We had no budget so I had Mr. Canali give me a messy old construction site office. It was a wooden shack. We fixed it up as best we could. I brought some furniture from my home to make it look nice, and of course we had to give it a fresh coat of paint out front, so I chose my favorite color, which was blue."

Berlusconi pauses for effect.

"So I am out there on the ladder, with paintbrush in hand, it is a hot July afternoon and I am stripped down to the waist, hoping to catch some rays while I paint, and then suddenly this middle-aged couple appears. They tell me that they have a daughter who is about to marry, and that they live nearby, just up the road in fact, and how nice it would be if they could find an apartment for their daughter right here. They ask me if I can give them some information or a contact. I figured that I couldn't really tell them that the fellow with the paintbrush in his hand was also the managing director of the firm. So I made a funny voice and I asked them to wait a moment while I called the boss. I rushed inside the little office and I quickly cleaned up and put on a shirt and tie. Then I went back out there and pretended to be the sales manager. That is how I sold my very first apartment. Of course, sometime later, when I got to know this couple as my first customers, the man said to me, 'You know, when I first visited the construction site I saw a kid who looks almost exactly like you. He was outside doing the painting.'

"I told him that he must have met my cousin, who looks a lot like me but who is not very bright," he recalls, laughing. "Anyway the point was that the first apartment was sold. My second customer turned out to be the mama of my friend Fedele Confalonieri.

"I took her around on a tour of the site. I showed her where each of the houses would stand. I showed her where the garden would be. I measured out the distance, step by step, to where the courtyard and the garage would be. I showed her every detail. She liked everything but the garage. She ended up buying four apartments, an entire floor."

After the initial success in the Via Alciati, where he sold about twenty apartments, Berlusconi was ready for a bigger challenge. He already had Canali as a construction partner and he already had proof of concept and reliable bank loans and guarantees. So he decided to think bigger.

In 1963, he was ready to make the leap from building four

apartment buildings on a city block, as well as residential homes, to constructing an entire little "new town" for four to five thousand residents. This he would do on the northern outskirts of Milan, in a town called Brugherio that lies in the direction of Monza, famous for its Formula One racing. This was something of a quantum leap for a man still in his mid-twenties, and Berlusconi was already seen as a fast-rising star on the thriving Milan real estate scene, an aggressive newcomer with plenty of ambition.

"I began to think about a bigger project, where we could have a fully functioning and perfect model apartment on the site, as well as the sales office. We would build four times as many apartments as Via Alciati. I wanted to create something new, a new form of urban planning. I went back to Mr. Canali. He came in and then we got some more shareholders to join us, and we ended up forming a company called Edilnord and we called the development the Centro Edilnord. I didn't really like the name Edilnord, but my partners were old-fashioned and they wanted it."

The name of the company translated roughly into "Northern Construction," with Canali as a minority stakeholder, and Rasini again helpful with more bank financing for the new project. The bulk of the capital for the first Edilnord project would come, however, as had some of the funds for the original Via Alciati project, from a Swiss fiduciary trust that was located in the discreet and scenic little town of Lugano. The shareholder structure of these projects tended to be a cobweb of cross-holdings, often featuring Berlusconi's family members as shareholders of holding companies. Later in life, when Berlusconi had already become a billionaire, he would face unpleasant questions from investigators about the Swiss origins of his initial seed capital for Edilnord. He would deny any irregularities with vigor and venom.

Berlusconi would also be dogged by suspicions about how he had obtained the necessary permits and authorizations from local city councils for all his real estate projects. He himself remembers well the jungle of bribe-taking local officials who populated Milan at the time.

"The Edilnord project was not an easy one, but it was in a town located outside of Milan because I had sworn that I would never build anything again in Milan, which was impossible because of the politics and the bureaucratic complexities."

Berlusconi looks down at his hands with a mixture of embarrassment and distaste as he recollects that era.

"In Milan, in those days, in order to obtain the various authorizations needed to build a house, you had to make the rounds. I used to say that you had to make the rounds with a cash-stuffed envelope in your mouth. To get the permit at the office of sewers and drainage systems, you had to pay someone. To get the right permits for street signs, you had to pay, and then for traffic lights, another payment. It was endless, and so with the project at Brugherio, I was happy to finally find some honest people."

At the time, however, Berlusconi was facing an even greater challenge. Construction work on the new project was getting under way just as the real estate market was collapsing. It was the end of 1963. The 1960s boom was proving itself a bit choppy in Italy, and the construction sector hit a cyclical recession, a downturn.

"We had a very tough time right from the start of this project. It was very challenging," recalls Berlusconi. "It was getting very hard to sell a new home. My partners wanted to quit."

By 1964 Berlusconi found himself facing a clutch of impatient investors.

"My partners basically said to me that it would be better to halt work on the project, given the depressed state of the market. They said it was pointless to continue. But I was young and this was important to me. This was only the second business venture of my life and I did not want to throw in the towel," recalls Berlusconi. "So I asked them if they would give me three months to come up with a solution, to find a single buyer for the whole thing. I wanted to experiment with a new idea that I had. If I couldn't sell the apartments one by one in the retail market, then maybe a big pension fund would buy them all as a single block investment, and rent them out to families. I wanted to try the pension fund route and I wanted to try to sell the whole project. My partners said okay, that I had three months to sell all the apartments. They said that if I failed, they would put the company into liquidation."

He clearly loves to talk about how he did it.

At the time of the ultimatum Berlusconi had already identified the right contact at the right pension fund, in this case a corporate managers' pension fund that had just elected as its president a commercial director he knew over at the Manzoni advertising agency in Milan. This was the same agency that only a couple of years before had given Silvio a prize worth 500,000 lire for his award-winning college dissertation on the contractual aspects of advertising slots. Contacts everywhere and constant networking. Both are hallmarks of the Berlusconi style.

"I went to see the president of the pension fund over at Manzoni and I presented my idea to him," Berlusconi recounts. "He liked me a lot and actually he had been one of the examiners during the oral exams for my dissertation. So we had a good rapport. But he told me that while it was true that his pension fund bought apartment blocks, they only bought them in Rome. Not in Milan. I argued. I made the case that Milan was an important city, that it would be good for his pension fund to diversify its investments. He told me that it was nearly impossible, that he had only recently taken over as president of the fund, and he didn't have much of a power base. In Rome the pension fund had board directors who were all pretty tight with the Roman construction industry, that they were a tough bunch and it was a closed shop. He was pretty dubious. But I pressed him and insisted. I asked him if he could at least send one of his managers to view the property. He muttered something about it being a colossal waste of time but he finally broke down and sent me to see his director-general. That fellow was really tough. He looked like a giant."

Berlusconi now makes a show of cowering, with one arm raised above his head in fear of an imaginary giant.

"His name was Dodet, and he actually came to visit the construction site and he liked it. He said that it was well done but he said it would be difficult to persuade the pension fund to invest in

Milan rather than in Rome. He was pretty hostile. I begged him to at least bring his Rome-based board members to see the project, to have a look. A week later he called me and said he could schedule a visit in a month and a half or so. Then I was informed that they would show up in less than three weeks. I was screwed. All I had to show was a partially finished building site. I don't think I ever worked harder in my life than in the days and weeks that followed. For those next three weeks I hardly slept."

During those three weeks he rounded up all his architect friends, his buddies from college, his construction crews, and, as usual, a smattering of aunts and uncles and cousins and other family members. He put them all to work, day and night, round the clock.

"None of my workers slept much during those three weeks," recalls Berlusconi. "We were on three shifts a day, three eight-hour shifts. But when the pension fund's twelve board members arrived from Rome, together with that giant guy, Mr. Dodet, they couldn't believe their eyes. They found a huge green lawn because I managed to buy an entire soccer pitch of lawn from the Salesian fathers. I had uprooted the whole thing like Astroturf and had it transported and replanted right there at the construction site. It was like a new invention at the time. I had birch trees shipped in from Holland. I replanted bushes and trees from a friend's garden that were twelve or thirteen meters tall. I put them along the walkways. I scattered pots full of flowers everywhere. I lined the paths. We finished the exterior sidings of the houses with the best tiling. We furnished each of the show apartments; each one was decorated in a different style. One was English style, one was contemporary modern. They were all different, for every taste. We brought in pieces of furniture from the homes of my architects, from my family home, from my aunt's house. We brought in blankets and sheets for the bedrooms, towels for the bathrooms, plates and glasses for the dining room, the works."

Now Berlusconi's voice gains a conspiratorial tone as he recalls a little piece of trickery, a little Berlusconi touch.

"I even persuaded a friend of mine from Florence," he confides, "actually a baron from Florence, to play the role of concierge, sort of an old-fashioned hotel-style concierge out in front for when the board members arrived, a hotel porter complete with a uniform, a hat, and a visor. At the entrance to the site I had installed a plaque with words engraved in Latin that meant 'Today we should party. Tomorrow we work. Welcome to this home.' Everything was perfect, it was all done to utter perfection."

With Berlusconi's early career in the balance, and the future of Edilnord depending on this deal, he was keen to make a good impression on the severe-looking board members who had descended on the residential project. So the twelve men from Rome, who had come against their will and only at the explicit request of the president of their pension fund, began their tour of the Edilnord project. Berlusconi offered them drinks and canapés but it was not easy to win them over. He remembers a conversation he had with the vice chairman, who turned out to be the most hostile of them all. The vice chairman had strolled out onto a terrace of one of the houses, where he stood for a while smoking an Astor, a popular cigarette in elegant Roman society at the time.

"We were standing out there on the terrace," recalls Berlusconi, "and it was one of my personally designed terraces, all kitted out with a Ping-Pong table, with motion detectors, and even an infra-red modern heating system that allowed you to sit outside in midwinter. The vice chairman was standing out there, chain-smoking these Astor cigarettes. He would use the butt of each cigarette to light the next one. He beckons me toward him, and he says 'As you can see, I like my cigarettes. So tell me, my boy, if I wanted to go out and buy a pack, how many miles would I need to travel to find the nearest tobacconist?' And he bursts out laughing. He is really being cruel. But I answer him immediately. 'If you look over there,' I tell him, and I am pointing out into the distance, 'on that corner over there, we are planning to build the first combined tobacconist and bar.' He sort of sniffs at this but he let me off the hook, because after that I told him a pretty hilarious joke about Naples."

Despite his being ever the showman and entertainer, it was not easy to explain away one aspect of his plan to give the impression that the development was popular among the locals. The point was to cajole the skeptical board members from Rome into agreeing to purchase a real estate project that was less than half built, and in the middle of a recession.

"I am always a perfectionist," says Berlusconi, "I wanted to make a good impression and I also wanted to prove to these people from Rome that there was a lively market for rentals here in Milan. I wanted to show them a crowd of eager customers. So I telephoned my mother and all my relatives and I asked them all to show up the next morning at the Edilnord site to visit the apartments. And all of my relatives came. Lots of them. They wandered around, they admired the apartments, and at one point they all ended up on the same terrace where I was standing with the Astor-smoking vice chairman, the nasty fellow. He turns to me and says 'There is something odd here. I feel like I am at a funeral, or maybe at a wedding. A pretty girl has just arrived, and she seems to know all the other buyers and she is going around kissing and hugging all the other buyers as though they were family members.'"

"I could no longer hide the truth. I was busted," Berlusconi says, laughing. "She was the only cousin I had forgotten to call, and she had only decided to come because she had heard from another cousin that I was having 'a family gathering' at the Edilnord building site. So of course when she arrived, she kissed and hugged her family members."

Berlusconi screws up his face with mock chagrin.

"I had no choice but to confess the truth to the vice chairman and the board members, that I had invited my entire family to see the houses, and of course I insisted that they were all very curious to see the houses, which was true. When they left, the board members were all very nice and some were even complimentary. But a few days later the president of the pension fund told me that there was still one key executive, a certain Mr. Mancuso, who was still bitterly opposed to the deal, probably because he was part of the Rome circuit and only wanted to do business with his buddies there. This Mr. Mancuso could stop the deal."

Having charmed the board of directors, notwithstanding his little family pantomime, Berlusconi was not about to give up because there was one last holdout. The plan he set in motion was worthy of Agatha Christie. It was an example of his persistent and obsessive ambition, and his ability to scheme a deal through both strategy and tactics. Berlusconi had, and has, a profound conviction that just about any problem can be solved if he is able to get in front of his adversaries, and then charm and wheedle and schmooze them into an agreement.

"The first thing I did was to go to Rome and ask my friends to try to find the secretary of this Mancuso and get me her phone number. Then I go to Rome and I manage to 'bump into her' and then to charm this secretary. You could even say that I courted her for a while."

A smile appears on Berlusconi's face.

"Once I had charmed her, I explained to her exactly what I needed done, and I persuaded her to book me a ticket on the train her boss would take every fifteen days, the train that went from Rome to Milan. It would leave at five in the afternoon from Rome and arrive at midnight in Milan. So I got this secretary to book me on the next train with Mancuso, and to call me to inform me when she had done it. She called me. I took a plane down to Rome the next day, and just before five o'clock that afternoon I boarded the train. I sat in the dining car, at a table where I would be seated directly in front of Mancuso. I first saw him arrive from a distance. He had a scowl on his face, I remember that. I got a bit frightened and I picked up my newspaper, the *Corriere della Sera*, and I hid behind it so that when he sat down he could not see me. A few minutes after the train had left the station, I lowered my newspaper and made believe I was surprised. 'Oh, dear sir, what a coincidence,' I said. He gave me a nasty stare and said, 'Oh. My enemy!' That is the way our conversation began. It was pretty tough at first but the train journey was long, it was seven hours long, and I guess I

managed to seduce him, to eventually win him over. By the time
we rolled into Milan we were best friends. He had told me his life
story and we had talked about everything under the sun, including
the real estate project. He was completely sold on the deal, and he
became one of its staunchest defenders. Shortly after that train ride
the pension fund bought the whole project. The deal was done."

Berlusconi punctuates his point with a mimic's sigh of relief.
Phew!

Being lucky is part of making your fortune. By 1968, when the
Edilnord project at Brugherio was entering its final construction
phase, the real estate market had improved again, and all of the
apartments that the pension fund had bought were rented out. Berlusconi's gamble had paid off. He was making a name for himself.
But as usual, he was restless for a bigger deal.

Now he had grand new designs for bedroom communities
he wanted to build around Milan. He had proven that he could
undertake a medium-size real estate development and even manage to unload it onto a big investor during a downturn. Not bad
for a young man who was barely thirty. Ever the ladies man, he
had meanwhile started a whirlwind romance with a modest girl
from the suburbs, Carla Elvira Dall'Oglio. The two were married
in 1965 and had two children together, their daughter, Marina, in
1966 and their son, Pier Silvio, three years later. Berlusconi was
prospering, and like a true son of the Milanese bourgeoisie, he was
setting up his first family.

When the Edilnord project was finished in 1968, Berlusconi
formed a new company, Edilnord Residential. This time he registered it under the name of a cousin of his, a certain Lidia Borsani.
The thirty-one-year-old cousin was the daughter of his mother
Rosa's sister, and the company she owned on paper was financed
by a variety of Italian and international investors, including once
again the Swiss fiduciary trust companies in Lugano. The point
was that Berlusconi himself did not appear as the owner in the
company records. Berlusconi formed the new company initially as
a special-purpose vehicle for a new venture because he had made

another deal. He had bought a 180-acre chunk of land on the eastern outskirts of Milan for 3 billion lire (about $2 million at the time), in an area not far from the city's Linate Airport. It was here that Berlusconi had decided to take his next leap. From building apartment blocks in and around Milan he would now become an innovator, and bring to Italy the Northern European concept of satellite cities. The trend was growing in the late 1960s in Britain, the Netherlands, Germany, and France. Berlusconi decided he would build a little suburban residential community for fifteen to twenty thousand inhabitants, and he would kit it out, Berlusconi-style, with every modern convenience known to man. This time though, he would control it all with vertical integration: he would be the builder-developer *and* the owner-operator.

"I wanted to continue with my dream of building new towns," says Berlusconi. "There was plenty of demand in the market. By 1968 there was euphoria. I had learned from the first Edilnord project that if I wanted to build a really great new town, then I had to first get planning permission for everything, for a complete and self-contained locality that had schools and shopping centers, parks and gardens, piazzas, churches, and hospitals. My idea was to achieve this with a very modern style of urban planning for the time that included lots of green, lots of bicycle paths, roads, and walkways. We had to build a place where a young mother could send her kids to school without worrying, where you could live and work and shop and pray and go to the sports club and use the tennis courts and swimming pools and have everything that a family could desire. My idea was to make it possible to do everything at Milano Due so that you never had to leave."

Milano Due (Milan Two) employed copious doses of capital, starting with the first 3 billion lire that were paid to acquire the land. But the project became a landmark innovation for Italy. By 1973 Berlusconi would inaugurate the first stage of Milano Due, and he would shoot to national fame as the man who had built a truly modern and luxurious garden city for ten thousand residents in Milan. A few years later he would receive the Italian equivalent of a knighthood for services to the nation in the building of Milano Due. It was no longer plain old Silvio. From now on he was *Cavaliere* Berlusconi. The title stuck in title-loving Italy, where the uncrowned king of the Italians was Gianni Agnelli, the former playboy who had just taken over the helm at Fiat, his family-owned automobile company. Agnelli was known by his law degree, as the *Avvocato*. Berlusconi would be known as the *Cavaliere*.

From a commercial point of view, the Milano Due project was a big hit. Families arrived by the dozens each weekend, flooding the sales staff with questions and eager to see the face of residential modernity. They lined up to inspect the new apartments. Berlusconi sold out his initial stock in no time. He was making his fortune. He was getting rich.

There was just one last commercial and political hitch toward the end of the project. Thanks to the local zoning arrangements, Milano Due was located just under the flight path of Milan's main airport, Linate. Planes were taking off every ninety seconds at rush hour, and that was not contributing to the appreciation of the value of the apartments at Milano Due. If only, somehow, these flight paths could be slightly rerouted away from Milano Due, well, the value of the apartments in Milano Due would surely skyrocket.

It was highly fortuitous at this time for Silvio Berlusconi to meet a priest who turned out to be his salvation. The priest was also a businessman; some would say he was a visionary while others would call him a rogue. Like Berlusconi, this priest-turned-businessman was also a builder and a seller of dreams, and of buildings. He was as capable a schmoozer, and every bit as ruthless in business, as Berlusconi.

Enter Don Luigi Verzé.

This fast-talking priest was a mover and shaker in the late 1960s and early 1970s when he first met and worked with Berlusconi, something of a local legend. Verzé spoke in the name of the Lord, but he sure liked his property deals. The two men hit it off from the start. Don Verzé was a munificent man and a philanthropist in the eyes of the people, a builder of hospitals. For his critics he was a treacherous Cardinal Richelieu, a wily and powerful man with a dome-sized ego.

In the early 1970s Don Verzé wanted to build an innovative nonprofit hospital right next to the 1,800 acres that Berlusconi had bought for the Milano Due development. He had already bought an eleven-acre chunk of land, where he was planning to build the San Raffaele hospital complex. Don Verzé wanted to name the hospital after the patron saint of health and healing, the Archangel Raphael.

The two men, when they met, understood immediately that they had the same problem: Berlusconi did not want airplanes flying over his new real estate project and Don Verzé did not want planes flying over his clinic. After some discussion they came to a meeting of the minds: Edilnord became a partner in the San Raffaele project. They filed a joint petition, on behalf of the patients of San Raffaele and the residents of Milano Due, to the Ministry of Transport in Rome asking for the flight paths to be changed. The two men went to Rome on numerous occasions, where they met officials of the military, the civil aviation authority, the airline Alitalia; and back in Milan they met city and suburban local officials, the regional governor, and the health and urban planning authorities. They joined forces in one huge lobbying effort, and in the end they got what they wanted. A government directive dated August 30, 1973, established explicitly that "the new flight paths will avoid overflight of the area Berlusconi-don Verzé."

Berlusconi recalls meeting Don Verzé and immediately finding common ground.

"I first met him because I was looking for the right person to build a hospital near Milano Due," recalls Berlusconi. "We liked each other and we became friends, and we did a lot of things together for the hospital, starting with the hospital's water purification system. We did many things over the years and we were always friends."

Berlusconi's face is suddenly somber.

"We also had a project that we worked on for many years.

Unfortunately it was not completed because Don Verzé passed away. We were building an organization that would study how to live until the age of a hundred twenty years, and with an excellent quality of life. We had everything planned. We bought some land near Verona, and we began the project. We brought in the most famous gerontologists, the best and the brightest. And then Don Verzé died."

Back in 1973, with Don Verzé still very much alive, Berlusconi's new real estate empire was thriving. It was in April of that year that he persuaded his childhood friend Fedele Confalonieri to come and work for him. Confalonieri had been struggling with a small textiles firm, and he was ready to team up again with his old friend Silvio. The alter ego from the Salesian college had returned home.

Berlusconi was now a famous real estate developer and construction magnate on the Italian national scene. Milano Due was raking in the kudos from architectural and urban planning critics. It was also causing plenty of controversy. The rerouting of the flight paths around Linate airport had not gone down well with the local city councilors and the community in nearby Segrate. Allegations that local politicians in Segrate received bribes to help them decide on the flight paths would dog the Milano Due project for years.

"I did not pay bribes," insists an adamant Silvio Berlusconi. "I battled hard for my urban planning permits. I had endless discussions and debates with the entire local council of Segrate. I held meetings with plenty of citizens' groups. I was even physically attacked by a group of protesters who were rallying against the project. But I never paid a single bribe."

Bribes or no bribes, it was undoubtedly the Milano Due project that made Berlusconi a wealthy man. He had been doing well in the 1960s but the completion in 1973 of the first phase made him rich. It was also the moment in which he began to live the high life. In 1973, using the services of another controversial friend, in this case a lawyer named Cesare Previti, he acquired the luxurious seventy-room Villa San Martino in the village of Arcore. Berlusconi was now becoming a full-fledged national figure, a bit flashy—like an Italian version of Donald Trump—rather flamboyant, but then, that was part of the package.

He moved into the Villa San Martino in 1974, which came full of furnishings and expensive works of art, and he registered the property in the name of a company that functioned as a holding vehicle for various other houses. The move would later raise questions. By now a flourishing Berlusconi had his childhood friend Fedele Confalonieri at his side, plus his younger brother, Paolo Berlusconi, who began helping out with the management of Milano Due, and subsequently the Milano Tre project that followed, as well as an assortment of shopping centers and office blocks.

Berlusconi, according to Confalonieri, was a bit bored at this point. He was restless and ready for something new, and began expanding his holdings. He bought a downtown Milan theater called the Teatro Manzoni. He bought into a national newspaper that was edited by a legendary figure in Italian journalism, the wry Indro Montanelli. He set up more companies for the new real estate projects.

Berlusconi the deal maker had already become a real estate tycoon. But he was clearly not content with newfound money and newfound fame. He wanted a different challenge, and he would find it back at Milano Due, in the makeshift closed-circuit television services he was providing to the residents.

"This is where my television adventure really began," says Berlusconi. "First I had a local closed-circuit TV service for the residents that would allow parents to watch their kids from home, to see them at school or at the playground, or at the swimming pools. We set it up so you could even watch the local mass in the church. People really liked it. And I liked it, too. So after I had acquired some experience with the TV channel and with the studios and equipment, I began to look around at the local television market and what it could become."

Back in 1974, a key indicator of what could happen in the state-run television industry in Italy came in the form of an Italian Constitutional Court ruling on the obscure case of a local cable TV channel in the Piedmont textiles town of Biella. The court allowed the TV channel to continue broadcasting via cable, independent of government control. The ruling hit Italy like an earthquake. It may have been the 1970s but Italy was still a country where the only television broadcasts that were allowed came from the giant state broadcaster that was known as RAI.

"Berlusconi followed that court ruling very closely," recalls Fedele Confalonieri, "and for the first time back then it looked like it might be possible to challenge the monopoly of the state broadcaster. That was when Berlusconi had his biggest intuition. He immediately saw this as an extraordinary business opportunity. So he took the established local cable service at Milano Due, and then in 1978 he bought the frequency of a small TV channel. He put it all together and launched TeleMilano 58 as a local commercial TV channel. You cannot imagine how radical it was back then. The law still did not allow local channels to transmit live broadcasts or to report the news. But by 1979 Berlusconi was already getting ready to challenge the government-owned television system. That meant not only television. That meant politics. It was courageous but it was wild."

Berlusconi, as usual, had an ambitious plan. He would pit his wits against the entire apparatus of the state.

"For us in Italy, like everywhere else in Europe, public television was the only TV available," recalls Berlusconi. "It was a state monopoly that nobody ever thought of taking on. To make matters worse, the TV channels were all controlled by the political parties. You couldn't find an employee of public television who wasn't the brother, or cousin, or relative, or intimate friend of some politician. It seemed impossible to scale this Mount Everest, impossible to take on the state broadcaster. I guess you could easily call the battle which ensued an 'epic' battle."

The battle would indeed be epic, it would be highly controversial, and it would make Berlusconi into a billionaire. Berlusconi lunged into a furious buying spree and snapped up local TV stations around the country. When he owned a string of them, he was ready to make his next move. He was ready to take on the state, ready to make the jump from real estate tycoon to media mogul.

In the process he would invent the first large-scale private and commercial television network in Europe.

CHAPTER THREE

———

The Media Mogul

U ntil we made our move," says Berlusconi, seated on a plush couch amid the baroque splendor of his drawing room at the Villa San Martino, "there was nothing but state-run television in Italy, like in many other parts of Europe. The channels would shut down at midnight and there was nothing in the morning for housewives to watch. It was pretty boring."

In 1976, when he first decided to take advantage of Italian Constitutional Court rulings that allowed free-to-air broadcasts by local private commercial TV stations, it was a fairly black-and-white world. Italy was still only a decade into its postwar economic boom and the country was still industrializing. The full introduction of color TV was years away. State television was largely educational; it was pedantic and pedagogic. There was a famous show on RAI called *It's Never Too Late* that featured an elementary school teacher named Alberto Manzi who literally taught viewers how to read and write. Many of the workers from the agrarian provinces who streamed into cities to work in factories were still illiterate. So this kind of programming had a social function and helped many Italians who had until now never learned the basic skills of reading and writing. Italy was still a country of workers and their feudal overlords. Euro-communism was on the rise in Italy and across Europe. In Rome, the Kremlin was helping to finance the Italian Communist Party while the CIA operated behind the scenes to prop up the Christian Democrats, as a counterweight to what the Soviets were doing. The country was meanwhile under siege from Red Brigades terrorists, hard-left militants who were like the Baader Meinhof terrorists in Germany or Action Direct in France. The influence of the Roman Catholic Church was also seen in the world of politics, and on a daily basis

The Vatican opposed the idea of legalizing divorce and meddled in the affairs of state as though it were an Italian political party, preaching family values and allying itself with the Christian Democrats. The staid programming of the time reflected the values of a largely family-centered Christian work ethic. Italians might be party animals. They might be flamboyant or colorful. But the political overlords in Rome who controlled the RAI state broadcasting network preferred a shade of institutional gray.

At midnight the state broadcaster ceased programming and channels would sign off to the strains of Rossini's "William Tell Overture." Then a pattern containing the RAI test card would appear in a freeze-frame that remained fixed upon the screen all night, accompanied only by occasional static or a single excruciatingly loud tone that reminded sleepy viewers to turn off their TV sets.

The same relatively gray and institutional aesthetics prevailed in much of the rest of European television, except for Britain and Luxembourg, which had already allowed some commercial channels to compete with public television.

In Europe in the late 1970s, television was considered a public utility like water, electricity, or the fixed-line telephone. In Italy, as in France and Germany, it was part of the package of public goods and services controlled by government-owned companies on behalf of the state for its citizens. The state TV channels also served, through the nightly news broadcasts, as a megaphone for the politicians who governed.

In Italy, this mission and mind-set meant that RAI carried almost no advertising. What little there was did not come in the shape of thirty- or sixty-second spots but in a quaint little format. Once a day, at a few minutes before nine o'clock in the evening, Rai Uno, the national flagship channel, would broadcast about twelve minutes of advertising, bundled into a container called "Carousel" and consisting of a handful of two- or three-minute sketches that featured famous actors and singers. These sketches were a primitive form of TV advertising, part celebrity endorsement and part product placement. In one memorable ad for an artichoke-flavored liqueur called Cynar, an actor sits down at a sidewalk table outside a crowded bar. He extols the energy-giving benefits of the drink and then orders his favorite aperitif by name, just once. That was the entire ad.

"The advertising on public television did not increase sales for the advertisers. This was because most of the advertising was really institutional and staid, it just showed the brand once or twice. We used to say that watching those ads was like pissing in your pants," says a deadpan Berlusconi. "You get a kind of warm sense of well-being, but nobody notices anything."

Berlusconi has never tried to hide his scorn for the state-run broadcaster.

In 1977, having filled his TV studios at Milano Due with musical contests and quiz shows, he was ready to expand his operations. He bought a local TV frequency, installed an antenna high atop the Pirelli skyscraper in Milan, and he began beaming his TV station to the entire city and out to the suburbs. The channel was now called TeleMilano 58.

Berlusconi's eldest daughter, Marina Berlusconi, was twelve years old when TeleMilano 58 made its debut in 1978. She remembers watching the very first show that was broadcast on the new channel, which happened to be a Betty Boop cartoon shown at eight o'clock in the evening. She was in the company of her younger brother Pier Silvio, who at the age of nine was known by his nickname of Dudi.

"My brother and I were seated there on the couch together, in the living room downstairs at Arcore," says Marina. "My father was at a business dinner and so it was just the two of us watching the Betty Boop cartoon. I remember that my father must have called us thirty times. He kept calling us every five minutes to make sure we were sitting on the couch and watching. He wanted to know if the signal was clear, if the broadcast image was good, if the sound was audible. He was really excited. He truly believed he was creating something new and he was very nervous that night."

Marina also remembers the way her father would do his own market research, mainly by asking the opinions of close family and friends.

"At the beginning of his adventure in television, Silvio Berlusconi did not trust the marketing agencies or market research. He would talk to us about the programming, he would ask his children what they liked, he would consult friends and family, he would ask those who were around him."

Marina lets slip a chuckle at her next recollection.

"The thing I remember the most," she says, the chuckle now escalating into a laugh, "is that he must have been the only parent who was actually *happy* for his children to watch television! When he came home in the evening, around eight p.m., he wanted us to be in front of the television watching. He even persuaded my mother to let us eat dinner in front of the TV. We were his main test audience, and he would ask us which channels we were watching and what programs."

Like many self-made men who came from nowhere to invent and then dominate entire industries, Berlusconi didn't trust the system. He ignored the advice of his closest advisers and his experts. He liked to do things his way. And that meant big and splashy.

By 1979 he had lured an American-born celebrity quiz show host with a funny name away from RAI and made him the first big star of his new TV station. This star, a cheerful showman named Mike Bongiorno, began to draw viewers. For the state broadcaster in Rome, this competitive and ambitious Berlusconi up in Milan was starting to be an irritation. In fact it was to be the battle for advertising dollars that would eventually prove decisive in Berlusconi's attempt to challenge the state and carve out market share for private TV channels. From the beginning Berlusconi proved himself an exceedingly aggressive competitor to RAI.

"With TeleMilano 58 on the air, we began to go after local advertising," he recalls. "We were very innovative and we pursued clients very differently from the way RAI did. Back in those days you had to have special connections just to be able to buy some airtime, some advertising space on the state channel. Only a handful of companies were allowed to place ads on RAI. And to get into the RAI system you needed contacts, mainly political contacts."

Berlusconi sits forward on the couch.

"There used to be this colonel who ran the RAI advertising concession, Sipra. His name was Giovanni Fiore. He was the undisputed boss of all advertising. A friend of mine went to see him to buy some advertising space on the nightly Carousel. Fiore told my friend to return in a month. When he went back a month later Fiore told him, 'I am very sorry, but based on the information we have been able to collect, it seems that you are not a good Catholic.' My friend asked him what he was talking about. Without batting an eyelash, Fiore told him that according to his informants the businessman in question did not regularly attend mass in church on Sundays. So he waited another month. Then he went back to Fiore again and this time Fiore told him, 'Yes. I can confirm that you have indeed been attending mass, but it seems you have never taken Communion.' After that my friend went back to church and took his Communion wafer and finally the colonel at RAI allowed him to buy fifteen ads on Carousel."

Berlusconi has the look of a man who has made his point as he finishes recounting the story. But he has not finished saying what he really thinks of RAI.

"RAI, like every state broadcaster in Europe," says Berlusconi, "was considered the private property of the politicians. The only people who had access to television were journalist friends and the cronies of politicians, and businessmen who had a good relationship with the political parties."

In 1979, with his first commercial TV station already causing a stir in Milan, Berlusconi was buying up a string of stations around Italy. He was not going to play ball inside that system. He was going to change the rules. He was going to do things his way.

"When the court rulings came, Berlusconi had this intuition about challenging the state broadcasting monopoly," recalls Fedele Confalonieri. "He thought the liberalization of the market represented an extraordinary business opportunity. But to do that back in 1979 you needed to have a lot of courage. That was when Berlusconi decided he was going to try to compete with RAI. He understood that the deregulation meant opportunity at the local level, but this was not enough to achieve critical mass in terms of the business and revenues. So he put together a number of local and regional stations. The law did not permit either live broadcasting or news broadcasts. But it did allow prerecorded shows. So Berlusconi's challenge was how to attract big advertising revenues if he only had a string of local and regional stations that commanded lower prices."

The answer was to go for the bigger bucks by offering his advertisers a nationwide demographic instead of just a local market. Berlusconi would unify local stations and simulate the programming of a national TV network.

Using motorbikes, trucks, trains, and on occasion even light aircraft, Berlusconi created the illusion of a national television channel by getting the same master videotapes to each of the local and regional stations in time to synchronize the broadcast of a particular soap opera or other prerecorded show, and eventually the entire broadcast day. This resulted in the impression that up and down the Italian peninsula you were watching a single channel, even though you were actually watching a nationwide simulcast by local stations.

"By prerecording the master tapes and distributing them to the local stations, we created a de facto national network, and we could sell spots to the big advertisers like Coca-Cola," says Berlusconi. "To get a piece of the big bucks in the national advertising spend,

I invented a form of live television that wasn't really live. It was just taped as live and each station had to transmit the master tape at precisely the same moment so it looked to the viewer at home like it was a live broadcast."

This taped-as-live and simulcast system allowed Berlusconi to approach advertisers with a value proposition. But the advertising agencies, set in their ways and used to ruling the roost on the media scene, were proving an impediment. They were not buying the Berlusconi plan. So once again he changed the rules of the game. In 1979 he formed a company called Rete Italia and started buying up Italian TV rights to Hollywood blockbuster movies, soap operas, game shows, and sitcoms. He was forming a library of entertainment content that would soon compete against RAI. Then he cut out the agencies by creating his own in-house advertising agency, a company called Publitalia. He went directly to the advertisers and he offered a full package of sexy TV programming and modern spots that he would also produce for the advertisers.

"The agencies were taking big fat fees but they were only throwing us breadcrumbs," says Berlusconi. "It was the agencies that decided everything. So I decided to turn things upside down. It was pretty tough, fairly slow going at first. It took about three years to really break through. I used to come up with special introductory offers. One of them we called 'Operation Risk' in which we took the risk, gave an eighty percent discount to big advertising clients, and promised them their money back if their sales did not increase once they started advertising with us."

Berlusconi was now offering nationwide coverage that could be measured by national Nielsen audience ratings and other market metrics, and he was offering a one-stop-shopping service to produce and strategically place the spots where they would work best in the program schedule. It was here, in the strategic approach, the nationwide broadcast coverage, and in the new style of content, that he revolutionized the market. Gone were the old-fashioned black-and-white sketches and routines with actors endorsing products. In their place were Madison Avenue–style spots of the sort one would see on American television, punchy, in-your-face, and full of pretty women and lots of razzamatazz. Berlusconi made sexy and compelling advertising, he bundled it together with the biggest consumer brands on the market, and the Italians loved it.

Berlusconi knew what he was doing. The former cruise ship crooner turned real estate tycoon turned out to be a natural impresario in the world of show business and television. He had his finger on the pulse of the national taste, even if some of these tastes were more base than tasteful. In 1979 he recruited more of his former schoolmates and some of the veterans of the Milano Due project, and sent them to Hollywood to begin buying up movie rights. He began challenging RAI for the rights to live soccer matches. He even managed to outbid RAI for the Italian rights to the hit TV show *Dallas,* and he got Coca-Cola to become a key sponsor. He added soaps like *Dynasty* and *Beautiful,* and fashioned a lavish Saturday night variety show that featured scantily clad chorus girls and working-class humor. It was working.

In 1979, now armed with a string of regional TV stations, he registered a new trademark that would eventually prove his most valuable property: a television channel called *Canale 5,* or Channel 5. Pretty soon the master videotapes that were being shuttled around Italy with the latest hit TV episode also carried a little logo in the corner of the screen with the Canale 5 brand. The logo, which would become the general logo of all of Berlusconi's future ventures, took its inspiration from the eleventh-century family coat of arms of the aristocratic Visconti family of Milan. It featured a serpent eating a flower. It was already the symbol of Milan, with a version in use even on the grill of new Alfa Romeo cars. Now the serpent would become the symbol of Berlusconi's growing media empire.

In the late 1970s Berlusconi bundled his television interests into a new family holding company named Fininvest. But his closest collaborators remained the same. Fedele Confalonieri, whom he had met at Salesian College at the age of thirteen, was always at his side. Marcello Dell'Utri, from university days, was put in charge of the new in-house Publitalia '80 advertising agency that came after Rete Italia. But there was one man who made Berlusconi's dream of a national TV network into a reality. Today this man is better known in the world of soccer as the long-serving boss of the AC Milan soccer club. At the time he was a small entrepreneur from the Brianza farming region of Lombardy, a businessman who specialized in supplying equipment for broadcasters and in building and maintaining transmitters and repeaters for TV channels. His main client was a little broadcaster based in the principality of Monaco that was called TeleMontecarlo. The man who transformed Berlusconi's dream into a reality was Adriano Galliani.

"My first meeting with Galliani was in November 1979," recalls Berlusconi. "He had a company called Elettronica Industriale and they were specialized in this kind of work. He came to pitch me his technical services. I guess we found each other very *simpatico*. We had really good chemistry. Adriano Galliani was a real Brianza businessman, an extraordinary and very talented fellow. So we found ourselves in perfect synch."

Galliani, a jovial and bald-headed man in a natty blue suit and yellow tie, remembers that first meeting with Berlusconi on the afternoon of Thursday, November 1, 1979. It was All Saints' Day, a cool autumn day darkened by thick banks of low-hanging fog that surrounded the driveway leading to the Villa San Martino at Arcore.

"It is a day that is etched permanently on my memory," says Galliani. "I was supplying some high-voltage equipment for the TeleMilano broadcasts and one day I was invited by Berlusconi to come to see him at his villa at Arcore. I had read about him, and he was a client, but I had never met him before. I didn't know what he wanted. Fedele Confalonieri was also there. We were in the Room of Couches at Arcore. I had flown in to Milan from Tokyo the night before, where I had been attending an electronics convention, and so I was pretty jet-lagged. Berlusconi sat me down and he asked me flat out if I was capable of building him a broadcast transmission system for three national TV channels. His reasoning was that since RAI had three channels and he wanted to compete against RAI, he would also need to mount a challenge with the same dimension. I told Berlusconi that I could do it, and he immediately said that he wanted to buy fifty percent of my company. He told me to name my price and he would pay it. I looked at him for a minute and then I just said the figure of one billion lire. He said 'Fine!' It was done. Then we shook hands and I left the villa and that is how my adventure started. And soon after that we built Canale 5 as the first nationwide commercial TV channel."

Galliani did not actually build three new channels from scratch; Berlusconi would buy two others and then Galliani would grow them. But he was the key man on Berlusconi's team who helped create a national network. In 1982 Berlusconi managed to buy a second channel, Italia 1, from the Rusconi group, a struggling magazine publisher in Milan. He began applying the Berlusconi touch. Next came the purchase of a channel named Rete 4, this time also for a song because the legendary Mondadori book publishing empire needed cash and could not afford to compete with Berlusconi's bells-and-whistles extravaganzas on Canale 5. The stuffy publishing elite of Milan knew how to publish best-selling books but they had no idea how to run a commercial TV channel.

By the autumn of 1984, less than five years after his first meeting with Galliani, Silvio Berlusconi had achieved his goal. He was the proud owner of three national television channels, just as many as RAI. Canale 5 was the flagship, but the garish mix of sitcoms, showgirls, and soaps was proving a winning formula. Italia 1 and Rete 4 were also garnering market share.

In 1980 Berlusconi's had a 13 percent share of the Italian national audience, and state broadcaster RAI had more than 80 percent. Two years later RAI's audience share had slipped to 63 percent. By 1984 Berlusconi could boast not only nationwide coverage but an audience share almost equal to RAI's. Advertising revenues at Publitalia were soaring. The advertising arm of the Berlusconi empire racked up an average revenue growth of 48 percent a year throughout the 1980s. Revenues soared from $6 million in 1980 to $455 million by 1984. They would double again within the space of four years.

In Italy, as in America, Britain, and much of Western Europe, the mid–1980s was a period of newfound prosperity, of rising consumerism, fueled by the dreams that were advertised in TV spots. Berlusconi was selling an alternative lifestyle, of *Dallas* and pretty girls, of glitz and kitsch. He made a fortune as consumer advertising exploded alongside the "me generation," creating an army of newly rich yuppie consumers who would watch Canale 5 and Italia 1 and Rete 4. Just as London Weekend Television and ITV had challenged the primacy of the BBC in Britain, Berlusconi was offering a colorful alternative to state television in Italy.

By 1984 Berlusconi was an influential and significant player on the national scene. He was still an outsider, still a maverick, but he was becoming powerful. He was challenging the state broadcasting monopoly and he was conquering market share with a network of regional stations, despite the fact that they still could not broadcast live or offer news programs. From a strictly legal point of view, Berlusconi was not breaking the law, but he was getting around the law that placed in RAI the sole national broadcasting authority.

Culturally, he was splashing the new color television screens with huge gobs of pastel and Technicolor. The American-style commercial TV, adaptations of game shows such as *Wheel of Fortune* (hosted by the American Mike Bongiorno), and Hollywood films filled a tremendous void for an Italian public hungry for entertainment. Berlusconi's television was pure escapism, though all of this earned him the wrath of fashionable intellectuals and the guardians of radical-chic culture.

Confalonieri acknowledges that some of the early programming was garish, but he says it was radical for a time when everything else had been so dull.

"You have to understand the context, the way things were back then," says Confalonieri. "By the 1980s Italy had been living through years of recession and austerity and Red Brigades terrorism and the strong and continuing influence of the Italian Communist Party on society. In that context it was pretty revolutionary for Silvio Berlusconi to launch his commercial TV challenge against RAI. He was going against the prevailing culture and mind-set of the Italian establishment. He was offering an alternative lifestyle. That, in itself, was a political act."

Confalonieri traces the start of Berlusconi's political career to this moment, when his flamboyant and shamelessly commercial television began to really take hold in Italy, posing a challenge to the keepers of the traditional Christian Democrat mind-set.

"Berlusconi launched a television that exalted consumerism. It was full of flashy advertising spots. It was feel-good television. It was optimistic. It was pro-American. It was that great and energetic American kind of optimism. It was the exact opposite of the austere mind-set of the time, with all due respect to Communists and Catholics. So the real political revolution, not just cultural but political, began with television."

Despite Confalonieri's perspective on the revolution that Berlusconi unleashed, for the snobbish Italian business and financial establishment in Milan, Berlusconi was still a nouveau riche, an arriviste, an outsider. He might have become a billionaire media mogul, but he had not been born to riches. To the older families of cozy Milan society he was the object of derision and scorn. He was considered crass and inelegant.

Berlusconi did, however, have exceptionally good relations with at least one man in the Italian establishment who truly counted. In 1984 he was on highly familiar terms with the newly installed prime minister of Italy, a lanky Socialist named Bettino Craxi.

The new prime minister, broad-shouldered, stubborn, bespectacled, and bald, was a dear friend of Berlusconi's. He was a forceful man who presided over a complicated and rancorous five-party coalition government that was known as the *Pentapartito*. But Craxi was a pro-business Socialist, a full decade before the emergence of Tony Blair in Britain.

The two men had been friends for some time and Berlusconi was considered something of a sponsor or business supporter of

Craxi. In fact, one could say there were exceedingly close ties between the Craxi and Berlusconi families. In the summer of 1984, Prime Minister Craxi became the godfather of Berlusconi's daughter Barbara, who was born out of wedlock in Switzerland to Berlusconi's mistress, an actress named Veronica Lario. When Berlusconi eventually divorced his first wife and married Veronica, it was Craxi's brother-in-law, Paolo Pillitteri, the long-serving mayor of Milan, who presided at the wedding in Milan's City Hall. Berlusconi's best man was Bettino Craxi and Veronica Lario's maid of honor was Craxi's wife, Anna.

Craxi had taken office as prime minister a year before in 1983, and was already encountering the wrath of the Communists because he seemed willing to open the state-centric Italian economy to more private-sector competition. Berlusconi by now of course owned substantial interests that could be affected by government regulations and broadcast laws. As it turned out, his friendship with Craxi would prove decisive in protecting and nurturing these interests.

Berlusconi needed the help. In addition to being derided by Italian intellectuals as a purveyor of garish American sitcoms and soaps, he had an array of politicians and intellectuals against him, and he was despised by the state broadcaster and by competing newspaper publishers who feared he would drain away too much of their advertising revenue. Even worse, his foes were arguing that by effectively broadcasting on a nationwide level, he was breaking the laws that gave this privilege solely to RAI, the state broadcaster.

"There was great resentment in RAI and in the world of Italian politics. There was lots of hostility toward me," recalls Berlusconi. "I remember in the early 1980s having this terrible phone conversation once with the head of RAI, a man named Willy De Luca. He was furious that we were making inroads, taking audience share away from RAI. He told me I was crazy, that the politicians would destroy me. He even threatened me. 'Any day now,' he told me, 'the tax inspectors will come and get you.' I remember putting down the phone after that and my knees were shaking."

In Italy it is not unusual for investigating magistrates and prosecutors to coordinate their actions against a political foe or a judicial target. In the space of three days in October 1984, with Berlusconi clearly in their sights, magistrates in Rome, Turin, and Pescara ordered the blackout of his three TV channels. They cited illegal nationwide broadcasting as the reason. The move was a coordinated attack, and Berlusconi remembers it very well because it almost put him out of business.

"It was the start of a long war, with no holds barred," says an indignant Berlusconi. "The judiciary decided to move against me in 1984 by ordering the sequester of our broadcast transmitters. They shut us down because RAI filed a complaint, saying that our channels violated an article in the Constitution that gave public television the monopoly for nationwide broadcasting."

The ensuing legal and political battle pitted RAI, backed by the old warlords of Italy's Christian Democratic and Communist parties, against Berlusconi. Craxi, the Socialist prime minister who relied on the Christian Democrats to support his government coalition, was immediately dragged into the fray. Berlusconi asked for his help, and he got it. Within four days of the shutdown, Craxi had signed an emergency decree ordering that the broadcasting be resumed. This first decree became instantly known as the "Berlusconi Decree." It was highly controversial.

Perhaps the most surprising aspect of the judicial saga that autumn was not the blackout ordered by the magistrates itself but the popular protests that it triggered across Italy. Berlusconi's 1980s dream world of aspirational kitsch had struck home with a nation, with millions of families, and especially with mothers and their children. And they were angry. For one thing, the much loved and favorite program of many schoolchildren, *The Smurfs*, had been taken off the air. Gone were *Dallas*, and *Dynasty*, and *Wheel of Fortune*. Viewers were suddenly deprived of Richard Chamberlain in the miniseries *The Thorn Birds* and Robert Mitchum in *The Winds of War*. Italy was in an uproar. In an age well before Facebook and Twitter, Italians would express their anger by flooding the switchboards of newspapers with thousands of telephone calls. The true impact of Berlusconi's media power was clear when he ordered his TV channels to fill the screen with a card that contained the phone numbers of the offices of the magistrates in Turin, Rome, and Pescara, the number of the main switchboard at the Rome headquarters of RAI, and even the number of the prime minister's office. The viewers hit all of these numbers with a barrage of calls. Berlusconi's loyal viewing public was now in a fever, telephoning their protests across the nation. He had understood what the masses wanted. He had given them bread and circuses. And now they wanted it back.

"We were teetering on the brink of disaster when they shut us down," recalls Berlusconi. "But then the public rebelled. There were children protesting in the streets, carrying placards that read 'Give Us Back *The Smurfs!*' We had entered into the lives of the ordinary people and we had become part of the family life of millions of Italians. When we started our channels, the state broadcaster only showed programs in the evening. We were the first to broadcast shows in the morning, in the early afternoon, late at night. So we began to have a profound impact on the habits of the Italians, especially on the housewives who were at home and for the first time enjoyed the comfort of watching TV during the morning and daytime. But our biggest supporters were the companies that advertised on our channels, and the business associations. They put a lot of pressure on the politicians to reverse the ban, and they told Craxi and the others that without the ability to advertise on commercial television their sales and production would be affected. This was perhaps the strongest argument in our favor."

Craxi's decree putting Berlusconi's TV channels back on the air was so controversial that it was declared unconstitutional when he tried to get it approved in parliament a few weeks later, in November 1984. Craxi did not give up. He presented a second "Berlusconi Decree," which was eventually approved in February 1985. But this law expired at the end of the year, so Craxi had to introduce in June 1985 a third "Berlusconi Decree." This one would finally be signed into law, but only on condition that it eventually be replaced by full and proper legislation governing the regulation of television broadcasting and advertising in Italy. That would take a further five years, until 1990, and even then it was considered so controversial that five ministers of the government of the day resigned in protest, among them the current president of Italy, Sergio Mattarella, who at the time was minister of education. The entire left wing of Prime Minister Giulio Andreotti's governing Christian Democratic Party stormed out of the government in protest at the legalization of Berlusconi's private TV empire. But Craxi, no longer prime minister in 1990 but still the powerful leader of the Socialists, who were part of the ruling coalition government, had maintained his steadfast support.

There is no doubt that Craxi played a crucial role in saving and legalizing Berlusconi's television empire. Friendship has its benefits.

"I would say that yes, my friendship with Craxi helped, and played a part in his decision," says Berlusconi. "But I had also explained to Craxi in great detail how commercial television was fundamental for the economy, and that there was nothing for the political world to fear from commercial TV channels which were not even allowed to do news broadcasts. I was certainly grateful to Craxi for what he did, but I would also say that he had enough backing from his coalition partners to act."

Not everyone thought that Craxi signed this string of decree laws simply out of friendship for Berlusconi or because he was a more modern and pro-business Socialist. Berlusconi faced allegations that he had bribed Craxi, that he had paid him with slush funds and transferred money into offshore bank accounts. Italian magistrates opened investigations, they brought charges, and they alleged that Berlusconi-controlled companies had paid the equivalent of about $15 million into Craxi-controlled offshore bank accounts. Craxi and Berlusconi would be charged and convicted of illicit financing of political parties, but ultimately the guilty sentence would be canceled when the statute of limitations expired.

Berlusconi repeatedly denied all the charges, claiming they were only a "theorem" devised by left-wing magistrates.

"I never engaged in this kind of relationship with any politician," Berlusconi declares gravely.

Craxi would face a galaxy of corruption charges before he was convicted in absentia and died in exile at his vacation home in Tunisia.

"As for Craxi, who was accused of having made money out of political career, this is a man who left his wife and family in absolute poverty when he died. He left his wife destitute, with a mortgage to pay on the house in Tunisia and a mortgage to pay on his apartment in Milan. And believe me, I know all too well... because..." Here Berlusconi stops for a moment as though he is trying to decide how much more to add. Then he his eyes close for a nanosecond as he assumes a priestly face of piety.

"Let us say," adds Berlusconi in a very quiet voice, "that somebody intervened to help sustain the Craxi family, who were by then without any other financial means."

Berlusconi maintains his aplomb and seems to stare out at something in space as he continues his recollection.

"I remember on one occasion that Craxi spoke to me about the way his party was struggling financially, and I told him that I was there for him if he needed something. He sort of froze up and stared me in the eye and he said: 'You are my friend. Don't ever make such a proposal to me again or it will destroy our friendship.' That was the real Bettino Craxi. That was the much reviled Bettino Craxi. Sure, as he himself admitted in front of parliament, he needed money to finance his Socialist party. Just like the Christian Democrats needed money. And the other parties. They were all facing powerful competition from the Italian Communist Party, which was very well funded by Moscow. When they finally opened the KGB files it was clear that sixty-three percent of all the Soviet Union's funding of parties in Europe had gone to the Italian Communist Party. The other parties were struggling, and so they naturally looked to the private sector for help."

In the 1980s, the financing of political parties by private lobbies and business interests, whether through offshore bank accounts or by way of a cash-stuffed envelope, was considered to be a quite normal practice in Italy. When new laws were promulgated a few years later to tighten up on the financing of political parties, the Bribesville (*Tangentopoli*) scandals that erupted would sweep away half of Italy's political class. It was amidst the hurly-burly of the Tangentopoli scandals, as the magistrates unleashed a revolutionary attack on all the major political parties of the day, that Berlusconi started to nurture the idea of taking a stab at politics himself. But for now he was happy to be a man in full. He had morphed from being a real estate developer into a billionaire media mogul. His ties with Craxi and all the other politicians? It came with the territory.

To his critics, Berlusconi was now a much despised merchandiser of trash, the man who had killed Italian cinema with his commercial television, and the man who had only managed to keep his media empire together thanks to political help from Prime Minister Bettino Craxi. To his fans he was an innovator, an impresario, and a marketing genius with perfect intuitions and an unusual empathy for the common man. He was selling an aspirational lifestyle; he was giving pure, brazen, and escapist entertainment to a famished Italian public. He was selling dreams.

Or, as he once told a friend back in the 1980s, "I sell smoke."

From the beginning, Berlusconi had understood the ingredients that made for big-time television entertainment in Italy. Movies, soaps, variety shows...and sports. He bought soccer rights, lots and lots and lots of soccer rights. The soccer-crazy Italian public was grateful. RAI was as furious as ever. Berlusconi was constantly outbidding them for match rights. It was therefore not surprising that once he had legalized his commercial TV empire of three national channels, Berlusconi would start thinking about buying a soccer club. He could see the match between sports and broadcasting. And what better soccer club than AC Milan, the team that he had adored as a small boy in the stadium with his father.

Being Berlusconi, you don't just buy the soccer rights.

You buy the soccer team.

CHAPTER FOUR

———

Apocalypse Now

A TTACK! ATTACK!"
Silvio Berlusconi is screaming at the top of his lungs. He is standing in the corner of the locker room of the elite AC Milan soccer team, flanked by a high-strung and rather nervous coach.

The lithe and fragile Filippo Inzaghi, a former player who has been in the job only a few months, most of them terrible, is trembling. Berlusconi is jabbing him in the arm.

"So tell me, what does the coach shout from the bench?" demands Silvio Berlusconi. "Come on, say it! I can't hear you! Louder!"

Inzaghi was once a striker, a key player for both Juventus and Milan, one of the most prolific scorers of all time. But today he is like a rookie before his first professional match. He almost shivers as Berlusconi eggs him on, clearly uncomfortable.

"Attack!" he responds weakly, his voice seeming to fail him now as Berlusconi stares at the faces of the bemused players seated on benches around the room.

"No. No. No," scoffs Berlusconi. "Is that the best you can do? We are in a stadium. Let me show you how it's done." Berlusconi puffs out his chest like Popeye and screams at the top of his lungs the word "ATTACK!"

Volume up.

In Italian the melodic howl that emerges from Berlusconi's throat sounds like a cross between a bullhorn and an opera singer's baddest bass note.

AH-TAH-KAH-RAY!

The coach of AC Milan looks down at the floor and Silvio Berlusconi rubs it in.

"There ya go!" taunts a grinning Berlusconi, now grabbing poor Inzaghi's hand for a triumphant handshake. "Who knows how to do it better? Me! I am always *Numero Uno!*"

On this particular day, Numero Uno had arrived an hour earlier at Milanello, AC Milan's historic training camp. As usual, he had come by helicopter.

Milanello is located some fifty kilometers from the city, in the lush Lombard countryside. For Berlusconi, a man whose political fortunes were to be built on a party whose name (Forza Italia!) sounded like a soccer cheer, the weekly visits with his beloved soccer team, Milan, were and remain essential, even fundamental, for his psyche.

The use of the chopper on the way in and out is, of course, very Berlusconi.

On this autumn day, a Friday afternoon in early October, 2014, the blooms on the bushes are still bright and a warm breeze is blowing across the treetops. The branches begin to rustle further with the arrival of Berlusconi's Agusta Westland twelve-seater, the Mediaset logo emblazoned across its tail.

The helicopter touches down on what is in fact a basketball court converted into a helipad. Adriano Galliani, the soccer club's vice president, comes bounding out of a white luxury sixteen-seater Volkswagen Crafter van with tinted windows that is parked just beyond the radius of the chopper's still-whirling blades. The nervous coach Inzaghi follows in his trail. As Berlusconi and his bodyguards emerge from the helicopter, both men rush forward to welcome the boss.

As always, Berlusconi and his aides board the van with the vice president and the coach, ride the three or four minutes over to the clubhouse, and once there Berlusconi ambles in, all smiles, shaking hands and schmoozing the kitchen staff as he tours the players' dining room. While Berlusconi goes to the restroom, Inzaghi and Galliani settle into the president's dining room, where places are set on a plain white tablecloth adorned in simple fashion, with bottles of olive oil, balsamic vinegar, salt and pepper, two silver baskets filled with rolls and grissini, and two varieties of mineral water, one sparkling and one still.

When Berlusconi returns, the immediate focus of all the diners is on the prosciutto and melon, or, in Galliani's case, on the prosciutto and figs. This is followed by a delicate saffron risotto that Berlusconi cannot resist, even though he tells his guests it will ruin his diet.

Inzaghi sits at the head of the little table, fingering his food gingerly, sipping mineral water, and keeping his eyes trained on Berlusconi. Galliani seems to enjoy his food, and helps himself to seconds. He is affable and jocular, except when making derogatory remarks about "the arrogance" of Juventus, a recurring and understandable leitmotif for a man who had built Milan into a world power in soccer, always in the shadow of Juventus. In other words, Milan had a bit of an inferiority complex when it came to the team owned by Gianni Agnelli, Juventus.

Once he finishes his risotto, Berlusconi gives his coach a penetrating look and begins the interrogation. He has seen the last game, and he has studied carefully the players and their moves, he tells Inzaghi. He wants to talk formation, he wants to know who will start in the next day's match and who will remain on the bench. He wants to talk about Inzaghi designing a more offensive game.

Turning to Inzaghi, Berlusconi poses the first question.

"Who would you suggest we start with?"

"I would go for Muntari, because we need his strength," replies Inzaghi.

"Why not Poli?" shoots back Berlusconi, not losing a nanosecond.

It is not lost upon the nervous coach that he is seated at the same luncheon table where Berlusconi and Galliani have discussed—on countless other occasions and with his predecessors—the next game, the midfield, the defense, the attack, the state of health of some of the players, the playing order. This is the room where the positioning of players on the pitch has been discussed with legendary Milan coaches, with Sacchi and Capello and Ancelotti, with coaches who won no fewer than twenty-six cups. So Inzaghi chooses his next words with care.

"Poli is a good guy but he won't last until the ninetieth minute. I would not use him at the beginning," suggests the coach.

Berlusconi immediately changes the subject. He asks after the health of Mattia De Sciglio, another player, and then he asks, rather insistently: "But tomorrow who will be our midfielders? Shall we begin with De Jong?"

Inzaghi doesn't seem to like the idea but he nods his head in assent and mumbles something about De Jong being "essential" for the game. Seeing the coach in some difficulty, Galliani makes a joke about Inzaghi being a lady's man, about how Inzaghi is a man without vices except for his weakness for beautiful women. The coach smiles sheepishly. The tension seems to break. But there is no mistaking what has just happened. Berlusconi is speaking to his coach in an exceedingly direct manner. He has not just suggested the starting formation; he has requested it in unmistakable terms.

"Berlusconi," as his old friend Confalonieri once put it, "likes to be in charge."

Thanks to Galliani's levity, the air soon clears, lighthearted small talk returns, and then, after lunch, it is off to the changing rooms, to the gym and locker rooms, to meet the team.

The trio of Berlusconi, Galliani, and Inzaghi trudges across the green, across the first of seven soccer fields at the sprawling Milanello complex, the one adjoining the clubhouse and leading directly to a beige set of structures that house the changing rooms, the physiotherapy area, the extensive gym, and the swimming pool.

Inside the locker room the entire team is waiting, each player seated on a little steel fold-out stool, each player's name stenciled in black on a piece of white paper with the Milan logo that is pasted across the door of each locker, and on top of each locker sits the same regulation black duffel bag with the names of sponsors Adidas and Emirates emblazoned in white across each bag. The players rise in unison as Berlusconi sweeps in and greets each one by name.

"Here we are. How are ya? Doing well?" Berlusconi asks a bemused Stephan El Shaarawy, a striker.

"Are you feeling better?" he asks Jérémy Ménez, the French forward. "The papers said you were not so well."

"How is your wife?" he asks Fernando Torres, the center-forward. "And the kids? And the new house? Everybody is settling in then? No problems? Great."

"Happy birthday again, by the way!" he tells Cristián Zapata, a Colombian-born defender, usually center-back.

"You all healed now?" he asks Alex, a defender from Brazil. "Back in the game this week, huh?" Alex nods yes, he is fine and will be able to play again.

Now it is time for Berlusconi to rally the troops. He positions himself in the back of the locker room, with Coach Inzaghi at his side. He assumes a slightly professorial pose.

"So I watched you in the last two matches," he begins. "You succeeded in developing a harmonious game; it was entertaining, it was absolutely worthy of a great team. I saw that you did quite well during the corner kicks. I would like to remind you that you have to come together in the penalty area when the ball is already in the air, so that the instinctive reaction of defenders, who cannot look at both you and the ball, will be to try to block you directly in front. I have been given a lot of penalties with this system, but it must be well executed. And I remind you that fifteen or twenty minutes before the end of the match always remember: 'Keep possession of the ball!'"

The amused but respectful AC Milan team is smiling as Berlusconi proceeds with his little sermon. Adriano Galliani, standing in the corner of the locker room, stares at Berlusconi with a mixture of wonderment and concentration. Inzaghi nods his head in agreement with the boss.

Now Berlusconi turns to Inzaghi and starts jabbing him in the arm again. "So tell me, Coach, at this point, what does the coach shout from the bench?"

Inzaghi almost whispers the word "attack" and Berlusconi rolls his eyes.

"You have to say it louder," he tells the coach, and now Berlusconi bellows out the word again: "Attack! It means you attach that ball to your foot and you keep possession of the ball, and you swing around backwards and play the ball. Okay, Coach, now you try and let's see if they can hear you."

Inzaghi tries again. "Attack!" he cries out weakly.

"Louder!" says Berlusconi.

"I don't have any voice left," moans the hapless coach.

"Louder!" repeats Berlusconi. "We are in a stadium."

Inzaghi looks embarrassed but he makes another attempt. "Attack. Attack," he cries out, but the words still seem feeble.

"I can't hear you. Louder!" commands Berlusconi.

"Attack!" shouts the languid coach, but his voice is still a tenor.

"Oh, come on," taunts Berlusconi. "Let me show you how it's done." And then he lets loose a battle cry, a bass note so deep and resonant that it could have easily come from his days as a cruise ship crooner who had played the upright bass with Fedele Confalonieri.

AH-TAH-KAH-RAY!

"So who does it better?" asks a grinning Berlusconi as he grabs Inzaghi's hand in a half shake and half salute. "Me of course! I am always Numero Uno."

Then, as the players rise to salute Berlusconi, he says his farewells and continues his one-by-one tour of the team.

"Ciao. Ciao. Ciao and thank you to everybody," says Berlusconi as he pumps the hands of the players on the way out.

"Hey, congratulations on last week's goal, bravo, bravo," he tells Japanese player Keisuke Honda. It will be Honda who scores the key goal in the match a day later.

The last player Berlusconi greets on the way out is Sulley Muntari, the powerful midfielder from Ghana.

"Hey, when are you going to introduce me to your wife?" he asks a startled Muntari. "I would just like to meet her, just to see her. I am old, so I can't do anything anymore. But I would love to meet her because everyone says she is the most beautiful girl."

Muntari smiles. Berlusconi smiles. Inzaghi smiles, and he accompanies Berlusconi to the door.

Then, with one final wave, an ebullient Berlusconi whooshes out of the locker room and heads off to greet the staff in the gym next door. The players file out to the pitch and get ready to train.

Later that day, back at the clubhouse, when asked by a guest if he had ever dictated a formation to one of his coaches, Berlusconi is all smiles.

"Have I ever dictated a formation? No. Have I suggested one? Sure. Very often. I always have discussions with my coaches, and we have spoken often about the formation on the pitch, about individual players and before every single match. Sometimes I disagree with the coach, and in this case the coach always wins. So I have never really abused the fact that I am the owner and the president of the club. I have never tried to be superior to the coach. After all, he is the man responsible for the team's results. With Sacchi, for example, we invented the formula for a Milan that would always take charge of the pitch, we invented a team that would enjoy playing the game, that would respect its adversaries and that would be applauded by the fans for this, and I think that by now this concept is deeply embedded in the DNA of Milan."

Galliani, who has watched Berlusconi interact with countless coaches over the years, smiles knowingly.

"He may not have dictated the formation," says Galliani, "but Silvio Berlusconi certainly does love to talk about the game, the technical and tactical aspects of the game. He loves to talk with the coaches, sort of in the way the owner of a newspaper likes to speak with his editor. The owner appoints the editor and the editor is free to decide his editorial line. But the owner can change the editor if he wants to. Same thing with the owner of a club and his coach."

It is now late in the afternoon, and Berlusconi and Galliani are seated on comfortable white couches in the living room of the clubhouse, strips of fading sunlight streaming through the white lace curtains that frame the floor-to-ceiling glass walls that look onto the pitch. Across the green, in the distance, are the changing rooms and gym.

Galliani is a playful sort, as well known a lady's man as the coach he had been teasing before. He is always full of stories and anecdotes. He is also the ultimate Berlusconi groupie, a sincere fan, a real friend, a serious business partner, and his right-hand man when it comes to AC Milan, as he had been in the early days of commercial television before. In the life of Berlusconi, Galliani is one of the man's most important alter egos, almost on a par with Fedele Confalonieri in terms of closeness and friendship. He watches intently now as Berlusconi speaks about what brought him to buy Milan back in 1986, and about the real meaning of Milan in his life.

"You know," begins Berlusconi, "for me it was like a dream come true to walk in here, to arrive in Milanello the first time as the president of the club. That was a dream I had lived together with my father. You have no idea how many times I would go to the stadium with my father and we would lose and I would cry afterwards. Dad would always console me, and he would always tell me: 'You'll see. Milan will win next time. You just have to keep wanting to win.'

"The real significance of Milan for me," says Berlusconi, "is that Milan reminds me of my childhood, and it reminds me of my father. My father and I would talk about Milan almost every night when he returned home from work. After asking me about my homework I would always steer the conversation to Milan. It was not a great team at the time, and it never won anything. But in that soccer team I saw myself transported somehow. I identified with individual players. I fantasized. So when I was first contacted in 1986 about the possibility of buying Milan, I immediately thought of my father, and I went for it. This is at least part of why I bought Milan, even though at the time it was a pretty mediocre club with lousy results and a terrible losing streak."

Confalonieri, Berlusconi's other major alter ego, remembers discussing the potential purchase of Milan as far back as the late 1970s. The snobbery toward Berlusconi back then did not help his cause.

"Silvio and I had been Milan fans since we were kids," recalls Confalonieri. "I would go to the stadium with him all the time, and especially with his father, who was a major fan. The first time Berlusconi thought about making an offer to buy Milan was at the end of the 1970s. Milan was a bit of a mess back then, and the captain, Gianni Rivera, did not like Berlusconi at all, and he managed to block the deal from going through. You can imagine, having an owner like Berlusconi is not so easy. From the moment he walks in he takes charge. I remember in the early 1980s that Milan continued to be a disaster, losing all the time, getting demoted to Serie B on two occasions, a complete disaster. So when Berlusconi started talking about buying Milan again in the autumn of 1985, several of us were opposed to the idea. I even remember Galliani having doubts. Galliani had experience in soccer. He had been vice president of AC Monza, and he was saying that the financial accounts were not so clear. We were afraid that after buying Milan we would discover some secret hidden bank debt or some other unpleasant financial surprise. But Berlusconi was determined. He wanted to buy Milan, and in my opinion it was mainly out of passion."

Galliani remembers the crucial moment of decision as being between Christmas and New Year's Day, at the end of 1985.

"We were together at Berlusconi's house in St. Moritz," recalls Galliani. "It was the place that had previously been owned by the shah of Iran, Reza Pahlavi. And it was there that Berlusconi decided to buy Milan. I advised against it because I knew how much money it can cost to own a soccer club. So I told him that it was a beautiful idea but would cost him an endless ocean of money. Berlusconi didn't answer me. We left St. Moritz and on the private jet he was silent all the way back to Milan. It was just me and him and Confalonieri. Then, as we are landing at Linate Airport in Milan, after a forty- or fifty-minute flight during which Silvio Berlusconi remains completely silent, he suddenly speaks. All the way down from St. Moritz he has been thinking about my warning that he should be very careful about the deal, and he has been thinking about the enthusiasm of his childhood friend Fedele Confalonieri, the big Milan fan, who at this point is all in favor of doing the deal, and then just as we were landing, just as we are rolling down the tarmac, Berlusconi announces his decision to us: 'Let's go and take Milan!' he says."

On that day Berlusconi sent his team in to make the final arrangements. On February 20, 1986, the deal was signed. Silvio Berlusconi, the real estate tycoon turned media mogul, now owned AC Milan. As if this was not enough, on the same day, or more precisely later that evening, Berlusconi and Galliani and Confalonieri boarded the private jet and flew from Milan to Paris, in order to be present for the launch of Berlusconi's first French commercial general entertainment television channel, La Cinq.

"It is a day I will never forget," says Galliani. "We flew to Paris to launch La Cinq, the first on-air broadcast from our new French TV channel. It was the first commercial TV network in France. It was an amazing day that began with the purchase of AC Milan and ended with Berlusconi conquering France. We celebrated that evening at the restaurant Le Jules Verne at the Eiffel Tower, with plenty of Champagne, and with a Bordeaux by Mouton Rothschild that I can still remember. It was very excellent."

Having bought the team, Berlusconi now wanted to make a spectacular debut in the world of soccer.

"Since I came out of the world of show business and television," Berlusconi recalls, "I figured we needed something splashy, something that would make news, something different. When we were planning to present the team in the Arena stadium in Milan,

I remember thinking about that scene in *Apocalypse Now* where the helicopters swoop in from on high. We had this idea: The players would emerge, elegantly, from the helicopters and they would wave to the crowds, and I would make a speech about how proud I was."

Galliani well remembers the arrival of the helicopters, the Wagnerian moment of three choppers arriving at the stadium while speakers blared out thunderous waves of *The Ride of the Valkyries.* "We wanted the public to be wowed. So Berlusconi landed in the middle of the stadium, and out of the helicopters came the entire team," says Galliani. "The small stadium was full of Milan fans, nearly ten thousand people."

Berlusconi's carefully planned and audacious *Apocalypse Now* moment was nearly rained out as a summer thunderstorm hit Milan on that morning of July 18, 1986. The downpour was brutal, and the Milan fans were drenched. They did not seem to mind as the players streamed out of the helicopters on the pitch: Massaro, Tassotti, Maldini, and the captain of the team, Franco Baresi. Silvio Berlusconi's Milan has arrived in the heart of Milan, in the stadium where Milan originally played.

At forty-nine years of age, Berlusconi on that day fulfilled another one of his dreams. After the relaunch and reset of AC Milan in July 1986, Italian soccer would never again be the same.

The key to Berlusconi's revival of AC Milan was spending lots of money on players and coaches and management in order to build the brand, and especially in order to develop a more offensive and attack-oriented team. The strategy was clear. The cost was astronomical.

"AC Milan is not quoted on the stock market," says Galliani, "and so we don't disclose this information, but I think it would be fair to say that since 1986 Milan has cost a few hundred million euros. Passion is a very expensive luxury."

Over the ensuing years, Berlusconi might have spent a cumulative total of a few hundred million euros, but he also built a team that had at least a few hundred million euros of value. The team of

Berlusconi and Galliani seemed to have the right intuitions about the buying and selling of players, and about winning trophies. One of the keys to this was the choice of a succession of coaches, all predecessors to Inzaghi, who seemed to come from nowhere and yet frequently proved to be world-class winners. The first such choice was Berlusconi's recruitment in 1987 of Arrigo Sacchi, who had been coaching the modest Serie C and Serie B team of Parma, and who for the Italian sports press seemed to lack credibility. Berlusconi recalls having hired him shortly after his team, Parma, had beaten AC Milan at the group stages of a Coppa Italia match.

"I thought Sacchi would be the right coach for Milan because I had been observing how his team played, a team that was not playing defensively, like so many Italian teams," recalls Berlusconi. "For many years Italian soccer was a game that was played defensively, as though a tied score was good enough. Sacchi was exhorting his team to play hard and to win, to want to attack. I remember first meeting him for lunch, together with Galliani. I liked him a lot even though he seemed to be a difficult character."

Sacchi joined Milan on July 1, 1987, and he began showing his mettle immediately, thanks to his force of will, his strategic brain, and his intelligent use of Berlusconi's money. He was able to sign the Dutch trio of Ruud Gullit, Marco van Basten, and Frank Rijkaar. These legendary stars would give Milan the attacking power they were looking for. Stars and management in place, the club began to rack up victories. Milan won the *scudetto* for the 1987–88 season, and the Champions League trophy, the European Cup for 1988–89, which it won a second consecutive year in 1989–90. It appears that Berlusconi did not succeed in imposing a formation very often with Sacchi.

"Sacchi had a very strong and decisive character," says a diplomatic Berlusconi. "It was hard to change his mind about anything. He was a proud man, very determined. But he turned out to be a very good choice. We launched a buying campaign together and we succeeded in making Milan a more offensive, a more aggressive team."

Galliani concurs.

"We had four good years with Arrigo Sacchi, winning a *scudetto* and lots of cups. Everything was perfect. Then Sacchi decided that he wanted to become coach of the Italian national team. But we got lucky. After Sacchi we had another legendary coach, another one of Berlusconi's intuitions, Fabio Capello. He had been a great player but at this point he was a TV commentator and he was managing our volley and rugby teams. So what happens if you take a manager who is not involved in soccer anymore and you stick him on the bench as the coach? What happened was that Fabio Capello won the *scudetto* of 1991–92, and again the *scudetto* for 1992–93, and again the *scudetto* for 1993–94. Then he enjoyed three back-to-back Champions League final appearances between 1993 and 1995, winning the cup in 1994, and then he won the *scudetto* again in 1996. With Capello as the coach of Milan it really was like *The Ride of the Valkyries*."

"I first met Capello when he was a player," recalls Berlusconi, "and I always thought he would make a good manager of a club. So I asked him to attend management school and he did that. Then I asked him to supervise three or four of our teams, which were hockey, rugby, volleyball, and baseball. He did a pretty good job and so when I needed a new coach I thought of him. We had the entire press against us with the newspapers claiming that I wanted to be the real coach and that I had just appointed Capello to be my *maggiordomo*. But that wasn't the way it was. Capello proved himself immediately with his many successes. He was a very good guy, very concrete, very positive. It was a pleasure to work with him."

After Capello, the duo of Berlusconi and Galliani scored again when they hired their third great coach at AC Milan, Carlo Ancelotti, who led the team to some of its greatest successes in the early years of the twenty-first century.

"Ancelotti was a hard worker, and he was always open to new ideas," says Berlusconi. "We were always in total harmony, in total synch about the formation. He also had an excellent rapport with the players. A great coach is not just technically competent but someone who acts almost like a father to the team. A great coach inspires and brings out feelings of respect and sympathy in his players, even feelings of affection. Ancelotti did this extremely well. I used to call him the father of our team. And when you come to think about it, that first trio of legendary coaches we had at Milan—Sacchi, Capello, and Ancelotti—well, that would be pretty hard to replicate any time soon."

Indeed for AC Milan, after the departure in 2009 of Ancelotti, things would never be the same again. With twenty-eight cups and trophies, Milan had become the second-most titled club in the world, but gone was the *Apocalypse Now* spirit, and in its place was a string of neophyte coaches, some with a really short tenure. Ancelotti was followed by a Brazilian named Leonardo, who had been a midfielder at Milan under Ancelotti. He lasted twelve months. Then came Massimiliano Allegri, who won the Serie A championship in 2011 but then went on a losing streak that lasted for more than two years before he was replaced by Clarence Seedorf of the Netherlands. But Seedorf was sacked by Berlusconi after less than six months and replaced in 2014 by the youthful Inzaghi, himself a former striker for Milan. These men, like Capello, did not always have experience as Serie A coaches; in fact, Berlusconi seems to positively thrive on choosing less experienced and novice coaches for AC Milan. Regardless of what he claims, he clearly wants men who will listen to him.

"For me this is not about a strategy or particular vision of the game, it is more about the man, about choosing one's collaborators. If you hire an older coach, certainly you have the advantage of his experience. But hiring a younger coach means he may be leaner and hungrier, more enthusiastic, and he may be more open to advice and to suggestions, to indications that are given by the executive management of the club."

Unfortunately for Berlusconi his latest hire of a younger coach, the inexperienced Inzaghi, would not work out too well. Inzaghi would later end up being replaced by a tough older coach from Serbia named Sinisa Mihajlovic.

Berlusconi can harp on endlessly about the tactics and strategy of a game, and on the need for elegance and style in the world of soccer. He may have bought and sold some of the world's most expensive players, including some of the more eccentric and troublesome stars from the pitch, but he remains a traditionalist, with an old-fashioned sense of the beautiful game. That includes his own personal brand of what he calls "Milan style," which is not so much about fashion as about looks and behavior.

"Milan style is about good behavior, both on and off the pitch," says Berlusconi. "It is about being a loyal adversary, about remaining cool no matter what happens. It is also about the way you present yourself, physically. Today, for example, so many players are covered in tattoos and have strange haircuts. In my days, and I am sorry to put it this way, I used to double-check my players personally to see if the knots of their ties were tied properly before they went on TV to make a statement."

Berlusconi likes order. He likes neatness. He does not like tattoos. And he does not like star player Mario Balotelli, who once played for AC Milan but was seen as more of a showman than an effective scorer.

"I guess," he says with a heavy sigh, "that I am from another generation. The truth is that I cannot stand either tattoos or piercing, nor do I like the strange haircuts of a player like Balotelli. I would like to see my Milan return to the elegance and style that was once part of its history."

In the main room of the clubhouse the light is no longer streaming in through the curtains; the day is now fading. Berlusconi is talking excitedly. He makes repeated reference to the team as "my Milan." He is a fountain of recollections, of memories and of moments of great emotion in the stadium. He seems transported somehow as he relives some of the team's greatest victories and defeats. Now he is speaking of one of his happiest moments, of the moment in Barcelona when the team scored a historic victory over Steaua Bucharest on the evening of May 24, 1989. There were 80,000 Milan supporters in the stadium.

For millions of Milan fans, that game with Steaua Bucharest was an epiphany, a defining moment in the evolution of the new AC Milan.

"That night, that victory in Barcelona, marked the first time we scored a victory on the international stage. Milan played an extraordinary game, and for a moment Milan seemed like the strongest team in the world, with a practically perfect playing technique. All day long, on the streets of Barcelona, you could see nothing but waves and waves of Milan banners and armies of Milan supporters. It was such a beautiful stadium that night, and it was really great when at the end of the match the Milan supporters in the stands all lighted candles in unison; it was like a paradise of stars that lasted all night long."

Without a trace of irony Berlusconi recalls further details of that victorious night.

"We went to the hotel and I even made a speech from the balcony. I felt like a young Mussolini," he says with an embarrassed giggle, "and the Milan fans called on me to come out and celebrate the victory with them. Anyway, it was our first big Champions Cup victory, and it will always stay in my heart, and in the hearts of all Milan fans."

Berlusconi's memories of Barcelona may be exuberant, but he scowls when he recounts the most painful moment in his history as owner of AC Milan. That, he says, was during the quarterfinal Champions League match in Marseille on March 20, 1991, when Milan played against the home team at the Vélodrome stadium. The night the lights went out.

This was Milan's return match with Olympique de Marseille; it had drawn 1–1 with Marseille just two weeks earlier in the first leg. Milan was the defending champion and this was the quarterfinals. It was a contentious match, with the referee issuing no fewer than five yellow cards, three to Milan and two to Marseille. Not a single goal was scored until well into the second half, when Marseille finally took the lead with a seventy-fifth-minute goal from winger Chris Waddle. With little more than two minutes of time remaining, in the eighty-seventh minute of play, and with Marseille leading 1–0, the game was suddenly halted because of floodlight failure. The lights, quite literally, went out. Some fifteen minutes later, when the lights came back on, Milan refused to resume play, arguing that the lighting was still not working well enough and that television crews and Marseille fans had disrupted the game by going onto the field. Galliani had personally halted the match. He had come out onto the pitch and ordered the team back to the benches. He had taken Milan off the field.

In the end, the Union of European Football Associations (UEFA) gave Marseille the game by forfeit, ending Milan's hopes of winning a third straight European title. Marseille was given a 3–0 automatic walkover. AC Milan was then banned from European club soccer for a year, charged with having refused to complete a Champions Cup quarterfinal match. Galliani would also suffer, and in more ways than one. UEFA barred him from all official functions for two years.

Silvio Berlusconi remembers it with a grimace, with evident distaste. He puts the blame squarely on his alter ego.

"It was all Galliani's idea, although he made that call after a series of taunts and provocations from the bleachers, and from the referee and from the Marseille players. It was an extremely tense moment. Everyone was very nervous. Galliani was sick and tired of all the irregularities he perceived in the course of the match and he let himself go and he made this decision, which cost us, of course. But it was Galliani's decision, and he has always owned up to it. He has always accepted full and complete responsibility for his actions."

Galliani now seems a bit uncomfortable as he leans forward on the couch. That decision ranks as his personal Vietnam. He remembers it with a pained and solemn look on his face.

"It was three, four, maybe five minutes before the end of the match, and suddenly the floodlights go out," says Galliani, trying to brave a smile. "Everything suddenly went dark. You couldn't see properly on the pitch. Some of the fans thought the game was over and came running onto the field. I managed to get on the field and I went to the referee and I told him that this was all highly irregular, with the public now lining the inside border of the field and half the floodlights still out. The referee said we had to play. I insisted and told him to get the public off the field. The referee said we had to play and I said again that it was irregular and I argued. And then I took this decision, I made what was definitely a mistake. I attribute it to a moment of unbridled emotion, but I really believed that there was not enough light to play properly, and that we could not play with the Marseille fans on the playing field, screaming and taunting. That's how it ended. It is absolutely true that I made this decision. Milan ended up getting disqualified for a year, and I was disqualified for two years, but only internationally and not back in Italy. And Silvio Berlusconi kept me in my job, and right after that we began to win the *scudetto* again in 1992, and the Champions League in 1994."

So no regrets?

Galliani takes off his glasses and comes up smiling.

"Regrets, sure, because this episode was not very elegant, certainly not in line with Milan style. But I figure that this was twenty-four or twenty-five years ago and so by now the statute of limitations has expired for this particular murder."

Galliani may have outlasted the statute of limitations at Milan, but the game of soccer has changed. The market has become global as new moneyed investors fueled by petrodollars have become the latest rich men to dabble in owning soccer franchises and developing the brand.

Berlusconi describes a world of soccer that has changed almost beyond recognition, a globalized sports marketplace that places prohibitive prices on the buying and selling of major players, whether they play for Real Madrid or Chelsea or Milan. Berlusconi speaks of a world peopled by Asian and Arab billionaires, of new investors and sheiks who have come forward to acquire clubs across Europe. He worries about his ability to compete in a world made of sheiks or clubs with mega-budgets like Real Madrid and Barcelona.

"In the case of Real Madrid and Barcelona, these are clubs with venerable traditions and deep roots in their respective cities. These are real cooperatives where the fans are the shareholders, and they both have rather deep pockets. As for the Middle East and Asian investors, it is getting very hard to compete with club owners who have petroleum in the ground."

Berlusconi now shifts again on the white couch. It is past six in the evening, and he seems ready to leave. Soon he will head back to his chopper for the fifteen-minute flight back to Arcore. The day at Milanello seems to have revitalized him. He has been talking soccer. His passion. Indeed Berlusconi's lifelong obsession with soccer is one of the defining elements of the man's psyche. It informs his approach to business, to entertainment, to politics, and to life in general.

"I think of soccer as a universal metaphor for life," says Berlusconi. "It is not only a national passion in Italy but around the world. It is a contrast between good and evil, between friends and enemies, and there is a referee who must be impartial. Just like in life. There is an adversary, and you have to face him, and you have to want to be better than him, and you have to beat him with elegance and style, you have to play beautifully and not in a careless manner. You have to convince everyone who is watching that you are the best of them all, just as one must do in life."

Italy, of course, is a soccer-crazed country, so Berlusconi's occasionally serendipitous flights of fancy about soccer and AC Milan have a context.

But in his life, being the president of Milan was more than just a dream come true. He was no longer just an *arriviste* real estate developer from Milan who had made a lot of money. He was no longer the property tycoon who had invented commercial television and had made his second fortune in media. He was now the owner of a proper soccer club. He was a player. He was a folk hero. And he owned a powerful set of brands and communications tools, spanning the worlds of entertainment, media, and sport. The billionaire media tycoon now owned the rights to a soccer cheer that could unite millions of Italians. To the ears of Milan fans, and not only Milan fans, the sound of "Forza Milan" was inspirational, optimistic, and cheerful. But in the hands of Silvio Berlusconi the soccer chant of "Forza Milan" was about to morph into the political battle cry of a new political party named Forza Italia. He was about to take his act onto the national stage, transforming himself one final time, from billionaire businessman into founder of a political party. And he would do it all in the idiom of soccer, exploiting the notoriety and fame bestowed by his ownership of Milan. At a time when Italy's entire political system was imploding, in the wake of the scandals, suicides, and corruption trials of the early 1990s, Silvio Berlusconi would decide to take the field. He would do so by inventing a new political party that was named after a soccer chant and staffed initially by the marketing team of his television network.

This time the stakes would be far higher than any Champions League match. This time Berlusconi would face the battle of his life.

CHAPTER FIVE

The Billionaire Prime Minister

Everyone told me not to do it. My closest friends and advisers and my entire family warned me not to go into politics. They were all against it. My mother was bitterly opposed to the idea. She said that if I went into politics I would end up hurting myself, my family, my children, and my businesses."

Silvio Berlusconi is sitting at a lacquered teak table in the garden of the Villa San Martino. He is reliving those early days in the spring and summer of 1993, in the run-up to his videotaped announcement in early 1994 that he would run for public office. Like a proper soccer fan, he would tell the nation that he had decided to "take the field." It would be an audacious launch, complete with a meticulous marketing plan worthy of Madison Avenue. The product being offered to the Italian public was Berlusconi himself, together with a new political party that he had invented and named after a soccer cheer. The party would be called Forza Italia.

By the early 1990s Berlusconi was already a big deal in his native Italy. He was also becoming known across European politics and business. He had launched commercial TV channels in France, Germany, and Spain that sought to replicate the success of Canale 5 and his Italian network. He had done battle with politicians and regulators across half of Europe in his quest to grow his media empire.

By now Berlusconi was close to being Italy's richest man. He was a newly minted billionaire and very much at the top of his game. He was Europe's answer to Rupert Murdoch. He had made it onto the list of the world's leading billionaires that *Forbes* compiled each year, the global rich list. But he was controversial.

Aside from the TV empire, which would be rebranded as Mediaset and floated on the Milan stock market with an initial value of $5 billion, he had expanded and diversified the empire still further. He now had interests that spanned media, insurance, personal finance, property and construction, department store retailing, and publishing. He had taken over the Mondadori publishing group in a controversial deal and now controlled 40 percent of the Italian magazine market. He had bought into a center-right national newspaper called *Il Giornale*, which had been founded by a legendary libertarian journalist-intellectual named Indro Montanelli. Then of course there was the trophy-winning soccer club, AC Milan, which brought him millions of fans across the nation.

By 1993 Berlusconi had become quite famous, or, if you were a critic, quite notorious. For the left he had become the bogeyman, a fierce anti-Communist entrepreneur with lots of media power.

His commercial television empire remained under fire from left-wing commentators, politicians, and intellectuals. They kept his TV channels in the spotlight, claiming that he was debasing culture and grabbing too much of the national advertising pie. The legalization of his media empire after the Craxi decrees of the 1980s had only just been finalized, thanks to the new law in 1990 that would establish a de facto duopoly in the Italian media market, with Berlusconi allowed to keep his three channels alongside RAI, the public television network. In order to comply with the new legislation, he had to divest his newspaper holdings; this was not a problem, since he simply transferred the equity stake to his younger brother, Paolo, who alongside cousins and other family relations had in any case been part of the Fininvest shareholding structure for years.

By 1993, in his native Italy, Berlusconi was no longer just a billionaire media mogul. By virtue of his spectrum of holdings, he wielded political power. He had clout. But not all was well in the Berlusconi empire. The recession of the early 1990s and the drop in advertising revenues had hit him hard. His television empire was growing but so were its debts, which now amounted to more than quadruple his net equity. His bank lenders, part of the Milan establishment, put the screws to Fininvest and forced it to install a professional outside manager named Franco Tatò. His job was to cut costs and reduce the company's debt. His work proved so successful that within twenty-four months the media empire's debut on the Milan bourse was hailed as a stock market success and by the end of the decade was worth more than $30 billion.

In addition to the financial problems, in 1992 and 1993 Berlusconi began to attract the attention of a growing number of adversaries in the Italian judiciary. A small band of Milanese magistrates and judges had begun to place Berlusconi's business interests under intense scrutiny. In little more than a year, they opened nearly a dozen separate investigations into his real estate, media, and construction businesses in Milan and Rome.

Berlusconi remembers this period all too well because it was the start of a series of major corruption scandals that would rock the Italian political establishment and would lead to the disgrace, exile, and eventual conviction of his friend Bettino Craxi. It was the beginning of a judicial earthquake in Italy known variously in English translation as either Kickback City or the Bribesville scandals, and in Italian as Tangentopoli.

For more than two years a handful of Milan magistrates had led the investigations, characterized by the arrest of armies of bookkeepers and bagmen who would be imprisoned until they named names in exchange for lighter sentences or plea bargains. The magistrates made fulsome use of dawn raids and surprise tax inspections. They made dozens of arrests and detained some of Milan's leading corporate executives and entrepreneurs, almost all of them accused of the illicit financing of political parties or making bribes to win contracts. They uncovered a systematic network of bribery that implicated just about everybody in Italian business and politics.

The probe became known as Operation Clean Hands, and it washed away an entire generation of party leaders. It caused the overnight collapse of much of Italy's political establishment. A number of entrepreneurs and businessmen who had been arrested committed suicide in prison. The air was rife with intrigue in Milan, with tales of envelopes stuffed with bribes being handed to politicians and rumors of who would be the next celebrity arrest. The newspapers were filled with stories of offshore bank accounts and money laundering. Employees turned against bosses, the magistrates tightened the screws, and those who traded information for plea bargains set off a chain of still more bribery and corruption scandals.

Berlusconi speaks of this period as a time of "terror" and "anguish" for him.

In 1992, his brother, Paolo Berlusconi, came under multiple judicial investigations. He was indicted on charges of bribery and corruption in both Rome and Milan. In April 1993 Berlusconi's chief lobbyist in Rome, a vice president of Fininvest named Gianni Letta, admitted to having personally stuffed an envelope with about $35,000 in cash and sent it across Rome, by messenger, to the leader of a small political party. That spring the tax inspectors descended again on Berlusconi's corporate headquarters in Milan. They raided his offices at Milano Due. In June 1993, Fininvest put out a formal denial of any wrongdoing and took pains to note that the company's offices had been raided by the tax police no fewer than fifty-seven times so far. The investigating magistrates did not stop at Berlusconi's television and property companies; they also investigated what they said was a pool of slush funds allegedly being used by Berlusconi's associates to buy and sell players at his beloved AC Milan.

The anti-corruption campaign driven by this tiny band of Milan magistrates was having a widespread impact on Italian politics and society. It was driving a truck through the old established order, decimating the careers of dozens of politicians and business-men in its trail. The comfortable salons of Milanese finance were filled with paranoia, while in Rome the leaders of each and every one of the five governing parties were systematically indicted and disgraced. They went down like bowling pins, one after the other.

"When the Bribesville phenomenon occurred, the five parties that had been governing Italy at the time were simply erased from the political scene," recalls Berlusconi. "What began to emerge from the investigations was the impression that the political leaders were all personally profiting from the party financing, which was true in some cases. But soon it was pretty clear that in the majority of the cases, starting with Bettino Craxi, the money had been used mainly to finance the functioning of the political parties, and not for personal gain."

Berlusconi argues that these private-sector contributions had become the norm in Italy in the absence of alternative or public funding for political parties.

In other words, everybody did it. Or, as they say in Italian, *cosi fan tutti.*

Bettino Craxi, symbol of the Old Order, later sent written testimony to the investigating magistrates in which he specified that his political party, like others, had regularly received money from Italy's biggest corporations, including Fiat, Olivetti, and Fininvest.

"There simply was no other financing of the parties at the time," recalls Berlusconi. "There were no other options, with the exception of the Italian Communist Party. They were always very well funded. They got tons of illegal and secret financing from the Soviet Union and they controlled business cooperatives up and down the country. They also had their own party newspaper. The Italian Communist Party was very powerful, very well funded back then. So when the scandals swept away the moderate parties, I began looking around, searching for an alternative to the Communists. I was trying to put together an association of parties that could stand up to the Communists. I was worried that if there was no other party or moderate political force in Italian politics, then the Communists would end up winning the next elections virtually unchallenged."

It was in this cauldron of fear and loathing that Berlusconi made his decision in the summer of 1993 to go into politics. He began using the marketing team at his television empire to conduct focus groups and opinion polls. They studied opinion polls and voter preferences the way a marketing team studies the promotion of a soft drink. In July 1993, Berlusconi denied in a newspaper interview that he planned to go into politics. The public's reaction was carefully analyzed by his team. Meanwhile, he went to see the few political leaders left standing and tried to convince them to form a united front, a coalition. But the Italian political landscape was a desert by the summer of 1993.

In Italy, most people would agree that Berlusconi went into politics to save his businesses and to achieve parliamentary immunity from investigation. That is the widespread belief. That is obviously not the way Berlusconi sees things. He claims he had no other choice. He says he decided to jump into the political arena after the Operation Clean Hands probe had transformed the landscape of Italian politics into scorched earth.

What was striking was that even though the Berlin Wall had fallen four years earlier, in 1989, and even though the Italian Communist Party had changed its name to the Party of the Democratic Left in 1991, Berlusconi still saw the main threat to himself, his businesses, and his nation as the risk of being governed by the newly renamed but old-fashioned Italian Communists. He had then, and he still has today, a visceral hatred, an almost corporal dislike for the hard left. It is reciprocated.

The word "communist" in Berlusconi's rhetoric is an umbrella term for everything he despises.

"The left-wing prosecutors were going crazy," says an agitated Berlusconi, tapping his left foot repeatedly now, up and down. "They were going especially crazy at the Milan prosecutor's office. As a result, the five political parties were erased from the map. That left a big opening for the left. For the first time in fifty years it looked like they could win power and remain in power for who knows how long. For me, all of this represented a tragedy, but not just for me. The threat of the Communists taking over Italy scared lots of businessmen because we all knew what Communist ideology represented. Let's just say that we did not exactly think that a victory of the Italian Communists would bring about the creation of a terrestrial paradise."

It was at this moment in 1993 that the Milan prosecutors who had been investigating the Bribesville scandals began to train their sights on Berlusconi. They began picking off his top managers and putting the spotlight on his company accounts. Fedele Confalonieri, his longtime friend, was by that time installed as head of the television empire. He was among the first of Berlusconi's lieutenants to be called in for questioning by the investigating magistrates from Operation Clean Hands.

"In April 1993, the tax police raided our offices and the magistrates came after us. My assistant and I were both questioned by the magistrates," recalls Confalonieri. "The investigators were accusing us of illicit financing of the Socialist Party because we had participated in the summer parties of the annual conventions of the Socialist Party. We had our corporate stands up at these gatherings. When I told the magistrates that we also had our stands at the annual Festa dell'Unità summer conventions of the Italian Communist Party, they told me that they would open a separate investigation into that."

Confalonieri laughs grimly at this.

"But in the end I was declared not guilty and in fact they never even put me on trial," recalls Confalonieri with a bit of a smirk. "I tried to explain that the reason we did all this was to promote ourselves, to get in front of the political parties who controlled our regulatory destiny as a broadcaster. Most of our corporate advertisers also showed up at these party gatherings. It was simply the thing to do."

Berlusconi does not deny that by 1993 he had become a target of the Milan prosecutors. But he speaks with plaintive tones when he answers the allegations that have dogged him throughout his career. All his life he has been accused of going into politics only to save his business empire and to achieve immunity from prosecution. He utterly and categorically denies that he was forced to go into politics or run for office in order to save himself by achieving parliamentary immunity or because his media empire was debt-laden and on the edge of bankruptcy.

"These are absolute lies," he declares, with only the slightest hint of discomfort. "This is the opposite of reality. I would have done a greater service to my companies if I had remained on the job, if I had not gone into politics. Instead, by entering politics all I got was a record number of attacks by the magistrates that would go on for many years."

Confalonieri, as one would expect from Berlusconi's fiercest defender, is even more vehement.

"Sure, we had big debts, but we were also a big group, with TV interests, publishing, retailing, insurance, lots of different businesses. But we had large assets, we had substance. The beef was there and the proof of the beef was that we were valued at around five billion dollars just two years later, in 1996, when we went public. The idea that Berlusconi was forced to go into politics because of the investigations or because our business was collapsing is completely false. It is untrue, it is fake, and it is the first brick that was laid in the construction of a huge castle of lies against Berlusconi over time."

How Berlusconi decided to go into politics is an open question. On April 4, 1993, according to one story, Berlusconi held a "council of war" at Arcore with former prime minister Bettino Craxi. The discussion about going into politics began there, according to Ezio Cartotto, an embittered former Fininvest employee who served as a political adviser to Berlusconi in the early days. They discussed the idea of forming a new political party that could replace the vanquished Christian Democrats and Socialists, now no longer on the scene. At the end of this conversation, so the story goes, Berlusconi said he knew what he had to do.

Berlusconi denies this version of events. He does remember discussing the idea of getting into politics with Craxi, but not on April 4, 1993. And he claims that Craxi was on the opposite side of the argument.

"He counseled me not to go into politics," recalls Berlusconi. "He told me that politics was the ugliest world I could ever imagine, and he said it was even uglier in Italy because of the role played by activist magistrates. He was categorical. 'Absolutely not! Don't do it,' he told me."

Confalonieri also remembers the conversations with Craxi as well as the generalized fear that if Berlusconi were to go into politics he would become a target for the investigating magistrates.

"Back in 1993, there were huge risks for somebody like Berlusconi entering politics. The magistrates would put you under a magnifying glass until they had found something. Many of them were left-wingers and they supported the Communist Party," says Confalonieri, evidently convinced of what he is saying. "I was totally against the idea of Silvio going into politics. For one thing, I did not believe he could just start a party and win an election in one shot. So I argued that we would end up paying the bill for dinner but we would get nothing to eat. I remember the last time I ever saw Craxi, before he went into exile. I asked him what he thought and he said that Silvio might win six percent or eight percent of the vote at best, nothing more."

Berlusconi has always been obsessed with opinion polls and one of the trigger events for his decision to enter active political life came in July 1993, not long after a visit to Arcore by an obscure political science professor named Giuliano Urbani.

"Professor Urbani came to see me at my request," he recalls. "I asked him to bring the latest opinion polls that his university had conducted. It was clear from these surveys that in the next election, given the absence of center-right parties that had been eliminated by the scandals, the left could score a big victory. The numbers showed that the renamed Communist Party could win almost forty percent of the vote, and that would be enough, under the electoral system, for the Communists to control seventy-four percent of the seats in Parliament."

Berlusconi pauses, as though he can see the poll numbers before his eyes. If there was one thing he did not want to see happen in Italy, as a businessman, it was a victory of the leftist parties. That would be bad for business.

"That was the moment when I decided. Those polling numbers triggered my decision to actively seek a political alternative. First I tried to create a coalition of center-right parties, and when that proved impossible, I decided to create my own party."

During that torrid summer in Italian politics, Berlusconi also went to Turin to pay homage to Gianni Agnelli, the Fiat heir and the uncrowned king of Italy.

"I had dinner with Gianni Agnelli and I showed him some of the policy platforms and materials I was preparing," says Berlusconi. "We discussed the idea of bringing together different parties in order to compete with the Communists. I even showed him some storyboards for spots that our advertising division had prepared. He was very impressed and he said to me: 'I hope you succeed in putting back together again what is left of the previous governing parties.' After that dinner, I remained in close contact with Agnelli throughout the summer and at one point I told him there was no alternative but to create my own political party. He said I shouldn't do it, that it was too dangerous, that businessmen have a different mind-set from politicians. He tried to dissuade me."

A few months later, when Berlusconi made his big move, the notoriously cynical Agnelli would famously proclaim on behalf of Italian industry: "If he wins, then we all win. If he loses, then he loses alone."

By the autumn of 1993, Berlusconi had put dozens of sales and marketing executives from his television and advertising empire to work on a new assignment: the creation of a political party. Marcello Dell'Utri, who had become the head of Mediaset's advertising arm, and Cesare Previti, Berlusconi's most trusted lawyer and friend, were among the more vociferous in favor of starting a new party, and helped groom candidates. They put salesmen and advertising executives through weekly training on political organizing. They drafted representatives of Berlusconi's Programma Italia financial services subsidiary as candidates or local party organizers. In September 1993 Berlusconi told Dell'Utri, who was moving ahead to create a political movement, that he wanted to be able to field a full national party at the next elections.

By the end of 1993, a number of the advertising and marketing men, alongside the network of financial consultants, opened local Forza Italia clubs up and down the country. This would become the backbone of a national party whose strategists had carefully analyzed their target audience, created the content, and were now ready to unleash a blitz of television spots, as soon as the game was on. They were ready with the marketing plan. It was all straight out of the Mediaset playbook, and it marked the first time in Western history that a national political party had been designed, engineered, funded, and then launched from inside a major corporation.

"Berlusconi was always an entrepreneur," recalls Confalonieri, "and he took an entrepreneurial approach to creating the party. He analyzed the market, he saw what was lacking, and he created a product to fill the gap he perceived, the market gap. I remember him saying to me: 'In the political marketplace today there is only one product on offer, the left. Let's compare the left to a soft drink, let's say it is a bitter drink. What is missing in the market is an alternative, a sweet drink.' So he figured that if this alternative product did not exist in the marketplace, then we had to create a new product and offer it to the Italians. That was the way he thought of politics, like an entrepreneur with a marketing plan to launch a new brand."

Berlusconi was ever the salesman, but now he began deploying his legendary schmoozing talents in Italian politics.

Toward the end of 1993, Berlusconi began sending out signals of his impending political activism. Surprisingly for a billionaire media tycoon, he suddenly gave a very public endorsement to a right-wing mayoral candidate in Rome named Gianfranco Fini, a post–Fascist politician who still openly admired Mussolini. Berlusconi says he was simply responding to a question from a journalist, but across Italy the endorsement was seen as a message.

That was not all; he sent out feelers to another right-wing party called the Lega. This was a xenophobic and anti-tax party from Italy's hard-working north, a kind of Italian Tea Party whose proclaimed ambition at the time was the secession of the Northern regions from Italy. Berlusconi made the approach to this fringe party because he calculated he would need a broader center-right coalition to achieve power.

"I was desperately trying to get the remaining political parties to unite with me. There was also a party that had been marginalized because its origins were in the Fascist party, the MSI. It was very rough going for a while but in the end I was able to get people to see that the only way to stop the Communists was to create a new conservative political movement made up of moderates on the right, the free-market liberals who were the majority of the voters. I managed to forge an electoral alliance with the Lega, which in time gave up its ideas about secession, and with the post-fascist MSI, which eventually became a more moderate and democratic party."

On an evening in the middle of January 1994, Berlusconi gathered his family, his friends, and managers Gianni Letta, Fedele Confalonieri, and Marcello Dell'Utri, and his eighty-three-year-old mother. The agenda had one item: to establish Forza Italia.

"I invited them all to dinner and I gave them my assessment of the situation. I explained that I had tried and failed to find an alternative solution. I told them that I really felt I needed to do this," recalls Berlusconi. "They were ferocious in their reaction. Everyone told me not to do it. My closer friends and advisers and my entire family warned me not to go into politics. They were all against it. My mother was bitterly opposed to the idea. She said that if I went into politics I would end up hurting myself, my family, my children, and my businesses."

Berlusconi pauses as he remembers the way the evening ended.

"Their reaction was totally negative," he recalls. "I told them I would sleep on it and then reconvene another family meeting. My mother then got in the car to return to Milan, and when she passed our old family apartment, where she had brought up her three children, she asked the driver to stop the car, then she got out and stared at the apartment building for a long time. And then she asked my driver to bring her back here, straight back to Arcore."

Berlusconi pauses and gestures toward the window on the second floor of the Villa San Martino.

"She came up to my bedroom, the one right up there," he says. "Fortunately, I was still wide awake, staring at the ceiling. I was pretty upset. I was thinking about everybody's reaction. My mother came to the foot of my bed and I will never forget what she said: 'I have been thinking about this. And I am still bitterly against what you are doing. They will find a thousand ways to hurt you, your family, and your companies. But I understand that you feel strongly that you need to do this. So I guess that you would not be the son I taught if you felt you really needed to do something for your own freedom and for the freedom of your country and then you did not have the courage to actually do it.' Then she hugged me and got back in the car and went back home to Milan. Right after that, I resigned all positions in my companies and a few days later we founded Forza Italia as a political party."

When Berlusconi pressed the button, his army of marketing men turned parliamentary candidates was ready. But the Italians were not prepared for Berlusconi's new style of campaigning, complete with all the media saturation techniques and the straight talking and optimistic script. This was democratic populism in the age of television, with Madison Avenue technique and style. It was American. It was feel-good. It was like Berlusconi's TV channels, filled with dreams and aspirations and pastel colors. It was like Berlusconi's soccer team, and of course the *Forza Italia!* chant became a mantra. It also helped that the Berlusconi family owned half the country's main TV channels and lots of print media.

The way he did it, the way Berlusconi managed to win in just sixty days after his January 1994 party launch date, is the stuff of a political scientist's fantasy. It could have made for a Harvard Business School case study in branding and marketing.

Berlusconi not only piled on the razzle-dazzle media techniques, he also invented a new political language and a new series of symbols. He appealed to the Italian equivalent of what in American politics was once called "the silent majority." That term had been used many years before, by President Richard Nixon when he claimed that the majority of American voters were conservative and pro-business. In 1994, Berlusconi offered an unabashedly pro-business and free market set of policies, a mix of deregulation, tax cuts, and a chicken in every pot. For the exhausted Italian electorate, sick and tired of years of scandal and recession, Berlusconi seemed to offer the same quality that would later put Barack Obama in the White House: he offered hope to a desperate nation.

"I remember that we designed the campaign right here, in the living room and in the kitchen," says Berlusconi, brimming with nostalgia. "We were a relatively small group, working out of this house. This was the command center and there were only four or five people working on the campaign strategy here at Arcore. In a matter of a few weeks we put together a government program, including economic policy, right here. My calculation was that the majority of the Italians had lost their way and did not know who to vote for anymore. So Forza Italia satisfied that market demand, from a majority of Italians who did not want to vote for the left."

Berlusconi may have employed his media empire's resources to produce all the colorful new posters, the aspirational blue that was the color of Forza Italia, the campaign literature, the TV spots, and much more. But he was, as all those who knew him will attest, still very much a one-man band and a micromanager, with an obsessive, even manic, attention to detail. He prepared the brand launch and then he performed on the roadshow. He covered the thousand-mile-long Italian peninsula city by city, town by town, serving up the promise of a brighter tomorrow and staging flashy campaign rallies that could have come straight off the set of one of his television extravaganzas.

Berlusconi would personally inspect every detail, frequently turning up for a sound check or as the carpenters were nailing together the stage scenery for a rally. He ordered his team to paint the stage sets a brilliant and luminous white. It looked expensive. It looked happy.

"I was always very attentive about the way we presented ourselves to the public. I changed almost everything in the way politicians interacted with the public. For example, all the old political parties used to put their senior party officials on stage, standing shoulder to shoulder behind the party leader when he gave a speech. I decided instead on a single microphone and just one person on the stage rather than the old-fashioned formation of party hacks."

Ever the showman.

"I used to get personally involved in designing the scenery for all of our big TV shows," recalls a proud and smiling Berlusconi. "I always personally managed the architectural details of new real estate projects we were building. So it was natural for me to get involved in every aspect of our public image and our messaging. I supervised all the campaign brochures and the posters. I personally wrote most of our advertising spots as well as the speeches I would make. I got involved in every aspect of the campaign, and for those sixty days I guess I never slept more than three hours a night."

Aside from the manic obsession with brand positioning and imagery, Berlusconi also deployed an unusual method to unveil his new party. He made a slick nine-minute video message to the nation, filmed at his home office. He was seated presidentially behind a big desk, the bookcases filled with family photos behind his shoulders, and looking every bit the part in his smart blue tie, crisp white shirt, and double-breasted Brioni pinstripe. Actually he looked more like a Milanese business leader than a politician, and this helped his cause. Berlusconi then had the video transmitted on his own TV channels first. He received considerably less airtime in the nightly news programs on the RAI public television channels.

That videotaped speech became famous because of the way Berlusconi declared, "Italy is the country that I love" and then announced dramatically that he was "taking the field." The video marked the start of a campaign that would seduce millions of Italian voters. It would change everything in Italian politics. Berlusconi was trying to create a two-party system where before there had only been fragmentation and unstable coalitions composed of tiny parties. He was offering himself as a billionaire entrepreneur who was placing his experience at the service of the nation. Above all, he was pointing his biggest guns at the old-fashioned Communists, even though they had recently changed their party's name and given up the hammer and the sickle.

"The orphans of Communism are not only unprepared to govern but they come with an ideological baggage that is anathema for those who believe in a free market," declared Berlusconi, glancing only occasionally at the typed notes on his desk.

Berlusconi was staring straight into the camera, a terse and determined smile on his lips. The video address resembled an Oval Office moment, but Berlusconi's message was full of rancor.

"Those on the left claim to have changed," he said with an accusatory tone. "They say they have become Democrats. But it is not true. Their people remain the same. Their mind-set and their culture and their most profound convictions have not changed. They don't believe in the free market. They don't believe in private enterprise. They don't believe in profit. They don't believe in the individual. They don't believe in diversity. They have not really changed. In fact, they have no real beliefs. They just want to transform this country into one big noisy piazza with a motley crowd that simply screams out accusations and condemnations."

Here Berlusconi looked down at his desk for a second and then came back self-righteously.

"*This* is why we must fight them. Because *we* believe in the individual, we believe in the family, we believe in business, in competition, in progress, in efficiency, in the free market and in social equity, which comes from justice and liberty. If I have decided to take the field with a new movement, and now if I ask all of you to join me, right now and before it is too late, then it is because I dream of a free society that is made up of men and women who do not live in fear, a society where instead of class envy and class warfare there is generosity and hard work and solidarity and tolerance and respect for life. The political movement that I propose to you is called Forza Italia..."

Berlusconi now reeled off a long list of homilies and platitudes about freedom, modernization, transparent government, job creation, prosperity, a crackdown on crime, freedom of worship, help for the poor and pensioners, and even a cleaner environment.

Then he had his Martin Luther King moment.

"I have a dream," he declared, "a big dream that I believe we can realize together. I dream of an Italy that is more just, more generous toward those in need, more prosperous and more serene, more modern and more efficient, an Italy that takes its rightful place again as a protagonist in Europe and in the world."

Berlusconi's video address concluded with a rhetorical flourish that was worthy of Barack Obama's "Yes We Can" slogan, and more than a decade before Obama first became a presidential candidate.

"We can do it," he said into the camera, now slowing down the cadence of his speech and pronouncing each of his words with brio. "We can, and we must create, for ourselves and for our children, a new Italian miracle!"

Fade to black.

It was stirring stuff at the time, and it worked. Berlusconi shot to victory just sixty days later, riding a wave of national repulsion at the past and a vague hope in the brighter future offered by Forza Italia. He was sworn in as prime minister on May 11, 1994, just a week before it was learned that Bettino Craxi, now facing multiple corruption trials, had fled the country and taken refuge at his vacation home in Tunisia.

Berlusconi had done it. He had planned and executed the launch of a new political party and he had gotten himself elected prime minister. He had won more than eight million votes, and forged a center-right coalition that gave him majority control of the parliament. He had become Europe's first billionaire prime minister. But his background as a businessman did not prepare him very well for the rough-and-tumble of Italian politics. Berlusconi was, after all, a self-made and strident Milanese entrepreneur. He was used to running his own show. He was used to being the boss. The only problem was that things worked a bit differently in Rome.

"It was disastrous. I got really frustrated," he recalls. "I discovered that a prime minister has less power than you would actually think. Because of our country's Fascist heritage, our Constitution gives most powers to the legislative body and not the premier. But our parliament was just one big courtyard filled with gossip and secrets. There were very few members of parliament who worked hard, maybe about a hundred or so. For a businessman like me who was used to working from morning until night it was just disastrous, it was awful at first."

"Berlusconi was very impatient, very frustrated at the slow workings of government," recalls Confalonieri. "He thought he could just go in there and change everything. But he got mired in the swamp of Roman politics. It is no accident that in two thousand years of history the Romans have seen it all. They have seen and they have digested everything and everyone who came to command here, and they were slowly digesting Berlusconi. In fact, they kicked him out of office in just six months."

Confalonieri watched it all at close quarters.

"Never forget that this is the land of Machiavelli," he warns. "Everyone in Rome has read *The Prince* and even if they haven't read the book, they practice Machiavellian politics. It is in the red and white corpuscles of Italian politicians."

Whether it was a Machiavellian plot by left-wing magistrates and politicians, as Berlusconi has always claimed, or a mere coincidence of timing, the manner in which Berlusconi was brought down at the end of 1994 was unusual, to say the least.

On the morning of Tuesday, November 22, 1994, just six months after taking office, the billionaire premier was hosting a UN world summit in Naples on transnational efforts to tackle organized crime. It was meant to be a moment of prestige, although Berlusconi's critics would dine out on the irony of the summit's subject matter for some time. For Berlusconi it was a badge of honor to be on a par with international leaders, and for the second time in just a few months; he had already welcomed Bill Clinton and Boris Yeltsin along with Tony Blair, François Mitterrand, Helmut Kohl, and other world leaders to Naples the previous July for the annual G-7 summit, which had proved an historic moment, since it marked the first time Russia had been invited. On this day he was getting ready to meet the United Nations secretary-general and delegations from 140 countries.

At 5:40 that morning, Berlusconi was awakened by.a phone call from Gianni Letta, who had moved from Fininvest to become the gatekeeper in the prime minister's office. Letta did not have good news. He read over the telephone a spectacular front-page scoop in the *Corriere della Sera* newspaper. The headline said it all: "Berlusconi Under Investigation in Milan" and the strap line clarified that the prime minister was the target of a judicial probe into bribes allegedly made to tax inspectors and with Berlusconi's knowledge, payoffs by Berlusconi's companies.

The front-page article rocked the Berlusconi government. It soon emerged that Berlusconi was not only under investigation; he had also been sent a subpoena to appear for questioning before the investigating magistrates of Operation Clean Hands in Milan. He was going to be interrogated on suspicion of bribery and corruption in a case in which Fininvest attempted to explain that it had not initiated the offer of bribes; the payoffs, claimed Fininvest, had been demanded by the tax authorities who were extorting Fininvest in the early 1990s.

The premier's press office confirmed the existence of the legal notice and said Berlusconi had been asked to appear before prosecutors in Milan. Berlusconi declared himself "serene, because, as I have said many times, I have not committed any crime." But his Naples summit was ruined, and so was his spell as prime minister. He had been very publicly humiliated, in front of the entire world. His government collapsed a month later.

The subpoena, as it happened, was signed by one Francesco Borrelli, the district attorney in Milan. For many Italians, Borrelli was a hero, a crusading magistrate who had taken on the establishment in the Bribesville saga. He was also perceived as a left-wing sympathizer. In fact, Borrelli had fired an early warning shot of sorts, less than a year before the subpoena hit Berlusconi at the Naples summit. The warning came in late December 1993, when Berlusconi was still preparing to "take the field" and launch Forza Italia.

In an interview with the *Corriere della Sera*, the district attorney had spoken ominously of how "certain coincidences can lead to upheavals." He issued this warning: "Those who want to become political candidates should look into themselves. If they are clean, then they should go ahead serenely. But if they have skeletons in the closet, or any past embarrassments, they should open their closets now and stand aside from politics, before we get there."

In Italy, it was understood that while the prosecutor's words could be intended for any number of people, they were directed mainly at Silvio Berlusconi.

"From the moment I became prime minister," says a strident Berlusconi, "the militant magistrates of the left unleashed a string of actions against me. They created a continuous uproar. They sent me that subpoena right in the middle of an important United Nations meeting in Naples. What they were really doing was denouncing me in a manner that would have destroyed anybody's ability to stay in politics."

This perspective on the Naples affair is in sharp contrast with the view of politicians on the left who would later note that Berlusconi was actually convicted of bribing the tax officials in his first trial, even though he was later acquitted on appeal. The *Corriere della Sera*, under the evenhanded direction of a legendary editor in chief named Paolo Mieli, minced few words in describing the subpoena as the culmination of a lengthy battle that pitted the Milan magistrates against Berlusconi.

The investigation, said the newspaper, was part of a broader set of tax inspections that had for more than a year placed Berlusconi's empire at risk. "After months of skirmishes and controversy, the magistrates have struck their final blow," said the article that led to the collapse of Berlusconi's first government. "As always, in crucial moments of the Operation Clean Hands investigation," said the newspaper, "the prosecutors wait until elections are over and then they launch their attack."

The most ominous words, which would prove prescient, were that "as of yesterday the prime minister's situation has changed and a new phase begins in which it is hard to predict the next political and judicial developments."

In other words, Berlusconi's political future was now uncertain at best.

"It was a carefully piloted operation by the magistrates to get the news out," claims an aggrieved Silvio Berlusconi. "Instead of simply sending me a subpoena via official channels and without publicizing the news, this stuff was leaked and put on the front page. After this the president of the republic, who came from the left, called up my main coalition partner and told him: 'Berlusconi is finished. If you don't want to finish up in the same way, it is best for you to pull out of the government and bring him down.' And that is precisely what happened. It was an authentic coup d'état."

This would not be the last time Berlusconi would cry foul or accuse his opponents on the left of plotting his downfall. The language of plots and conspiracies would become a mainstay of Italian political discourse over many years, and in at least one later occasion Berlusconi's claims would be proven well grounded. But that occasion, many years later, would not be about domestic politics or a court case. Rather it would concern a genuine international intrigue during the height of the euro crisis and it would feature not just Berlusconi but a group of world leaders of the caliber of Nicolas Sarkozy of France and Angela Merkel of Germany, plus a most unexpected ally for Berlusconi: Barack Obama.

After he was placed under investigation on corruption charges, his government did not last long and he resigned as prime minister at the end of 1994. Berlusconi remained in the wilderness for six long years, or, as he called it, "my years in the desert." By 1995 he was considered a has-been. In 1996 he tried and failed to win the elections again. In 2001, after his time in "the desert," Berlusconi staged an incredible political comeback and began to rack up time as Italy's longest-serving prime minister. During his years in government in the early twenty-first century, he actively participated in or bore witness to international political events that became history: the aftermath of the 9/11 attacks, the war in Afghanistan, the nudging of Vladimir Putin into a form of détente and cooperation with the West, the euro crisis, and the taming of Libya's Gaddafi. Berlusconi liked being in the international arena even though he often came on like gangbusters, lacking a certain diplomatic finesse and being frequently prone to the most undiplomatic gaffes. His least known and perhaps his greatest foreign policy failure, however, was a surprising secret attempt to stop George W. Bush and Tony Blair from going to war against Saddam Hussein.

CHAPTER SIX

―――――

George Bush and the Attack on Saddam

"I will never forget the first time I met George W. Bush. We liked each other right away. There was a kind of feeling between us. There was good chemistry. I guess I felt myself attracted to him, to his vision."

Berlusconi recalls the moment his friendship began with President George W. Bush. The two men first met at a hectic NATO summit in Brussels on June 13, 2001. Both leaders were fairly inexperienced on the international stage. Bush was making his debut visit to Europe after just five months in office. Berlusconi had been sworn in as prime minister less than twenty-four hours before. This was Berlusconi's first great moment of international prestige following his political comeback in Italy's elections of May 2001. It was quickly apparent to the former Texas governor that in a Europe where most of his relations were poor or tepid at best, he would find in Silvio Berlusconi a man who would lend a sympathetic ear.

The Bush administration had already gotten off to a rocky start with its European allies. The decision to pull out of the Clinton administration's much-vaunted Kyoto agreement on global warming angered many in France and Germany. Bush's determination to speed ahead with a new and costly missile defense plan that some had dubbed "Son of Star Wars" had stirred further resentment in Paris and Berlin. His approach was not subtle. Tony Blair was already on board, but then that would prove the case with just about any request Bush might make of him. Blair was well known to be in awe of the U.S. president. But the French and Germans were opposed to Washington. Neither Jacques Chirac nor Gerhard Schroeder liked Bush.

Italy's foreign policy, meanwhile, was about to undergo a big change. Berlusconi was Italy's most openly pro-American prime minister. His support for Bush and the United States was a given. Even before taking office, Berlusconi had already signaled that he was ready to endorse the missile defense shield. And he would.

In Brussels, the body language of the two men said it all. They were spotted joking and making friendly small talk during the traditional "family photo" of the NATO leaders. Bush and Berlusconi seemed to have found each other, like two soul mates. Both men were ardently pro-business. Both had made tax cuts the centerpiece of their electoral campaigns. And both had been attacked repeatedly in the European media, for different reasons.

Bush was perceived as a caricature of an arrogant cowboy from Texas while *The Economist* magazine had recently put Berlusconi on its cover with a headline that seemed to sum up the sentiment of many in the European media: "Why Silvio Berlusconi Is Unfit to Lead Italy."

Both Bush and Berlusconi were strong and polarizing political figures. Both were loved and adored by millions of supporters. Both had attracted not just harsh criticism but genuine hatred from their opponents.

That evening, after meeting Bush at the NATO summit in Belgium, Berlusconi got back on board the prime minister's Airbus 300 and flew on to Sweden, where the following day he would meet Bush again, this time at the European Union summit in the town of Gothenburg. The U.S. president's rhetoric was meanwhile becoming increasingly muscular. Aside from the missile shield, Bush was calling for NATO expansion and for pushing the borders of Europe to the east. Neither sat well with many, stirring widespread protest and dissent across European capitals, and in this case also in the streets of downtown Gothenburg.

The anti-globalization movement was out in force. They lined the streets of Gothenburg, outnumbering the Swedish police.

Bush and Berlusconi were ensconced inside the summit talks with more than a dozen European leaders, including Germany's Gerhard Schroeder, France's Jacques Chirac, and Britain's Tony Blair, while the police were fighting pitched battles with angry protesters out in the streets, using horses, dogs, and water cannons. The anti-Bush sentiment was so strong, just a few months into his presidency, that it brought together the massed forces of Italian and Swedish anarchists in addition to the anti-globalization protesters from across half of Europe. The Swedish police, overwhelmed by the protesters, eventually opened fire, shooting and injuring three protesters.

All of this happened just as the summit was getting under way in downtown Gothenburg in the town's glass and steel convention center.

"Bush walks into a room, with that Texas cowboy walk of his, where most of the European leaders present really don't like him," recalls Valentino Valentini, Berlusconi's closest aide. at the summit. "So President Bush walks in and he sees Berlusconi smiling at him, one of the few people there who is really happy to see him. Bush shouts out: 'Hey, Silvio! Hey, Silvio Berlusconi!' He sort of sidles up to him. You could see that the two of them liked each other right away, talking and joking over drinks. At dinner Bush discovers that Berlusconi is the only leader at the summit who is willing to support the U.S. position, the only European prime minister willing to loudly proclaim his support for Washington. Bush seemed very pleased to have met Berlusconi. After all, Berlusconi is a tycoon. He is pro-American. He is pro-business. He is a natural ally. Of course they liked each other right away."

Berlusconi says he remembers being struck most by the straight-talking manner of the new American president.

"There are not many politicians like him," says Berlusconi with a nostalgic smile. "What I liked best about Bush was that his 'yes' meant yes and his 'no' really meant no, just like me. So we had a lot in common."

That Berlusconi's foreign policy would be heavily influenced by his personal relationships—true of Bush as it would be later on with Russia's Vladimir Putin—was not surprising. "He is, after all, a businessman, an entrepreneur, a tycoon. His whole world is built on his personal network of relations, and his style is to schmooze everyone," recalls Valentini. "In meeting Bush, he raised the profile of Italy in the world, he became a preferred ally for Bush, alongside Blair. That meant a lot to Berlusconi on a personal level but it also meant a lot to Italy."

At the Gothenburg summit, the chemistry with Bush must have felt good. For Berlusconi, who had just returned to power after six long years in the political wilderness, being on the world stage alongside the leader of the free world was more than just good chemistry. It was redemption.

The summit came at the start of a full five-year term in office for Berlusconi, an unusual feat in the world of Italian politics, where the average life span of a government tended to be around ten or eleven months.

More than six years had passed since the humiliation of November 1994, when the newspapers had reported that he was under investigation for bribery and corruption, and right in the middle of the United Nations summit on organized crime in Naples.

Now Berlusconi had just won a smashing electoral victory, literally rising from the political grave.

After the Naples summit his fate was sealed. A few days later Berlusconi was called in for questioning by the investigating magistrates in Milan, a first for a sitting prime minister. It implied that he was likely to be indicted on bribery and corruption charges.

In the local Italian manner, court officials traded quotes and secrets with the Milanese press corps, so that almost every suspicion, every whisper, whether investigated or not, was fair game. Everything leaked out and often the newspapers would publish details of investigations long before they were presented in court.

This drip-drip approach made for a new kind of torture for Berlusconi. He was now a sitting prime minister, thoroughly humiliated and very angry. His government coalition was falling apart and he was being interrogated by the crime squad in Milan.

He made one last televised speech to the nation, which was as usual videotaped in advance at his villa and then distributed to the media. He swore on the lives of his children that he was innocent of any wrongdoing and he pledged not to resign. He then managed to hold out for a little more than a week before the roof caved in.

His resignation came just three days before Christmas 1994. His allies had turned against him. The leader of his northern Italian coalition partner, Umberto Bossi, heaped abuse upon him in parliamentary statements and rallies, comparing him to Mussolini, attacking his control of half the television market in Italy, and claiming that his Fininvest group and sister companies were linked to the Mafia. Bossi also attacked Berlusconi's far-right coalition partner, a former Fascist named Gianfranco Fini.

When his government fell Berlusconi asked for a snap election, but President Oscar Scalfaro had already made his mind up. Using his constitutional prerogatives, he appointed Berlusconi's treasury secretary as the new premier, and Berlusconi was out the door. Italy is a country where the president is supposed to be bipartisan and above the fray. Since the president always comes from either the left or right, however, impartiality is rare among Italian presidents. After his resignation, Berlusconi and Scalfaro traded plenty of insults, neither man distinguishing himself in the process.

If 1994 was the year of his rise and fall as Italy's first billionaire prime minister, then 1995 was the year the magistrates really began piling on the charges.

In the space of little more than a year Berlusconi and his entourage faced a total of twenty-seven arrests and indictments. His younger brother, Paolo, was convicted of bribery. He himself was soon indicted and put on trial for bribery.

Berlusconi was now in disgrace. He was furious with the judges, because from now on, and for the rest of his life, his legal travails would always compete for his attention alongside his leadership of Forza Italia.

Politically he was unable to put the pieces back together again and struggled to rally the troops. Barely a week went by without the newspapers reporting investigations, indictments, witness questioning, gossip, or court proceedings related to Berlusconi. His war with the judiciary had been fully engaged. By the spring of 1995, with multiple judicial probes now underway, Berlusconi began to fear arrest. His brother, Paolo, was facing more indictments, as were his cousin, his lawyer, and some of his closest friends.

In the political arena a new center-left alternative to Berlusconi was being created. Romano Prodi, a jovial economist from Bologna, had just announced plans to form a social democratic political movement called the Olive Tree coalition. It was a new party that brought together former Communists, hard-left Marxists, and Christian Democrats. It was an unwieldy alliance of liberals and conservatives on the left and would only find unity in its opposition to Berlusconi. Nonetheless, the emergence of this alliance would threaten Berlusconi and his now fractured center-right coalition. In fact, it was an ominous sign for the media mogul turned politician.

Berlusconi claims, of course, that the prosecutors were out to get him and that they leaked damaging details of their investigations in a carefully orchestrated political strategy aimed at discrediting him. There is no doubt that at least some of the accusations were indeed leaked to the press just ahead of the elections, where Berlusconi fared poorly. Ahead of the 1995 local and state elections, when Forza Italia took a beating, Berlusconi was placed under investigation for allegedly cooking the books and falsifying company accounts in connection with a deal to buy a soccer star for AC Milan.

In October 1995, the Milanese prosecutors struck a body blow. They formally indicted Silvio Berlusconi and charged him, his brother, Paolo, four Fininvest managers, and five tax inspectors with bribery and corruption. Berlusconi recalls declaring for the first time (but not the last): "We are now living in a police state."

Things got worse a few days later when the news broke that the investigators from Operation Clean Hands had discovered a series of Swiss bank accounts that Fininvest had allegedly used to transfer slush funds to Berlusconi's old friend, former prime minister Bettino Craxi. Although the formal indictment would not come until the following summer, all the details appeared on the front pages of the Italian press. Berlusconi was now under formal investigation for bribing Craxi.

In January 1996, Berlusconi went on trial in a Milan courtroom for bribing tax inspectors. An even bigger blow came from Palermo, where word had leaked out that both Berlusconi and his closest collaborator at Mediaset, Marcello Dell'Utri, were being investigated for alleged ties to the Mafia. Although the investigation of Berlusconi was shelved by the end of the year, his friend Dell'Utri would now face multiple Mafia probes, and was ultimately convicted of being a go-between for Berlusconi and the Mafia. As for the prosecutor who originally placed Berlusconi and Dell'Utri under investigation in Palermo, he later became a hard-left politician.

In the Italian national election of April 1996, Berlusconi was beaten by the center-left candidate, Romano Prodi. His defeat followed a campaign during which the Milan magistrates had launched a fresh blitz, this time with truly suspicious timing. But the main reason he lost was that Berlusconi at this point could not get the other center-right parties to form an electoral pact.

"In that election I still managed to win nearly eight million votes, out of a total of more than 15.8 million votes that were cast for the center right," recalls Berlusconi. "But the fact that my coalition partners would not join forces with Forza Italia meant that we could not win."

By now Berlusconi was battered and besieged. The court cases were mounting, some of his closest advisers were pressing him to bow out of politics. His own former spokesman wrote a front-page article in a newspaper owned by the Berlusconi family that urged him to make "a dignified exit."

Electoral defeat was one thing. But money was another.

In the summer of 1996, Berlusconi turned his attention back to his media empire. He had found the time to hold talks with his friend Rupert Murdoch about selling Mediaset to the Australian media tycoon. But the two could not agree on a deal. Instead the billionaire former prime minister now managed to cut his debts and value up his own fortune by floating Mediaset on the Milan stock exchange. He also placed key equity stakes with Saudi prince al-Waleed, with German television mogul Leo Kirch, and with South African billionaire Johann Rupert.

Mediaset was now worth more than $5 billion, and by the end of the decade its value would rise to more than $30 billion. He was, in the eyes of the center-left government, a walking conflict of interest, a political leader who was also Italy's richest billionaire and a man with vast media holdings.

Fortunately for Berlusconi, the center-left government, instead of consolidating its position, was beset by internecine warfare and factional infighting. The former Communist leader Massimo D'Alema seemed to covet the job of Prime Minister Prodi. The crafty D'Alema would indeed replace Prodi as premier, and under circumstances that remain murky to this day. But first he would do something that no one could understand: In 1997 the leader of the largest left-wing party in Italy would invite Berlusconi, as leader of the opposition center-right, to join him in rewriting portions of the Italian Constitution. He invited the devil to dinner, and in doing so he would rehabilitate Berlusconi and pave the way to his political comeback.

Whether D'Alema acted out of personal ego and desire to be center-stage or because he truly believed this new initiative was needed for his country, the effect was the same. Berlusconi was suddenly catapulted from being a political has-been and target of judicial probes to being a newly recruited co–founding father of the revised Constitution of his nation. He was brought back from the political wilderness, thanks to the political miscalculation of his fiercest political rival, and perhaps thanks to his ability to schmooze and charm and seduce just about anybody, including his rivals.

Although D'Alema, a man of the left, may not have planned it, the result of Berlusconi's presence in such important constitutional talks (even if the effort would collapse after a few months) helped his image and helped him to reassert himself as the undisputed leader of the center-right. By 1999 Forza Italia scored a big victory in elections for the European parliament. A year later Berlusconi got his prickly coalition partners back together again and trounced D'Alema and the government parties in nationwide municipal and state elections. As part of the campaign, Berlusconi invented the idea of a lavish whistle-stop campaign tour, this time in a cruise ship around Italy's Mediterranean coast. He called it the *Ship of Freedom* and it worked very well. It was this victory in administrative elections that helped foster D'Alema's demise.

Then, in May 2001, Berlusconi staged an extraordinary political comeback, following a slick campaign that was heavy on the TV spots, celebrity endorsements from Mediaset TV stars, and the usual razzmatazz, including the mailing to ten million Italian families of a 125-page color pamphlet, starring Silvio Berlusconi. He promised the Italians that he would cut their taxes and create a million new jobs. Ever the showman, he clinched the election just five days before polling day when he went on state television, and, with a munificent flourish and the fawning cooperation of a popular pro-Berlusconi talk show host, he signed his promise to the nation of lower taxes and job creation in a document he called his "Contract with the Italians" an Italian-style version of Newt Gingrich's historic Contract with America.

His first act after being sworn in as prime minister was to fly off to the NATO summit in Brussels, where he would meet his new ally, George W. Bush.

If Berlusconi traces the start of his friendship with Bush to the experience the two men shared in Gothenburg just after that Brussels meeting, getting to know each other at a summit marred by riots in the streets, then their bonding would grow deeper a month later, during another summit of violence and protests: the G-8 summit in Genoa in July of 2001.

In Genoa, Berlusconi was once again happy to be back on the world stage. He was hosting the most powerful leaders on the planet, the G-7 heads, and, for the first time in history, the addition of Russia's Vladimir Putin for a formal G-8. It would be overshadowed, though, by protests, by violence, and by a tragic death.

On the morning of Friday, July 20, world leaders began to converge on Genoa. Canada's Jean Chrétien was the first to arrive; he landed early so he could have a bilateral meeting with Japan's Junichiro Koizumi, who had flown in from Tokyo the night before. German Chancellor Gerhard Schroeder was also already in the country, having his annual summer holiday in the countryside. Berlusconi had him picked up by Italian military aircraft from nearby Pesaro. Around eleven a.m., President Jacques Chirac landed at Genoa's tiny seaside airport. Britain's Tony Blair flew in from his country estate at Chequers, where he and President Bush had spent the previous night. As noon approached, Air Force One touched down, and President Bush, like the other leaders, was sped by motorcade to the thirteenth-century Palazzo Ducale, where Berlusconi was waiting to welcome his guests for an aperitif and opening luncheon. Vladimir Putin was not expected until later in the afternoon.

Drinks in hand, Blair and Chirac were admiring the frescoed splendor of the old Palace of the Doges of Genoa. Berlusconi was pointing out the magnificent ceilings as the world leaders sat down to dine. At almost exactly the same moment, troublemakers who had infiltrated the tens of thousands of protesters out in the streets were beginning a rampage that would turn downtown Genoa into a war zone. Before the second course of lunch had been served at the palace, the police were firing their first tear gas canisters.

Black-masked anarchists were throwing rocks and Molotov cocktails at the Italian police. By the time Berlusconi and his guests had gotten to the end of their lunch, a number of protesters were provoking the authorities by jumping over barricades and penetrating a top-security area ringed by steel-and-concrete barriers that was known as the "Red Zone."

At the end of the afternoon session, with Vladimir Putin's plane landing, Berlusconi came out to announce a new pledge of help for poor African countries and the promise of $1.2 billion to fund the battle against AIDS and other epidemics. By now, however, out in the streets the air was thick with tear gas, and nearly 20,000 policemen were fighting pitched battles with protesters.

Berlusconi had opened the summit meeting by telling President Bush and the leaders of Germany, France, Britain, Japan, and Canada that in the face of repeated protests now under way and looking back to the violence that had started at the Seattle world trade summit in 1999, it might be time to rethink the use of large cities as locations for future summit meetings.

He tried to defend himself against criticisms of police brutality, saying that his month-old government had sought to defuse the anti-globalization protests by establishing a dialogue with their representatives months before. But a small group of determined anarchists and anti-globalization protesters who were bent on violence had triumphed. Berlusconi was livid.

"Those who are against the G-8 are not fighting against leaders democratically elected in their countries," he declared. "They are fighting against the Western world, the philosophy of the free world."

Bush jumped in to shore up his new colleague. He told the White House press corps, crowded into a makeshift pavilion on Genoa's waterfront, that he regretted the violence but in Bush's opinion these protests would do a disservice to the impoverished masses of the world.

Then tragedy struck.

Just before six p.m., while Berlusconi was in the library of the

Palazzo Ducale with his closest staffers, an aide came forward with the news that a twenty-year-old protester had been shot in the head by an Italian paramilitary trooper. The victim, who had thrown a fire extinguisher at a police van, had been hit by one of the two bullets fired by the trooper. The image of Genoa that was being now broadcast to the world showed the youth lying in a pool of blood and covered by a white sheet. Inside, Berlusconi slammed his fist against the wall and let out a guttural sound of rage.

The death of this protester, along with the injury of nearly two hundred others, was ruining Berlusconi's dreams for this summit.

"The world had seemed so peaceful," he recalls. "How wonderful it was to sit as the host of a dinner with the most powerful leaders on the planet, with George W. Bush having a nice conversation with Vladimir Putin to my right. But of course the death of a young man was a human tragedy, even though it was later shown that the paratrooper was acting in self-defense. And of course everyone spoke with me and gave me their condolences, and especially President Bush."

At the end of the weekend summit in Genoa, Bush and his wife, Laura, remained in Italy, flying to Rome for a whirlwind state visit and a meeting with the pope. Berlusconi entertained the Bushes at a baroque seventeenth-century Roman villa, serving up an extravagant Italian lunch complete with an array of Italian wines and a red, white, and green pasta dish whose colors matched the Italian flag. The two men seemed to agree on just about every issue. They went for a long walk in the elaborate gardens of the Villa Doria Pamphili and they nearly got lost in the labyrinth. It was an unusual and unscheduled frolic for the American president and the Italian premier. They seemed to truly enjoy each other's company. Bush might be getting the cold shoulder from France and Germany, but he had found himself a staunch ally in Berlusconi.

The billionaire prime minister, already a virulent anti-Communist, was now leading an Italian government that was so pro-American that it was attracting major hostility from nearly all of the left-wing parties in Italy. Berlusconi was already hated by half of the Italians, just as he was loved by the other half. But the way he trumpeted his friendship with the much reviled Bush made him even more of a target of hate for the left. He didn't care a whit.

"I told George the reasons why I loved America and why I considered it the greatest democracy on the planet," recalls Berlusconi. "In fact, I told George how grateful all Italians should be to America, since we were liberated by American soldiers during the Second World War. I explained that for my generation of Italians the United States was still a kind of beacon of liberty. It was thanks to the generosity of the U.S. Marshall Plan that my country could emerge from poverty and achieve growth and prosperity after the war years. When we first met, I told him the same story about my father that I would later repeat in a speech to a joint meeting of Congress. It was about a moment in my life that had a profound effect on my thinking."

Berlusconi pauses for effect.

"When I finished high school my father took me to visit the American cemetery at Anzio. He pointed at the dates on the graves of some of the U.S. soldiers who were buried there."

Berlusconi now points a finger into space, virtually reenacting the scene.

"When we looked at the tombstones you could see that these were mostly kids who had died when they were just twenty-two, twenty-three, or twenty-four years old. My father pointed at the graves and he told me: 'These kids came across the ocean, from a democracy far, far away, and they sacrificed their lives for your freedom. I want you to now swear your eternal gratitude to them, to their democracy, and to their country.' He made me swear on the graves of these American soldiers that I would never forget their sacrifice. And I never will."

Berlusconi's eyes well with tears. A cynic would say that he is the world's greatest Method actor who has memorized and repeated the same story numerous times before. On this occasion, he appears to be speaking straight from the heart, with deadly sincerity.

Berlusconi pauses in his recollection. He glances around at the manicured lawn, recovers his composure, and then gestures to the old villa.

"I was here, you know, when we got the news of 9/11. I was right here at Arcore that very day in September 2001," he says, glancing at the house. "I was having a meeting with my staff and suddenly they started shouting for me to turn on the television.

The events of 9/11 would deepen the bonds between Berlusconi and Bush even further. After their baptism by fire that summer, amid the violence at the European summits, it was the destruction of New York's World Trade Center that would bring Berlusconi and Bush still closer.

"When I turned on the television I could not believe what I was seeing," recalls Berlusconi. "I thought I was watching one of those disaster movies. It was so unreal. It was unbelievable, unimaginable. I waited for several hours before telephoning President Bush, but I remember thinking that it felt like a spell had been broken. Until then, there really seemed to be peace in the world. Now it felt like the world's collective innocence had been shattered. Everything had seemed to be moving in the right direction. There was progress in the world, there was economic growth. But we were completely unprepared for the rise of this new force of global terrorism; it was a new threat to Western democracies. Of course after that terrible moment all the rest came quickly: the war in Afghanistan, the war in Iraq, the terrorism of al-Qaeda, the rise of Isis. It all came after 9/11. That was the date that changed world history forever."

Berlusconi pauses again. He looks down at his hands for a moment and then resumes his recollection. He is talking about the flurry of conversations he had with Bush and with Tony Blair in the months that followed.

"We had a kind of a continuous collaboration. It was nonstop. The bad news kept on coming, and we were constantly in touch with each other, either me and President Bush or me and Tony Blair, or one of them would brief me on what the other was doing.

There was a lot of coordinating and communicating. After all, this was the biggest problem we were facing, the challenge of all challenges, and in all of our countries domestic issues went on the back burner for a while. This was a challenge for all humanity and not just for the West. So we had lengthy discussions about how to fight the war on terrorism. Above all, we had one really big discussion, where we had a big difference of opinion. That was when the United States decided to go to war in Iraq."

It was in January 2003, sixteen months after the World Trade Center attacks, that the drumbeat of war would get steadily louder. By early February, when the hapless Colin Powell would go before the UN Security Council and wave around a glass vial that he claimed could contain a teaspoon of anthrax, it was clear that Bush intended to make war on Saddam Hussein.

"Frankly I was very worried," recalls Berlusconi. "I was worried and I wanted to see if I could change Bush's mind. I was looking for an alternative to the invasion of Iraq. I was thinking about how to find an exile for Saddam, a way out that would avoid war. So I began contacting Gaddafi and we began discussing the idea of his hosting Saddam in exile in Libya. We must have spoken half a dozen times between the end of 2002 and early 2003. And I was getting him to a point where he was almost willing to accept Saddam."

Berlusconi was scheduled to see Bush at the White House on January 30. In the weeks that preceded his visit to Washington, he engaged in a frenetic round of telephone diplomacy.

"It was a pretty crazy time and Berlusconi spoke to Gaddafi numerous times," recalls a close aide. "Bush was willing to accept the exile solution as long as it guaranteed regime change, but he didn't think we could pull it off. And Gaddafi was a wild man, unpredictable. He would call up Berlusconi in the middle of the night and we had to scramble to find an interpreter and we would tell him that we would call him back. It was pretty crazy."

While Silvio Berlusconi was getting ready for his visit to Washington and twisting Muammar Gaddafi's arm to accept Saddam in exile, Tony Blair was busy shuttling back and forth across the Atlantic so frequently that in the eyes of many the British prime minister began to look like a glorified messenger between the White House and continental Europe. Most of Europe was not interested in hearing Blair's message. The leaders of France and Germany were vigorously opposed to the idea of a war against Saddam Hussein. Aside from Blair, the few Europeans who would side with Bush were Spain's center-right prime minister, José María Aznar, and a handful of newly enfranchised Eastern European leaders who were just thrilled to be part of NATO and wanted to join the European Union. And then there was Berlusconi. At home he was walking a political tightrope with his vocal support for Bush. Some 75 percent of the Italian electorate was against the idea of joining Bush's "Coalition of the Willing." The Italian Constitution even prohibited offensive military engagements.

What the Italian public did not know at the time was that Berlusconi was still trying to dissuade his friend George W. Bush from the folly of war.

"The truth is that I wanted to stop the war," says Berlusconi, now staring intently at his interlocutor, as if to measure the impact of his words.

"I went to see Bush," recalls Berlusconi, "because I wanted to explain my opinion on Iraq, which is pretty simple. This is a country whose borders were drawn on a tablecloth. It is populated by three different ethnic groups which have ancient rivalries. Some sixty-five percent of the country is illiterate. This kind of country cannot be governed as a democracy, with a democratically elected government. This has to be a regime, preferably with a leader who is not a dictator, or at least not a bloodthirsty dictator. Iraq could not function as a democracy. So I wanted to avoid a war. That is why I kept trying to get Gaddafi to accept Saddam. Actually, Bush was receptive to this idea. He would have gone for it, if there had been enough time."

Berlusconi stopped off in London on his way to Washington from Rome.

"Berlusconi met with Tony Blair for a couple of hours at Downing Street. But Blair was distracted. He was having problems in the House of Commons over Iraq and it was not going so well," recalls Valentino Valentini, Berlusconi's aide. "Both Blair and Berlusconi shared the concern that any U.S. military action needed to have the correct kind of legal cover, at the national and international levels."

It was on that day, January 29, 2003, as Berlusconi returned to his plane to fly on to Washington, that Blair made one of his more controversial assertions about Saddam Hussein. He told parliament that based on intelligence reports "we know of links between al-Qaeda and Iraq."

On the morning of January 30, Berlusconi went to see Bush in the Oval Office. The two men seemed genuinely happy to be together, and Berlusconi spoke a few words of English for the cameras. Inside the Oval Office the conversation was all about Saddam Hussein and weapons of mass destruction, and the weapons inspections by Hans Blix of the United Nations. Berlusconi tried to press his case for the exile of Saddam to Libya.

"I remember telling President Bush about the talks I was having with Gaddafi," says Berlusconi. "He was very engaged and interested."

"Berlusconi was trying to be helpful," recalls former U.S. ambassador to Rome Mel Sembler, who was present for the Oval Office meeting. "He was being a good ally. He was looking for an alternative to war. The president listened to Berlusconi. He was open to the idea of Saddam going into exile, as long as he left Iraq."

After the forty-five-minute meeting in the Oval Office, Bush led Berlusconi upstairs for a private luncheon for the two leaders and their closest aides. Gathered around the table were Bush's National Security Adviser Condoleezza Rice, Secretary of State Colin Powell, Ambassador Sembler, and Andy Card, the president's chief of staff. Berlusconi was accompanied by his spokesman, his diplomatic adviser, and the Italian ambassador in Washington. Over a light meal of grouper with mushrooms and wild rice, accompanied by a California Chardonnay, Berlusconi and Bush continued their conversation about Iraq and Saddam.

Toward the end of the luncheon, just before an all-American apple pie was served for dessert, Berlusconi turned to Bush and spoke of the need for any military action to be well justified under international law. The discussion turned to the desirability of a fresh UN resolution to justify any intervention in Iraq. It was at this point that Berlusconi launched into the lengthy telling of a fanciful story, an allegory of his own making, to explain to Bush why he was worried about a war being launched without appropriate legal backing and justification that weapons of mass destruction had really been found. After all, the UN inspectors had returned empty-handed. France and half of Europe were bitterly opposed to an invasion. Now Berlusconi screwed up his courage, and puffed out his chest as he stared into the hard faces across the table.

"I wanted to find a friendly way of delivering my message," he says. "After all, I was telling the president of the United States that I was not in favor of military action. So on the plane while we were flying from London to Washington I had spent hours with Valentino Valentini trying to come up with a nice story, a fable, an allegory of sorts."

The story that Berlusconi then told took more than ten minutes to tell. It was long. It was complicated. It was a bit corny. To those who were in the room, Berlusconi appeared highly animated, playing the part of different animal characters, miming the scenes in an imaginary forest. The scene upstairs at the White House must have seemed slightly surreal.

"I told them a story about a lion and a wolf," recounts Berlusconi. "The lion in this story was Bush, who is the king of the forest. The lion doesn't like the wolf, meaning Saddam Hussein. But the wolf has to pass in front of the lion's house every day to get to his own home and every time he passes, the lion growls at him or punches him. So the wolf and the lion complain to the fox, who is the head of the General Assembly of all the animals in the forest. That would be Kofi Annan. The fox then tells the lion to stop picking on the wolf, but the lion says the wolf is a bad guy. 'What has the wolf done?' the fox asks the lion. 'He ate the three little piglets,' says the lion. But the fox wants proof of the crime, so the fox [Kofi Annan] sends the Swedish eagle [UN weapons inspector Hans Blix] to investigate the wolf. But the eagle returns without any proof of the crime. The fox then tells the lion that if he really wants to keep punching the wolf, he will need to come up with a good reason, some excuse. So the lion tells the wolf to run and get him a pack of Marlboro cigarettes. And when the wolf returns with the Marlboros, the lion tells him that he got the wrong kind of pack and he punches him anyway.

"In other words," says Berlusconi, now chortling about his own anecdote, "I was trying to find a way to tell him that he needed a really good reason and a plausible one if he wanted to take down Saddam Hussein."

When Berlusconi finished telling this lengthy and bewildering anecdote, a virtual cornucopia of mixed metaphors in the animal forest, the attendees at the White House luncheon laughed politely. Then everyone looked at the president and the air became still.

"Everybody was laughing at the end of my story," recalls Berlusconi. "Everybody except George..."

Bush was a man of few words.

"Yeah," said the president of the United States of America to Silvio Berlusconi. "I'm gonna kick his ass!"

What Berlusconi remembers following this statement of intent is another lengthy story, this one told by Bush, and this one not an allegory from the jungle but the story of how Saddam Hussein had tried to assassinate his father.

"President Bush had a particular, let us say a very vehement conviction, a genuine belief, that Saddam Hussein was a threat to all humanity and had to be destroyed," recalls Berlusconi.

As they left the White House, Berlusconi turned to his aides and said it appeared that Bush would not change his mind. He seemed crestfallen.

In his public remarks upon leaving the White House that day,

Berlusconi summoned up his strength and continued to give his staunch backing to Bush, as would Tony Blair when he turned up at the White House a day later.

That same evening Berlusconi and his team boarded their Airbus and returned to Rome. In his private diary that night, amid the general exhaustion and jet lag, Berlusconi scribbled a few notes about his failed mission. It had not gone as he had hoped.

A few days later, Colin Powell made his controversial appearance at the UN Security Council. After that it was clear that Bush really did intend to bring down Saddam. In March, when Operation Enduring Freedom was launched, Italy would provide logistical support and other non-military assistance to the war effort, even though Berlusconi remained convinced that the invasion of Iraq was a big mistake. He continued his enthusiastic support for Bush throughout the long war in Iraq, for years to come, and right up until the election of Barack Obama in 2008. His friendship would also blossom with Tony Blair, who famously vacationed with his wife, Cherie, at Berlusconi's fabulous villa on Sardinia's Costa Smeralda, enjoying the yachts and local watering holes in this billionaire's playground. But the friendship with Blair, whom Berlusconi perceived as the rightful heir of Margaret Thatcher, would never match the heat and intensity of the Bush-Berlusconi bond. Nor would the relationship with Blair ever come near to matching the warmth that Berlusconi would feel in the company of his other new ally, another world leader with a slightly macho disposition. He may have developed an instant rapport with Bush, but long after W. had left the White House and gone back to Texas, Berlusconi remained on the closest of terms with a man for whom he still professes the profoundest feelings of friendship. Who could this be?

"I am talking about my friend Vladimir," says a smiling Silvio Berlusconi.

That would be Vladimir Putin.

CHAPTER SEVEN

———

A Friend in the Kremlin

Silvio is a very appealing person," says Vladimir Putin. "What makes him so appealing? He is an extraordinary person. He is very direct. Of course, he is a diplomat and knows how to avoid sensitive matters, that is clear, but he is also a courageous man, and it is this courage that helps him to be blunt when expressing his point of view, his position. In my opinion, this is very important in politics, but it is even more important in life, and it is an important human quality. And that is where I think the appeal lies."

"Vladimir is the exact opposite of the image that is portrayed of him in the Western media. He is a really sensitive person, a man of profound feelings, always respectful of others. He is very gentle, a man with a delicate sensibility," says Silvio Berlusconi.

No other relationship has caused as much consternation, curiosity, or controversy as Silvio Berlusconi's effusive and abiding friendship with Russian president Vladimir Putin. The two men struck up their relationship in the early 2000s, when Berlusconi was playing an active role as self-appointed mediator between Putin and President Bush.

Four days after his White House visit, Berlusconi found himself in Russia for a meeting with Putin. On January 30, 2003, Berlusconi had failed in his attempt to get Bush to change his mind about making war on Saddam. But now he was Putin's guest for a bilateral Russia-Italy summit, and with Bush's knowledge he was also embarking on a little round of back-channel diplomacy over the mounting showdown with Saddam.

One of the official country residences of the president of Russia, the Russian equivalent of Camp David, is a sprawling dacha in the middle of the forest, near the city of Zavidovo, some sixty-eight miles northeast of Moscow. This is hunter's country, and out here on the tundra in winter it gets frighteningly cold. It was twenty-one degrees below zero on the evening of February third when a Russian military helicopter carrying Silvio Berlusconi and two of his aides landed at the complex in Zavidovo.

Putin laughs as he recalls the freezing cold weather.

"We were at a wildlife reserve that was created back in the Soviet times. It is a big one, some 124,000 hectares. I suggested that we have dinner there in the forest, and he agreed. We took a walk, we had dinner, and we sat for a while in front of the bonfire. I just wanted him to enjoy himself and I think he liked it."

The Russian president was indeed keen to show off some of the wonders of Mother Russia in wintertime. He had arranged a night camp for outdoor dining, reassuring the somewhat startled Berlusconi that the huge bonfire would keep them warm. Putin presented Berlusconi with a Russian winter fur trapper's cap, a huge Cossack-style affair with furry earflaps. A small convoy of four-wheel-drive SUVs pulled up to the front of the dacha, and the leaders drove off into the woods. Berlusconi's diplomatic adviser remembers the freezing cold, and he remembers Putin telling them that he would show them how real Russians lived, out in the wild.

"Putin was extremely hospitable," recalls Giovanni Castellaneta, who sat at Berlusconi's side that night. "He took us to this place where they had this raging fire going, but it was still freezing. Putin wanted to show us the beauties of nature in Russia, the vistas of endless steppes, the way hunters sit around a fire and eat and drink into the night. We were all bundled up even at the table, with our fur caps on our heads. The dinner began with a very excellent fish soup, and it was followed by grilled sturgeon. There was also plenty of vodka, although Putin himself doesn't drink much. The only problem is that at a temperature of twenty-one degrees below zero, by the time the waiters had brought the plates of sturgeon from the grill to the table, the fish was already cold."

Berlusconi, meanwhile, was in his element. He could certainly respect a leader who put on a good show. Thankfully, Putin did not make them suffer for too long in the cold, and eventually shepherded his shivering Italian guests back to the dacha, where they joined the rest of their delegations for a second, and rather more ceremonial, dinner that evening.

"At least it was warm back in the dacha," recalls Castellaneta. It was also a setting more amenable to the intense discussions about the looming war in Iraq. While Berlusconi conveyed to Putin the views of Bush, both he and Putin were against military intervention. Still, Berlusconi was trying to be a loyal ally to Washington while at the same time keeping lines of communication open with Putin. Former U.S. diplomats say that Berlusconi actually played a useful role as an occasional back channel for Bush and Putin, especially in the period after 9/11, and in 2002 and 2003.

With Bush, it had been love at first sight. Berlusconi's adoration of all things American had made that an easy relationship. There was also an unmistakable chemistry, which proved to be the case as well with Putin. Berlusconi always tried to help along the chemistry with his own salesmanship and bravura. He remained the inveterate deal maker and charmer, the natural-born seducer of his youth.

Berlusconi and Putin, from all accounts, liked and respected each other immediately. They made for an odd couple. Berlusconi was a virulent anti-Communist. Putin was head of the Communist Party in a virulently capitalist and post-Soviet Russia.

That Putin and Berlusconi should find solace in each other's company may seem surprising, but it was not. The two men proceeded to break all records in terms of bilateral visits between Russian and Italian leaders. Between their first meeting at the G-8 summit in Genoa in July 2001 and the dinner out in the cold of

Zavidovo in early 2003, they had already seen each other eight times in just nineteen months. And that didn't count the summer vacation at Berlusconi's luxury villa in Sardinia for Putin's teenage daughters or Berlusconi's annual visits to Russia each October for Putin's birthday parties. They would continue seeing each other at least twice a year, and more, for the next decade.

Berlusconi says he worked hard at the relationship with Putin because a personal connection is the most important starting point for his foreign policy.

"With my friend Vladimir and with other leaders I always try to be open. I try to establish a good rapport and a strong personal bond. This always helps when you have problems. It allows you to call each other at any moment and more easily resolve issues. But you also have to spend time together. Putin and Blair and various European leaders have come to visit and vacation with me in Sardinia. I think this is a good thing because among world leaders, as in any human relations, having a good rapport based on mutual respect, friendship, and trust means everything. For me, it has to be a bond that goes beyond the head and starts with the heart."

Putin, years after they had met, would call Berlusconi "the last of the Mohicans" and would laud him as being among Europe's greatest leaders, an opinion not universally shared. What did Putin mean by the expression?

"Well, I might be wrong," says Putin, "but in my view Mr. Berlusconi is a man who does not just think in terms of election campaigns and the next electoral cycle. He thinks more strategically. His life is not measured by electoral cycles: He has a strategic vision. The conversations we have had were not only about current issues. We do, of course, discuss them, but more often Mr. Berlusconi brings up strategic issues relating to Italy, Europe, and international relations in a broader sense. He is a man of great stature and vision, if I can put it this way."

According to Valentino Valentini, the Berlusconi aide who was present at every single one of the dozens of meetings with Putin over the years, the key to understanding the relationship between the two men is the way Berlusconi always goes for the human relationship before sitting down to do business.

"Remember," cautions Valentini, "that Berlusconi is a businessman, an entrepreneur. He may not be any good at diplomatic protocol and he commits plenty of gaffes, sure, but he has his own approach to international politics. First he wants to get to know you and connect, and then he proceeds with the business at hand. This is completely different from the American approach, where first you get down to business and then you decide if you like the person or not. In his dealings with Putin, the human dimension counted a lot."

In fact, Berlusconi's skills in salesmanship and marketing would come in handy as he and Putin developed closer ties. Putin, speaking about Berlusconi's life in an interview in the Kremlin, stressed the improvement in commercial ties between Russia and Italy.

"In 1994, when he became prime minister for the first time, the trade between Russia and Italy was $4.4 billion, and now it is $46 billion; so it has increased more than ten times," noted Putin.

While he remained a polarizing figure at home, Berlusconi did manage to connect in some primordial way with Vladimir Putin, perhaps more than he had with Bush. In some strange way, his unconventional manner and his larger-than-life aura allowed Italy to punch above its weight in foreign policy and to occasionally play the role of middleman between Washington and Moscow. That was the real value of Berlusconi's friendships with Bush and Putin.

Berlusconi's usefulness in transatlantic relations was most apparent in the spring of 2002, when he helped to accelerate talks that would lead to an agreement between Russia and NATO that would put a symbolic end to the Cold War.

On April 2, 2002, Berlusconi was a guest at Putin's dacha in Sochi, on the Black Sea. It was another in a lengthy series of visits, and the two men posed happily for the cameras as they drank Russian tea during a break in the talks. Just before dinner, Berlusconi and Putin sat down in a small room on the second floor of the dacha, accompanied only by close aides and an interpreter.

At that meeting Berlusconi was carrying a message to Putin

from President Bush about Russia's suspected supplying of sensitive technologies to Iran's nuclear weapons program. He was also urging Putin to speed up the talks that Russia was having with NATO about a cooperation agreement aimed at creating a new partnership council that would bring Russia and NATO together for the first time. Putin was understandably touchy about the subject, given that NATO was about to invite seven former Communist countries to join. He told Berlusconi that for political reasons he couldn't attend the planned NATO summit that year, alongside former Warsaw Pact countries who would be joining NATO. For the sake of appearances, Putin said the first priority was finalizing a new NATO-Russia partnership deal and holding a separate summit. This, Putin explained, would show the NATO-Russia relationship to be equal in importance to NATO expansion. That would work. Berlusconi agreed and immediately seized the opportunity. He suggested that Italy could host the treaty signing, to give it "an appropriate historic setting." Putin was delighted.

A few minutes later, Berlusconi's aides watched as Putin sat down with Berlusconi in the room upstairs at the dacha and phoned the White House. With interpreters on the line and Berlusconi at his side, Putin spoke with Bush. Putin urged Bush to speed up the negotiations on the new NATO-Russia agreement. He told him of Berlusconi's offer to host a summit and the signing in Rome in just a couple of months, at the end of May 2002. Bush did not agree immediately. He told Putin he would consider it. Berlusconi, who since the Genoa summit of July 2001 had been pushing Bush and Putin to try to put their differences aside, was thrilled by the phone call. He felt they had made progress and he wanted to stage a big show. He wanted to be the host of a summit in which the two most powerful leaders in the world, former enemies, would formally bury the hatchet and agree to cooperate.

Upon his return to Rome, on April fourth, Berlusconi summoned the American ambassador, Mel Sembler, to his office and briefed him on the meeting with Putin. As Sembler's own confidential cable report of the meeting reveals, at the end of the meeting, "Berlusconi pulled the ambassador aside to make a 'personal request' to President Bush on NATO-Russia matters."

Berlusconi asked the ambassador to tell Bush that Putin needed their help in building Russian public opinion on NATO enlargement. Putin needed to be seen to be part of the NATO family, Berlusconi argued. In addition, he emphasized his request for Bush to push for a speedy conclusion of the NATO-Russia agreement, which was still in the hands of bureaucrats and diplomats. He also reminded him of the big summit in Rome at the end of May, with Putin and Bush together in one room. Berlusconi asked Sembler to do his best with the White House.

Sembler cabled back to Washington for instructions, not quite sure if staging a big summit in Rome was more in Putin's or in Berlusconi's interest. But the answer came just a few days later, and it was positive. Bush called Berlusconi to say he had thought about it and had decided to accept the proposal to speed up the NATO-Russia deal so he could come to Rome and join Putin for the signing in May.

It was late at night on April twelfth when Bush called. The next day, after talking with Putin and NATO Secretary-General George Robertson, Berlusconi announced plans for the summit in Italy. Then, being Berlusconi, he did not call in his NATO experts. He called in his best television producers and stage set designers and architects and lighting technicians. He called in the A team from Mediaset, including quiz show producers and variety show set designers. To ensure maximum security and a spectacular sunset, Berlusconi chose as the summit location a military base just outside of Rome called Pratica di Mare.

"From the moment that Bush called him to say he was coming, Berlusconi started thinking of the media image that could be projected, the televised image of the end of the Cold War, a spectacular visual setting for Bush and Putin," recalls Valentini. "Sure, Berlusconi is a showman, and, sure, some of the American journalists made fun of the set he built, they said it was kitsch. But you have to understand that Berlusconi the prime minister was also a media and marketing expert, so he knew what he was doing."

What Berlusconi built, in record time, was a stage set worthy of the most lavishly produced TV show, a stage set placed at the center of a compound that would be complete with anti-missile batteries, fighter jets circling above in the sky, and Rome's airports closed to all traffic for forty-eight hours. Europe and the United States were still on heightened anti-terror alert. After all, 9/11 had happened only a few months before. Indeed the plan for the NATO-Russia Council had first grown out of Putin's willingness to align Moscow with the international alliance against terrorism in the period right after the September eleventh attacks.

Berlusconi deployed 15,000 people for enhanced security, including police officers, soldiers, and other security forces. He ordered ships of the Italian navy to clear a zone along the nearby Mediterranean coast. Inside the complex, he had carpenters build arches that were reminiscent of the Colosseum in the huge chamber where the government leaders would meet and sign the treaty. The structure, much of it in the style of faux marble, was actually made of plywood that had been painted to look like stone. To give it a more authentic feel, Berlusconi had Roman statues shipped in from an archaeological museum in Naples. The Rome correspondent of *The New York Times* called it "a sort of Cinecittà for world leaders."

By the time Putin and Bush arrived at the air base, it was completely locked down, a fortress on the outside with an inner core that looked like the set of *Who Wants to Be a Millionaire.*

For Berlusconi, what counted most was being at the center of it all as a witness to history, in a slickly produced and largely ceremonial meeting that lasted just five hours. Berlusconi was finally flanked by his friends Putin and Bush, with Blair and Chirac looking across the table as the document was signed.

"I guess of all the things I did in my life, this may be the one I am most proud of," says Berlusconi, now rummaging around in his study at the villa in Arcore. He comes upon a photograph of himself with Bush and Putin and smiles broadly. "This really was the moment that marked the end of the Cold War, you know. It really was an important moment in recent history."

In Putin's view, Berlusconi played a significant role in lowering tensions and fostering confidence between the former Cold War rivals.

"In the early 2000s, and especially in 2002, he pushed for signing an agreement between Russia and NATO, and in this respect he played a significant role in improving the situation in Europe not only in terms of relations between Italy and Russia, but also in the wider political process," says Putin.

The so-called Rome Summit Declaration that was signed by Putin and the NATO leaders in May 2002 at Pratica di Mare was indeed a piece of post–Cold War history, a moment lodged midway between the attacks of September 11, 2001, and the start of the war on Saddam in March 2003.

"At the start of the twenty-first century we live in a new, closely interrelated world, in which unprecedented new threats and challenges demand increasingly united responses," the declaration read. "We, the member states of the North Atlantic Treaty Organization and the Russian Federation, are today opening a new page in our relations, aimed at enhancing our ability to work together in areas of common interest and to stand together against common threats and risks to our security."

The summit marked the creation of the NATO-Russia Council, not exactly a household phrase but an important diplomatic channel in the early years of the century, when the leadership of Vladimir Putin still seemed to hold promise for Washington, when he seemed to be a modernizing influence in Moscow and a pragmatic partner. Bush had even announced that he had looked Putin "in the eye" and had gotten "a sense of his soul."

The council that emerged from this summit actually did serve a purpose over the years, and led to significant cooperation between NATO and Russia in Afghanistan as well as in the war on terrorism. NATO suspended the council's meetings in 2008 as a punishment for Putin after Russia's war on Georgia. But in early 2009, newly appointed U.S. Secretary of State Hillary Clinton made reviving the NATO-Russia Council a key part of her ill-fated "reset" policy with Moscow. The council's resumption was supposed to be part of the Obama administration's re-engagement of Russia in a constructive relationship. Clinton had already left the State Department when Washington joined the rest of NATO in suspending the council again, this time over Putin's landgrab in Ukraine, the annexation of Crimea.

Putin says that Russia will not allow the differences it has with the West over Ukraine to drag it back into another Cold War:

"There are some people who want to drive a wedge between Europe and Russia, or Ukraine and Russia. We understand this very well. And at times those who pursue such goals succeed. But this only suggests that our work is not efficient enough. We will not let anyone drag us into a new cold war of any kind. We will not allow that to happen."

Berlusconi, meanwhile, has consistently defended Putin's actions in Crimea and in Ukraine, so much so that his critics call him a mouthpiece for Putin. Yet for those who have heard both men speak about Ukraine and other subjects, it is clear that they share a common vision.

"On the issue of Ukraine," says Berlusconi, "I am in total disagreement with the policies of the European Union and the United States, and on the behavior of NATO. The people of Crimea speak Russian and they voted in a referendum to rejoin their Mother Russia. These sanctions on Russian individuals are the wrong policy. Expelling Russia from the G-8 is not the answer. Unfortunately, in my opinion, the behavior of Western leaders over the Ukraine could take us back to that isolation of Russia that existed before we signed the agreement at Pratica di Mare. Frankly, I see a complete lack of leadership in the West at this time."

Putin, in any case, recognizes in Berlusconi not just a friend and ally, but perhaps the man who did the most to help bring Russia in from the cold even back in the 1990s, when Boris Yeltsin was still in charge.

"A lot has changed for the better in our bilateral relations. Back in 1994 he invited President Yeltsin to the summit of G-8, which back then had been G-7. During his first term, which was not very long, his first term as the prime minister, he came to Moscow to sign together with President Yeltsin an agreement on friendship, on amity and cooperation between Italy and Russia. In the beginning of the first decade of the twenty-first century he was the one who initiated signing the treaty between Russia and NATO, and in this sense he played a very significant role in making the situation in Europe healthier, not only in the context of Russian-Italian relations, but also in a much broader context."

Throughout all these years, Berlusconi remained on extremely close terms with Putin, who clearly shows great understanding about his friend's political fortunes and even about the numerous indictments and court cases and scandals that Berlusconi has faced over the past twenty years. Has the Western media been unfair to Berlusconi?

Putin shrugs. "I do not think I have the right to indicate any mistakes of the Western media. Everybody makes mistakes, including politicians and mass media. I would like to note the following: If my memory does not fail me, Mr. Berlusconi became involved in politics in 1994. He went into politics for the first time in 1993, became a prime minister in 1994, but before that he had spent more than thirty years in business, and the law enforcement system, the law enforcement agencies, had never had any questions for him. But as soon as he became engaged in politics, almost thirty criminal cases were instituted against him during three years. Unfortunately, this is typical not only for Italy, but for the world in general," he says.

The Russian president speaks with genuine affection, referring ten times to Berlusconi as "Silvio" in a half-hour conversation. "Silvio," he says, "is a straightforward man, sometimes maybe too straightforward—he can offend someone and evoke responses from his colleagues, as well as from the press. So, you know, these are just elements of an open political struggle. Sometimes it does not go beyond the bounds of decency, sometimes it does. Frankly speaking, I do not have time to analyze what foreign media say."

The foreign media would play a role again in highlighting Berlusconi's friendship with Putin during the WikiLeaks scandal, with the release in November 2010 of a cache of more than 250,000 secret and confidential U.S. diplomatic cables. Included in the flood of documents were a few choice cables sent to Washington by American ambassadors in Rome. One of them was a secret memo entitled "Italy-Russia Relations: The View from Rome." It was written by U.S. Ambassador Ronald Spogli and sent to Hillary Clinton in late January 2009, just days after she arrived at the State Department.

Ambassador Spogli, a California investment banker and a big fund-raiser for Bush, tried his hand at analyzing the Berlusconi-Putin relationship. "Berlusconi," wrote the U.S. ambassador, "believes that Putin is his close and personal friend and continues to have more contact with Putin than with any other world leader. During the Georgia crisis, Berlusconi spoke to Putin on a daily basis for a period of almost a week. The basis of the friendship is hard to determine, but many interlocutors have told us that Berlusconi believes that Putin, a fellow 'tycoon,' trusts Berlusconi more than any other European leader. Berlusconi admires Putin's macho, decisive, and authoritarian governing style, which the Italian PM believes matches his own. From the Russian side, it appears that Putin has devoted much energy to developing Berlusconi's trust."

The most explosive part of the memo, which made headlines, concerned alleged business dealings between Berlusconi and Putin. While it was well known that the two men had pushed for deeper energy ties, deals between the Italian state oil company ENI and Russia's Gazprom, Spogli reported rumors of personal gain for Berlusconi. There was, he wrote to the secretary of state, "a more nefarious connection" between the two men.

Spogli reported that his contacts "believe that Berlusconi and his cronies are profiting personally and handsomely from many of the energy deals between Italy and Russia." He also raised pointed questions about Valentino Valentini, whom he described as "a member of parliament and somewhat shadowy figure who operates as Berlusconi's key man on Russia, albeit with no staff or even a secretary. Valentini, a Russian-speaker who travels to Russia several times per month, frequently appears at Berlusconi's side when he meets other world leaders. What he does in Moscow during his frequent visits is unclear but he is widely rumored to be looking after Berlusconi's business interests in Russia."

The former Berlusconi aide denies any wrongdoing and accuses the American ambassador of having gotten his information "from the newspapers and from gossip in Rome."

"This cable is complete nonsense," claims Valentini, "because there are no Berlusconi business interests in Russia. I have lots of friends in Russia and I have promoted Italian exports to Russia, but the rest of what Ambassador Spogli has to say is pure fiction, it is a figment of his imagination."

Berlusconi was furious at the allegations, especially as they were immediately seized upon by his opponents on the left and caused mayhem on the domestic political scene. Nor was he pleased to be described by U.S. diplomats as "feckless, vain and ineffective."

The subject of Berlusconi's relationship with Putin came up again in another cable, this one written later in 2009 by Ambassador David Thorne, an Obama nominee. Thorne quoted sources saying that "Berlusconi's frequent late nights and penchant for partying hard means he does not get sufficient rest."

"Sex scandals, criminal investigations, family problems and financial concerns appear to be weighing heavily on Berlusconi's personal and political health, as well as on his decision-making ability," wrote the ambassador.

The WikiLeaks cables were released to the world media on November 28, 2010. Ironically enough, Ambassador Thorne was tasked by the State Department with giving advance notice to Berlusconi's office that the cables were about to be published. Less than seventy-two hours later, on December first, an embarrassed Hillary Clinton found herself face-to-face with Berlusconi at an international security meeting in faraway Kazakhstan. Berlusconi had tried to laugh off the WikiLeaks cables in public, but he was being roasted by the Italian press and there was an uproar in parliament, with the opposition already calling for a special investigation of the alleged business ties between Berlusconi and Putin. Privately, he raised the WikiLeaks matter with Hillary Clinton as soon as they met at the security conference in Astana.

"I had a close enough relationship with Mrs. Clinton to be able to vent with her, so I demanded to know why these things were being said by American diplomats. I told her that America has no better friend in Europe, that I am the most loyal ally, the closest, with an eternal gratitude for what America did for my country," Berlusconi recalls. "After that she apologized and we went out in front of the cameras and she fixed things. She made a strong statement of support for Italy and for me. I am grateful for that."

Mrs. Clinton made the obligatory apology and issued the obligatory statement about warm relations with Italy, and it was done. Berlusconi thanked the secretary of state for her statement of support, which came in time to make the evening news shows back in Italy. Then he headed for the airport and boarded his Airbus, leaving Kazakhstan for his next destination, which just happened to be Vladimir Putin's dacha on the Black Sea at Sochi. In Sochi he could find solace.

Berlusconi denies to this day that he ever had any business interests with Putin, and continues to see his friend in the Kremlin as a strategic thinker, a strong leader, and a close friend. Putin appears to return the respect and admiration, and in some ways is effusive in his praise for Berlusconi.

"You know," says Putin, "he was the Italian prime minister for four terms. That means that people voted for him, it means that average Italian citizens found something very attractive both in his political agenda and in his personality. I believe there is positive chemistry between him and a large number of Italian citizens. He is a remarkable, straightforward, and very interesting person. All this taken together suggests that Silvio Berlusconi, as a politician and a man, will surely get the place he deserves in Italian history."

The challenge for Berlusconi, however, would not be whether he would make the history books as a politician. It would be how history would describe him as a man.

CHAPTER EIGHT

—

Women!

"Would you like to see the famous bunga-bunga room? Do you have the courage? Do you dare?"

Silvio Berlusconi is wearing a devilish smile. The syllables vibrate, they spark in the air like the sound of a bass being plucked: *Boong-gah! Boong-gah!* The words force one to smile, or laugh, with their insidiously onomatopoeic hint of erotic mischief.

Berlusconi grins like a naughty teenage schoolboy rather than a man of nearly eighty. He is perched in an overstuffed armchair in front of the marble fireplace in this, his favorite living room. He is dressed in his usual "at home" navy blue cashmere sweater and blazer. A black-and-white photo of a fatherly Berlusconi and his daughter Marina, encased in a gold frame, sits on the mantelpiece, just over his right shoulder.

It is late afternoon on a rainy winter's day at Arcore, the chill of December gradually creeping in from the surrounding woods. The night is falling fast. Out front, where the air is cool and moist, the stone façade of the eighteenth-century Villa San Martino is bathed in garlands of light. Here, inside the salon, in front of the fireplace, it is warm and comfortable, even toasty.

It is in this setting, in this sitting room with photographs of the family, the bas-relief by Luca della Robbia nearby, the Canaletto on the far wall, and the dainty collection of white porcelain on the long table, it is here that Berlusconi decides to open up and talk about the bunga-bunga scandal, about those infamous bunga-bunga nights, the wild parties, and the claims that he paid to have sex with a minor, the notorious and beautiful Moroccan girl Karima Rashida el Mahroug, a teenage nightclub dancer otherwise known to the tabloids as "Ruby the Heart-Stealer."

Now, with the devil-may-care abandon of a man who has been indicted on underage prostitution charges, tried in a spectacular court proceeding, convicted and sentenced to seven years in prison, and then acquitted on appeal, Berlusconi begins a guided tour of the bunga-bunga room. He rises from his armchair, summons up his best dramatic bravado, dramatically pivots left, and says, "Follow me!"

He strolls across another sumptuous living room, this one full of Old Masters in elaborate and ornate gold frames, he glances briefly across the portico at the green lawn of the villa's park, and now we are standing before a white door. Then, with a flourish worthy of the host of one of his own television variety shows, Berlusconi throws open the door and switches on a light that reveals an elaborate and high-ceilinged banquet room, a king's dining hall, at least sixty feet long and twenty feet wide. Berlusconi is no longer timid, or cautious, or carefully advised by his army of lawyers. No, he is alone at home, and he has become a one-man show, brimming with energy and humor, as he strides proudly into the magnificent frescoed chamber.

This was the famous bunga-bunga room? Not a bedroom but a supersize and rather baroque dining table surrounded by classic paintings and walls of mirrors and frescoes?

"Here we are!" proclaims Berlusconi, presenting a long table with thirty-six places set, as though for a state dinner, and a Christmas motif in the elaborate decorations and centerpieces, the table replete with miniature merry-go-rounds, tiny plastic mountain landscapes, miniature skating rinks, and a series of raging bulls.

The so-called bunga-bunga room seems to be just a big dining room.

"Of course it is, because this *is* a dining room, it is the room where the soirees took place," he explains with a big smile. "I sat over there and the orchestra was up there. The table is set just as elegantly as it was, and nothing has changed in all this time, and actually I have continued, and I continue to this very day to have these evenings, these parties right here, in this room, and with different types of guests."

But what about the first time that Ruby was here?

"On that particular occasion there was a significant number of beautiful girls, from the worlds of TV and cinema...I of course produce movies, I produce TV, and so they were all more than happy to visit the prime minister, the president of AC Milan, the cinema tycoon...Beyond that, I think one would have to admit that I am a rather amusing fellow, an anomalous sort of prime minister, if you will..."

Where did Ruby sit?

"Ah, I can't remember!"

Was she one of the guests?

"Yes, she was."

There was no sex, only dinners with music? Even though she returned here for nearly a dozen visits?

Berlusconi looks momentarily defensive, but only for a microsecond, and then he flashes that big Hollywood smile again. "I might add," he deadpans with an air of injured pride, "that even if there had been sex, here in a private house, it would not have been a crime. So where is the crime? What crime occurred here?"

Berlusconi may have been put on trial for underage prostitution, he may have been accused of having paid to have sex with a minor, but he has always maintained he was unaware of Ruby's real age.

"Ruby," announces Berlusconi, as he addresses the issue of her age, "well, first of all she used to tell everybody that she was twenty-four. And she certainly looked that age, because she was intelligent and smart, and because she had lived a hard life, but there was no possibility of there having been sex..."

No sex?

"Look here!" he adds, suddenly indignant, even defiant. "I have always said that I never touched Ruby, not even with one finger, and Ruby has always said the same thing, and nobody saw anything. So to prove that there had been sex you would need a photograph, or a video, or a credible witness. But there is nothing of the sort. It is pure invention."

He is smiling, relaxed and nonchalant, the billionaire tycoon turned politician who wants to be loved, admired, and entertained, who wants to entertain and charm all those around him. Perhaps he is still the original Silvio Berlusconi who became a television mogul in the late 1970s and early 1980s, the man whose taste in sexy and long-legged girls with curvy figures was shared by tens of millions of his fellow Italians as they watched his popular variety shows, his big extravaganzas on one of his commercial TV channels. Back in the 1980s, and ever since, Berlusconi has loved to host what he considers to be rather entertaining dinner parties. Personal taste and the definition of what may be described entertaining is always a subjective matter.

The Ruby case was, however, more than just a spectacular show; it soon proved a very serious matter for Berlusconi, and a political and personal embarrassment. As soon as the story broke, with publication of the first leaks from investigating Milan magistrates in October of 2010, Berlusconi found himself ridiculed in half the chancelleries of Europe. "Bunga-bunga" bars opened in many cities; from Moscow to Manchester, from Berlin to Bali, the words made Berlusconi appear to be half buffoon and half sex maniac, and in his native Italy his critics on the left were delighted at the new charges of abuse of office and paying for sex with a supposedly underage Moroccan nightclub dancer.

When Berlusconi was first informed he was under investigation in the case in late 2010, it looked at first as though the scandal might provoke a government collapse and early elections. Beyond the bunga-bunga story, Berlusconi was also facing a handful of tax fraud and corruption cases. These included the case in which Berlusconi was charged with bribing David Mills, his former U.K. lawyer and the husband of Britain's then minister of culture, to give false testimony about his media empire's finances. A Milan court had already convicted Mills of accepting the $600,000 bribe, even though both men had denied the charges.

As investigating magistrates shamelessly leaked to the Italian press a steady stream of wiretapped telephone calls, witness depositions, and stories of lavish presents having been showered on dozens of wannabe starlets and models who had attended the bunga-bunga evenings, Berlusconi was placed more and more on the defensive.

For the world's press it was all about Ruby. Aside from the sex charges, Berlusconi was alleged to have abused his position as a sitting prime minister by telephoning a Milan police station in May 2010 in order to get Ruby released from a holding cell. He wanted her released into the protection of a former dancer on one of Berlusconi's TV shows named Nicole Minetti, a former dental hygienist who was by then an elected county official in the Lombardy region for Berlusconi's Forza Italia.

Berlusconi apparently told the officer on duty that Ruby, a bit of a drifter who had been picked up shortly before by the police for allegedly stealing some money and jewels, was a relative of Egypt's President Hosni Mubarak, and it would be best for her to be released into the protective custody of Miss Minetti, who would be happy to pop by the station and pick up Ruby. Later, Berlusconi said he did not remember much about the call, but he denied abusing his power as prime minister by calling the police station.

Berlusconi also said at the time that he had helped Ruby financially when she was in difficulty. Both he and Ruby denied that they had had sex. But the newspaper stories and leaks persisted, and soon all of Italy was discussing allegations that the billionaire premier had kept a harem of thirty-two or thirty-three young girls, some of them housed in an apartment block that was part of Berlusconi's own Milano Due real estate development. Berlusconi, as always, ridiculed the whole business with self-deprecating humor. "I'm seventy-four years old, and although I'm definitely naughty, the idea of thirty-three girls in two months seems a bit much, even for a thirty-year-old," he said.

Unfortunately for Berlusconi, his sense of humor was not shared by the rather more buttoned-up prosecutors of Milan. He had once had to issue a public apology for another public joke he had made during a televised gala awards event, when he told Mara Carfagna, a former showgirl turned member of the Italian Chamber of Deputies: "If I wasn't already married, I would marry you right away!"

In Italy, such remarks may be offensive to some women, and in the specific case so it was for Berlusconi's second wife, who years later would file for divorce and win a monthly alimony of 1.4 million euros. But that was Berlusconi: The Man with the Golden Quip. "I am not a saint," he would say with a smirk. "I have been faithful," he once joked, "frequently."

In August of 2010, with news of the sexual scandals making for front-page copy across half of Europe, it wouldn't be long before Berlusconi became the butt of jokes, even to other heads of state. David Cameron, only recently installed at Downing Street, was leaving later for Rome for a state dinner with Berlusconi. That afternoon he had tea with his wife, Samantha, and with Ben Eine, a British graffiti artist. Mr. Eine recalled that the British prime minister was interrupted during the tea.

"We were sitting there chatting away, and his PA or assistant came in and said: 'David, we've got to go,'" Mr. Eine recalled. "He jumped up and said, 'Samantha, I've got to go off to Italy—dinner with Berlusconi. Don't worry, I'll get so-and-so to pull me out of the Jacuzzi before the whores turn up.'"

By the time the so-called bunga-bunga trial opened in April 2011, the story was no longer funny for Berlusconi.

"Say it ain't so, Silvio!" read the *New York Daily News* headline. The tabloid said Berlusconi would be tried "on charges that he paid for sex with an underage nightclub dancer and then tried to cover it up." A Swiss newspaper, *Le Temps*, wrote about "the decadence of Italian political life." *The New York Times*, rather more elegantly, reported that Berlusconi had decided not to attend the trial in Milan but would stay in Rome for a meeting on the crisis that was raging in Libya at the time. Newspapers around the world went crazy as the bunga-bunga trial opened. The *Observer* of London wrote of an "Italy in suspense as 'bunga-bunga' trial is poised to lift lid on Berlusconi's antics."

A total of 110 foreign reporters were accredited for the bunga-bunga trial in Milan's largest courtroom. CNN was running live coverage. Al Jazeera and the BBC were there. So were *The New York Times*, *Washington Post*, *Le Monde*, *Der Spiegel*, *Die Zeit*, *Liberation*, *El Pais*, and many others. Outside the courthouse dozens of paramilitary carabinieri police equipped with helmets, batons, and riot shields were on hand as pro-Berlusconi supporters clashed with the opposition camp. The protesters yelled out the words "bunga-bunga" while the prime minister's supporters burst into song with his unofficial anthem, "Thank Goodness for Silvio." In the courtroom the parade of two hundred witnesses included thirty-three alleged prostitutes and even testimony from Hollywood star George Clooney, who said he had spoken with Berlusconi's legal team and was happy to testify. Clooney revealed that he did spend one evening at Berlusconi's home in Rome, which he described as "one of the more astonishing evenings of my life." Clooney said he was taken to Berlusconi's bedroom to see the bed that Vladimir Putin gave him, and was then asked to stay for a dinner party.

Berlusconi smiles happily when he is asked about George Clooney.

"George Clooney came to a dinner party that I had in Rome, and afterwards he said: 'I went to a dinner and I had a lot of fun, and the host was very charming, but I had no bunga-bunga.' Of course he didn't, because the bunga-bunga was the dinner party *itself.*"

Berlusconi loves to pronounce the words "bunga-bunga" with a mocking bass tone that is so deep he sounds like Louis Armstrong saying, *"Boong-gah! Boong-gah!"* He explains the origin of the term, how it derives from an old joke, which has to do, he says, with his former friend, the late Libyan dictator, Muammar Gaddafi.

"Gaddafi always wanted me to come to visit Libya each year for the ceremony of the 'King of the Kings.' I couldn't go on one occasion, because I had a very important engagement, and so he asked me to send two delegates to the ceremony in Libya, which I did.

"Now here is where the story begins," says Berlusconi. "These two delegates of mine are captured by the most rebellious tribe left in Libya. They are tied to a pole in the center of the village, and all around them a tribal dance is performed. The tribe is crying out very guttural sounds, and the only word that they can understand is 'bunga-bunga.'

"The dance finishes, and the witch-doctor approaches Cicchitto, one of my two envoys, and asks him: 'Do you prefer to die or bunga-bunga?' And as anyone would have done, faced with a choice of death or bunga-bunga, he chooses bunga-bunga. And so all of the warriors of the village do him."

Even without any need of explicit terminology, Berlusconi successfully communicates the concept of his envoy being sodomized by members of the tribe. He continues now:

"The witch-doctor approaches my other envoy, Bondi, and he asks him: 'You want death or bunga-bunga?' Bondi, having seen what happened to his friend, says: 'Death!' The witch-doctor says, 'Okay, then, death it is, but before that, first a little bunga-bunga!' This is the joke that started everything," concludes Berlusconi, laughing heartily at his anecdote. He glides along the edge of the long dinner table, almost waltz-stepping, pointing out the elaborate Christmas decorations, and announcing that tomorrow evening there will be at least thirty-six guests gathered for dinner.

He pauses in front of an exceptional painting, from the high Renaissance, in the style of Da Vinci. What is most striking about this masterpiece, which sits upon an easel within a luxuriant frame of gilded wood, is that in the context of this notorious room the girl is partially nude, with the pale pastels of her breasts in full view.

"This is the *Mona Lisa*, from the School of Leonardo," says Berlusconi, pausing. Then, as though he can't resist the gag: "I have been accused of undressing her myself."

Gazing across the length of the bunga-bunga room, Berlusconi points out another Old Master, or a reliable copy, in this case the portrait of a beautiful but rather severe-looking courtesan or noblewoman, fully bloused, and known as *Antea*, by the sixteenth-century Italian Mannerist Parmigianino.

The two paintings, here in the room now known for its supposedly profane parties, offer a strong contrast in aesthetics between the sacred and the profane in Berlusconi's life, the sensuality of the bare-breasted *Mona Lisa* and the more austere feminine beauty of Parmigianino.

"I was also undressing the girl in the Parmigianino," explains Berlusconi with mock seriousness, "but then I looked her in the face and I said, 'I hope you are not like Ruby, who seems to be a twenty-something but then you find out she is seven months away from her eighteenth birthday.' So after that, I put her clothes back on."

Back in his favorite living room, relaxing with his political and press aides, Berlusconi is confessing that he finds it "difficult to speak of my feelings, of my emotions." He appears shy, and this time it is not an act. He is actually far better at making cocktail banter or joking about beautiful women than he is at looking at his own emotional life in the mirror. Everyone has had a first love. Even Berlusconi. Moving past bunga-bunga, he recounts the story of the first time he fell in love, and not as a teenager but in his mind's eye at an even younger age.

"I was seven years old, and my family was visiting the beautiful city of Lake Como. We went up to a very old castle called il Baradello, and I was brought to the very top of this castle, where there was a forecourt in the tower. We had this splendid panoramic view, and there were a few other people, and there was a girl, a little older than me, she must have been eight or nine, and she had this amazing hair. I looked at her and I immediately had this feeling of appreciation for this little girl. I spoke a few words with her and that was all, but for a long time she remained in my memory, and she remains in my memory today. That was the first time I paid attention to women."

Silvio Berlusconi as a schoolboy in Milan.

The Berlusconi family in 1947, with eleven-year-old Silvio, his four-year-old sister Maria Antonietta, and parents Rosa and Luigi.

Berlusconi (third from left in last row) at the Salesian high school he attended in Milan, circa 1952.

Berlusconi as a 1950s crooner.
He and Confalonieri formed
a band and played in postwar
Milan dance halls. Berlusconi
later sang on cruise ships and
worked as a tour guide.

Berlusconi on his
speedboat in the 1960s
off the Italian Riviera.
"I always said I was the
most handsome guy on
the beach."

Berlusconi in his Donald Trump
phase, as a Milanese real estate
developer, seated here next to
a model of his famous Milano
Due garden city development,
circa 1972.

Berlusconi the billionaire media mogul, photographed on the set at his flagship Canale 5 television network in Milan. He revolutionized Italian TV in the 1980s with brash variety shows, *Dallas*, *Dynasty*, and many other American sitcoms and soaps.

Berlusconi with his second wife, former actress Veronica Lario. Their messy divorce ended up costing Berlusconi $1.5 million a month in alimony checks, for life.

Berlusconi romping in the garden of his seventy-two-room villa in Arcore, on the outskirts of Milan, with two of his daughters, Barbara and Eleanora, in 1994.

Berlusconi and his five children from his two marriages, in 2005. From left to right: Eleonora (seated), Pier Silvio, Marina, Berlusconi, Barbara, and Luigi.

Berlusconi with Raisa and Mikhail Gorbachev at the villa in Arcore, during a visit in 1993.

President Bill Clinton and newly elected Prime Minister Silvio Berlusconi after a meeting during Berlusconi's short-lived first term in office, 1994.

Berlusconi at a Milan rally in 1998. His showmanship and charisma got him elected prime minister three times over a twenty-year period.

Vladimir Putin tosses a ball for Dudù to fetch during a visit with Berlusconi at his Rome residence, the ornate Palazzo Grazioli, in 2013.

© LIVIO ANTICOLI

Berlusconi offers a taste of Sardinia's "music paper" bread to his friend Vladimir Putin during a visit to Berlusconi's Villa Certosa on the Sardinian Gold Coast in 2003.

ROME SUMMIT

Putin, Berlusconi, a
George W. Bush at
historic NATO sum
at Pratica di Mare n
Rome in 2002, whi
led to the creation o
the NATO-Russia
Council. At the tim
Berlusconi had been
acting as a go-betwe
for Bush and Putin.

Christine Lagarde, the managing director
of the International Monetary Fund, who
was previously a slavishly loyal minister
to President Nicolas Sarkozy of France.
Lagarde was criticized for allegedly
behaving like a partisan politician instead
of a neutral arbiter in parroting Sarkozy's
anti-Berlusconi line at the height of the
euro crisis, during the G-20 summit in
Cannes in November 2011.

President Barack
Obama and Berlusconi
meeting in the Oval
Office. Obama was
standoffish in general
but ultimately took
Berlusconi's side against
Sarkozy, Merkel, and
Lagarde during the euro
crisis.

Berlusconi gives his nemesis, Sarkozy, a friendly strangle. Sarkozy led the attack on Berlusconi (with support from Christine Lagarde) at the G-20 summit.

Berlusconi with Hillary Clinton in late 2010. It befell the then U.S. secretary of state to apologize to Berlusconi for a raft of lurid and embarrassing WikiLeaks cables.

Berlusconi with his friend Muammar Gaddafi, having one of their many pow-wows in the colonel's tent. Together with Tony Blair, Berlusconi played an important role in steering Gaddafi from terrorism to cooperation in the early 2000s.

Berlusconi toasts his Naples-born girlfriend Francesca Pascale, who has been part of his life since the end of 2011.

"Ruby the Heart-Stealer," also known as Karima El Mahroug, the Moroccan-born prostitute and star of the infamous "bunga-bunga" parties at the villa in Arcore. Although he was acquitted of having sex with Ruby as an underage prostitute (for lack of proof), Berlusconi still faces new charges for allegedly having bribed her and thirty other escorts to perjure themselves at his trial.

With all the world's attention focused on his appreciation of sexy women, Berlusconi is not a man who has spoken much about his own understanding of love, or what he looks for in a woman, or even the way he met and fell in love with his first wife, or the pain he felt at the very public humiliations he endured during the breakup of his second marriage.

What is love, according to Berlusconi?

"I suppose I never really meditated on it, especially lately, since I have been distracted by so many other issues. Love is a feeling of deep attraction which becomes a feeling of the negation of one's own ego. It is to want what is best for the other so much, to love someone so much that in this love you find a mirror of yourself."

What, then, are the qualities that a man should look for, that Silvio Berlusconi looks for, in the perfect woman?

Berlusconi smiles a bit sheepishly.

"I am sorry if I seem superficial," he says, "but first of all you have to like her a lot. She must be beautiful, and she must be an object of desire. I can say that . . . even if this is a bit intimate, I can say that I don't think I ever went to bed, with either of my wives in the periods when we really loved each other, without desiring her, and without making love, and so I think this is important, basic. Then comes friendship, et cetera, but in the moment of love there is an attraction that is absolute. And there is another thing: you have to feel her attraction for you too, a real affection for you, and a sincere rapport, it has to be a feeling of shared loyalty; that is also a critical factor."

Berlusconi has called himself a "natural-born seducer" and he certainly has accumulated mountains of newspaper clippings in which his supposed sexual exploits make for good copy. In the Italian press, Berlusconi's sex life has been described over and over again and in lurid detail, with all sorts of allegations about the bunga-bunga girls, including claims of anal sex, sadomasoschism, and stories of girls dressed up as nuns and nurses doing lap dances. In the privacy of his home, however, he insists that he is actually a lot less exciting than most people might think.

"The popular descriptions of me are not accurate, really. The truth is I have always been pretty much a workaholic, and I have not devoted much of my life to the pursuit and seduction of the gentler sex. I have had an orderly life, I have had two marriages with two children the first time and three in the second marriage, and I was always a family man, trying to dedicate my free time, especially on the weekends, to my kids. So all of these other stories about me are just fantasies that are retold in order to disparage me, to damage me as a public figure. As a child, as a teenager, it is true, as my mother always used to say, that I was the most handsome guy on the beach. I sang and I played the guitar and I excelled in sports and so I was really attractive to the girls. But in truth, I would say that I was often the one who was seduced rather than being the guy who did the seducing."

Berlusconi was married for the first time in 1965 to the former Carla Elvira Dall'Oglio, with whom he had two children, Maria Elvira, known as Marina, and Pier Silvio, known in the family as Dudi. Carla Elvira was a not a public figure, and indeed she came from a humble background, having emigrated in the 1950s with her parents and two brothers from provincial Liguria, where her father worked as a maintenance man in the port of Genoa and her mother was a housewife.

At the time, Berlusconi had graduated from being a crooner on cruise ships and was just beginning to get into the business of real estate. He was young, not yet successful but highly entrepreneurial, always planning his next move, whether it was a question of business or even a personal desire. It was in 1964, when he was twenty-eight, that Berlusconi met Dall'Oglio. She was four years younger than him, and, unsurprisingly, the first thing Berlusconi recalls by his own recollection was seeing "the very graceful silhouette of a girl."

The manner in which Berlusconi met his first wife, and got her phone number, has been the subject of speculation for many years. According to Berlusconi, he saw her and fell for her in a train station, and he then engaged in an elaborate and improvised scheme, complete with elements of near slapstick, in order to attract the attention of the woman he would marry.

"I had been singing on a cruise ship back then, I was master of ceremonies, managing the games on the ship, doubling as a tour guide, I was doing many things, and I had this little flirt under way with the daughter of the ship owner who had traveled from Rome to visit me in Milan. When she had to return to Rome, I brought her to the train station, she hopped on board, and I waited until the train left the station. Suddenly, when I turned, right in front of me I see this very graceful silhouette of a girl, and she was also saying good-bye to her friend, and so she had also been abandoned, let us say, by her boyfriend, as I had been left by my girlfriend. I thought to myself: 'Well, I guess both of us are alone, and perhaps she would like a little company.'

"I lingered for a minute, and then I went to buy a newspaper. I went down the stairs and was heading out of the station and I saw her walking just ahead of me, and I admired her again. I went outside and got into my car, and as I drove by the bus stop there she was once more, with that silhouette that beckoned to me, that seemed to say 'Take me! Take me!' Now I thought to myself: 'Since this bus goes in the same direction I am going, toward my house, I am going to follow it, and I will see where she gets off.'

"Well, I followed the bus, stop after stop, and she didn't get off. But by now I was very focused on my goal, and so I followed the bus halfway across the city, to the other side of town. Then she got off, and I quickly parked my car and hopped out and started walking toward her. When I was in front of her I said to her: 'Wow, this is incredible! Excuse me, but weren't you at the train station just half an hour ago saying good-bye to somebody?' She kind of stared suspiciously at me, and said, 'Yes, that was me.' I asked her if she would give me her telephone number, but she said, 'No, you should not be under any illusion.' But then she gave me her number anyway, and from then on a love story began that brought me two children, thanks to this woman who I met in this rather peculiar manner."

Berlusconi's first wife proved to be not just a pretty "silhouette" but a reserved and somewhat timid woman, discreet and family-minded. After he met Carla in 1964, he romanced her in rapid, whirlwind Berlusconi style, and the two were married a few months later, in March of the following year.

A relatively stable family life ensued for two decades, and so did Berlusconi's rapid rise to fame and riches, as he moved from being a budding real estate tycoon in the 1960s to becoming the billionaire media mogul of his later fame in the 1980s. But Berlusconi was ever the restless man, ever the admirer of beautiful women.

In 1985, following twenty years of marriage, Berlusconi and Dall'Oglio met in a Milan tribunal and formalized their consensual separation, since they had already agreed on their planned divorce and the division of assets. The divorce would become final in 1990, five years later, but Berlusconi was already involved with someone else. By then, Berlusconi was already five years into a new relationship, this time with a curvaceous and sultry actress who had already borne him a third child. She was born Miriam Bartolini, but she had taken the name of Veronica Lake, a 1940s icon of Hollywood femininity, as the inspiration for her stage name of Veronica Lario (as she was known to the Italian theater-going public).

Lario and Berlusconi had first flirted in 1980, at Teatro Manzoni, a theater that he owned in Milan, a big hall located on one of the main boulevards in downtown Milan. She was twenty-four. He was forty-four. Berlusconi had only recently bought the theater, as he was at this point expanding beyond the business of real estate development and into television, theater, and cinema. On the evening in question he was attending a performance of a rather commercial comedy by Flemish playwright Fernand Crommelynck, curiously named *The Magnificent Cuckold*. Veronica Lario, playing the part of the wife of a pathologically jealous husband, lowered her top and revealed her breasts on stage.

The legend has it that Berlusconi bounded out of his seat and rushed backstage right after the performance, found his way to

Veronica's dressing room, burst in with a bouquet of roses, and romanced her straight into a major relationship, although a clandestine one at the time, as he was still very much married, with a wife and two kids at home. For a budding actress, starting a relationship with the man who would soon become Italy's most powerful media tycoon could have had its benefits. Veronica made a couple of films and then gave up acting and ended up having three children with Berlusconi in the ensuing years. Berlusconi's marriage to Veronica would wait until 1990, and it was finally celebrated by the mayor of Milan at City Hall. The presiding Socialist mayor, Paolo Pillitteri, was not only a close friend of Berlusconi's. He was also the brother-in-law of former prime minister Bettino Craxi, who in turn was present to serve as Berlusconi's best man.

For much of their marriage Veronica remained largely out of the public eye, sometimes the smiling consort of the billionaire Berlusconi, occasionally the smiling wife of Prime Minister Berlusconi, and more often simply invisible. This began to change in 2004 when she engineered a very public makeover of her image, confiding to a gossipy Italian journalist her life story, her views on the world, and all in a way that appeared to establish her new identity as an independent and modern woman, and not merely as the former actress who was the wife of Silvio Berlusconi. Maria Latella, the journalist chosen by Veronica to write her biography, approached her subject with kid gloves, and the project that emerged appeared to be innocuous enough.

All of that changed in 2007, when Lario became uncharacteristically outraged at reports of her husband flirting with women in public. Suddenly Mrs. Berlusconi appeared "shocked" at her husband's behavior, as though she had never known the real Berlusconi even though they had spent the past twenty-seven years together.

It happened in late January 2007, a few days after Berlusconi had attended the Italian equivalent of the Emmy Awards, which are known as the *Telegatti*, or TV Cats. At a star-studded party, filled with models, showgirls, actresses, and dancers, Berlusconi seemed to be enjoying himself. As he made the rounds, a two-time prime minister who was now leader of the opposition in parliament, he could not resist making some flirtatious remarks.

To a shapely Venezuelan model named Aida Yéspica, Berlusconi was heard to decree that "with you I would go anywhere." To others he was openly flirtatious, and with the television cameras filming every moment.

Whatever internal dynamic had governed the Berlusconi household up until now, it suddenly broke down. Lario, behaving like the archetypal scorned woman, suddenly did the one thing she knew would hurt her husband: She published a scathing front-page letter to the editor of *La Repubblica*, a left-wing newspaper that was a constant critic of her husband. She wrote that her dignity had been violated, and she demanded an apology from Berlusconi for having flirted openly with two women at a public event. What may have seemed petty under normal circumstances took on a whole new dimension with the players involved, and triggered a national shock and scandal. Berlusconi was publicly humiliated.

Lario made a melodramatic reference to a little-known Irish writer named Catherine Dunne, identifying herself with one of Dunne's characters, whose husband abruptly leaves her after a lengthy marriage. "I ask if, like the Catherine Dunne character, I have to regard myself as 'half of nothing,'" wrote Lario in the lengthy open letter.

Lario also demanded that her husband respond to her in public. Berlusconi did not wait to be asked twice. Faced with the implosion of his marriage on the front pages of all the Italian newspapers, he issued a public apology in less than twenty-four hours. One of Berlusconi's lawyers meanwhile called Lario and asked her what on earth had possessed her to pull such a stunt at a time when they were just beginning to have confidential discussions about a potential divorce settlement. Lario would have none of it. She had nothing to add. Unlike Berlusconi's first wife, this lady was not going to go quietly.

For the Irish novelist, Mrs. Berlusconi's public rant helped to boost book sales in Italy. At the time of Veronica's outburst in 2007, a friend called from Italy and announced to Dunne: "You're all over the newspapers!" As Ms. Dunne would later tell a London tabloid: "Eight hours later I got off the phone. It hadn't stopped ringing: radio interviews, print interviews. I was asked did I think Mr. Berlusconi should apologize. I said I certainly did! Veronica Lario was offended, hurt and humiliated."

"Berlusconi did apologize," Dunne added later, then a regular on the Italian book circuit, "but it wasn't much of an apology. I thought it was probably the first salvo in a rather expensive divorce campaign and so it has proven."

Dunne may have been right, but it took another two years before Lario launched an even more virulent set of attacks on her husband, including the formal announcement via the press of her intention to divorce Berlusconi.

The pre-divorce years would see Veronica resort on several occasions to public criticisms of her husband, press releases to news agencies, newspaper interviews with her biographer, and this created a great deal of unpleasantness all around. She appeared to see public humiliations of Berlusconi as her preferred instrument of torture, or perhaps, as she saw things, of self-defense.

The moment of greatest pain for Berlusconi came in 2009, when the premier was visiting Naples and attended a birthday party for a pretty and lithe eighteen-year-old lingerie model and wannabe actress named Noemi Letizia. Even though the party in question was attended by Noemi's own parents, the press would report that Berlusconi had known the young lady even before her eighteenth birthday. Veronica used the occasion to launch another salvo.

This time, instead of writing an open letter to the editor of a newspaper, Berlusconi's wife went nuclear, almost as though she were looking for a *casus belli* to use against her husband. Two days after the birthday party in Naples, with the Italian press in rhapsody at the idea of the eighteen-year-old birthday girl calling Berlusconi by the affectionate nickname of "Papi," Veronica pressed the send button and fired off a late-night press release to Italy's domestic news agency, ANSA.

It was an unorthodox move, to say the least. She railed at the idea, which had been rumored in the press, of her husband picking pretty former showgirls as candidates for Forza Italia in the upcoming elections for the European parliament.

Lario was essentially announcing that the marriage was over, and in a most public manner.

"I cannot stay with a man who frequents minors," declared Lario. "I am bringing down the curtain on my married life."

Lario continued her public war of words for some time, heaping opprobrium on the man who had brought a bouquet of roses to her dressing room. It proved effective. She filed for divorce and, years later, when she secured a billionaire-size divorce settlement, with lifelong alimony of $1.5 million a month, Veronica Lario seemed content to finally return to a quieter life of private luxury.

Today, Berlusconi still looks uncomfortable when speaking about his two former wives.

"I guess I would say that my rapport with my first wife, the mother of my first two children, has always been one of respect and friendship and affection, and this continues to be the case, without exception. With my second wife, there have been certain contrasts, certain positions that she has taken, perhaps suggested to her by others, that perhaps she would not repeat if she thought about it now. But we have gotten past all this—after all, she is the mother of three of my children—and now we have a rapport of respect and familiarity."

As for his relations with his five children, a subject that in the Italian press has meant speculation about how his multibillion-euro inheritance is to be divided, Berlusconi claims that everything is good.

"We have great affection and reciprocal love and respect, and they are always near to me. They write and say things to me that are moving, and I try to do everything I can to be worthy of them. But everything is good, very natural, there is nothing artificial in our relationship."

Talking about women seems to take a lot of energy for Berlusconi, and after more than an hour on the subject he seems hungry. It is well past six in the evening. He makes his way into the family dining room, and pushes open the door and into a smaller box of a room that leads into the kitchen. He pads over to a wooden table and sits down. His personal chef seems conscious of the need to keep Berlusconi on the strict diet imposed by his current live-in girlfriend, twenty-nine-year-old Francesca Pascale. But after consuming a healthy-looking centrifuged blend of mixed vegetables, Berlusconi still looks peckish, and finally a small plate appears, full of crackers dabbed with soft and pungent gorgonzola.

Berlusconi picks at the crackers, while outside it is dark, and a hard rain is falling on the gravel. The bodyguards are out front, smoking in the driveway, inside the gates of the villa.

Now Berlusconi is speaking of national politics, and of his pending court cases, and of the way he feels persecuted by politically activist judges, a familiar set of topics for anyone who has spent much time with the man. "The bunga-bunga case," he notes, "is only one of sixty-one separate trials I have had to go through in the past twenty years, and I have spent literally hundreds of millions on legal expenses." He is lamenting this enormous expenditure of time and money and energy in all of these judicial appearances, investigations, depositions, convictions, appeals, acquittals, and additional appeals. The case of Ruby and the bunga-bunga spawned nearly three dozen other potential cases, including one where the Milan magistrates, not content with the outcome of the first and second case, accused Berlusconi of bribing thirty-three separate defense witnesses to commit perjury.

"Could Berlusconi have been more discreet about his private life while he was prime minister?" asks his old friend Fedele Confalonieri. "Sure, he could have been more discreet. There are a few episodes he could have spared us. Sure. But what did Berlusconi actually do? This is the real point. What is he accused of? Inducing a minor into prostitution? Come on! Give me a break! The bunga-bunga parties? We all know that Berlusconi likes to sing, that he likes to entertain, that he likes to have lots of people around him. But let's be frank: He was alone in life. He no longer had a wife. He was in private, in his own home."

Confalonieri says the most disturbing aspect of all this is not the bunga-bunga parties.

"What is amazing is that for a very long time, thanks to the magistrates and judges, every single person who went to Arcore ended up having their phones wiretapped, placed under electronic surveillance as though they were Mafiosi. We are talking about more than 250,000 pages of transcripts of wiretapped calls. That is the big anomaly of this country, not that Berlusconi might like to have a few girls around him at dinner and do whatever he wanted, but that in this country of ours today the prosecutors can spy on your entire private life and on everyone as though they were gangsters."

Confalonieri's outrage at the way investigating magistrates went after Berlusconi suggests that if there is more to Berlusconi's rapport with women than the case of Ruby and the bunga-bunga parties, there is also more to his legal travails than a mere string of wiretaps. The lines in the sand were drawn early between Berlusconi and the magistrates of Milan. From the start of his political career, and even before, Berlusconi has faced more indictments and accusations than any other billionaire tycoon on the *Forbes* richest list or the Fortune 500. He is the world record holder among billionaires and former prime ministers for indictments. It is credible that he has spent hundreds of millions of euros on lawyers since first becoming prime minister in 1994. In Italy they call his endless battles with prosecutors and other magistrates of the Italian judiciary "The War of the Judges," and there is little debate about Berlusconi's innocence or guilt; it is a matter of faith one way or another, like religion.

This judicial war began back in November 1994, while Berlusconi was hosting world leaders at the UN summit in Naples. The stunning announcement on the front page of *Corriere della Sera* that Berlusconi was being investigated by magistrates in a corruption case was a fatal blow that would bring down his six-month-old government. It would also lead to an epic political struggle that would dominate Berlusconi's life and the life of his nation for the next twenty years. It was the first of many investigations and many prosecutions, all of which would begin with the very same words: *The People of Italy v. Silvio Berlusconi.*

CHAPTER NINE

———

Bribery, Corruption, and Mafia

I don't know if you have noticed, but I am not exactly having a good time here."

Silvio Berlusconi is not a happy camper. He looks tired and stressed. He is complaining that he did not get any sleep last night. It is nearly three in the afternoon and he has been sitting at the teak table in the garden of the Villa San Martino for nearly two hours now, patiently answering questions about the sixty-one investigations, indictments, and trials he has faced in Italy, on an extraordinary array of accusations that by now are all too familiar: bribery, corruption, money laundering, the illicit financing of political parties, false accounting, tax fraud, witness tampering, sex with an underage prostitute, and even alleged ties with the Mafia.

Berlusconi knows the workings of the Italian judiciary very well. He considers himself something of an expert by now.

The Italian judicial system is far more complicated than in the United States. Although there are no distinctions between state and federal prosecutors, there is a system dating back to the Napoleonic Code under which magistrates in the judicial system are divided into different types, starting with the investigating magistrates who can conduct investigations, subpoena documents, order wiretaps, and call in people for questioning. These same magistrates can then act as prosecutors and go to their superior, the Italian equiva-lent of the district attorney or state's attorney, asking for indict-ments. There is no use of grand juries; it is all in the hands of a few magistrates, the investigating ones and the ones who decide on indictments and trials. The Italians rarely use a trial-by-jury system except in serious crimes such as murder. Most defendants are usu-ally acquitted or convicted by a single judge in the first trial and then by a college of three judges in the appeals trial. Finally, there is the supreme court level, as in the United States.

The way Italians relate to the judiciary is also different from the American experience. In the United States a state's attorney who brings an important indictment against a politician or a Wall Street figure usually has a press conference and announces everything very clearly. In Italy, especially in the case of politicians who are being investigated, almost everything is conducted through sys-tematic leaks of a mixture of truth and rumor, of depositions and of wiretap transcripts which appear in the newspapers long before any indictment is brought, and often during an investigation phase. Most politicians do not even consider themselves guilty after a first conviction, and that included Berlusconi. This is because under the Italian system one is not considered guilty until all appeals are exhausted; they often get off on appeal or at the supreme court level. Cases frequently drag on for a decade or more, and the statute of limitations for a particular crime can run out during this period, as has also occurred for Berlusconi many times.

Now Berlusconi is trying to make light of a moment that for anyone else would be traumatic. How can he sit there with that same schmoozer's smile, making faces and occasionally letting out a sigh that speaks of exhaustion and frustration and discomfort? How can he face this barrage of questions that he has never been will-ing to submit to before, a chronological series of questions that will take him back to the worst accusations, that he and his closest cro-nies and advisers had ties with *Cosa Nostra*, with the Sicilian Mafia? How can Berlusconi deal with the emotional weight of reliving the darkest moments in his twenty-five-year-long battle with the Italian judiciary, and almost never flinch? Practice. The answer is practice. The man has had plenty of practice over the years in answering legal questions and he clearly believes his own version of events.

He swears he has nothing to hide but he wears a defiant look while birds chirp in the distance. He looks impatient. His face at times looks grim, at other times weary. He takes a sip of water from a small plastic cup. He combs his hair, adjusts his posture, and gets ready to begin the conversation. With the sound of the very first question, Berlusconi bolts upright in his seat. He flashes that million-dollar smile—or is it his mask? His cheeks go into some kind of default mechanism and his big smile seems to be saying that this is all a lot of nonsense, all of these criminal accusations.

He has a certain repertoire, and one of his key refrains is the mantra that all of the criminal cases ever opened against him— against his person, against his companies, his family, his advisers, his managers, his lawyers, and his friends—all of them are part of a long-running left-wing conspiracy of harassment by a group of militant and activist prosecutors in the Italian judiciary who are out to get him. There is no doubt that in his own mind Berlusconi genuinely believes this to be the exclusive truth, the only truth. In his most private moments with friends, he will talk about which prosecutors and which presiding judges in which cases against him were left-wing activists or politically influenced against him. He can tell you which Italian president named which judge to which court in which year. He will speak of how political signals on whom to indict or convict are sent to magistrates by senior judges and by politicians, from on high. Berlusconi has made a life's study of the dozens of magistrates who have come after him over the years. And their supposed political patrons. This is his obsession.

Legend would have it that all of Berlusconi's troubles with the law began during the UN Summit in Naples in 1994. But now Berlusconi sits back in his chair and proclaims with a sort of perverse pride that he was first placed under investigation long before he entered politics in the 1960s. He seems to wear his long-running battle with the judiciary like a badge of honor.

"If you go back to the days of Silvio Berlusconi the entrepreneur," says Berlusconi, "then you find that the judicial investigations actually started some fifty years ago, in the 1960s. We had loads of investigations from about 1965 onward. The magistrates always had a pathological obsession with me, at first when I was a popular and rising business star in Milan, and then later, when I became prime minister."

Later, in 1979, when Berlusconi was still a rising tycoon, becoming a billionaire for the first time thanks to the success of his Milano Due garden city project, some of his companies in Milan were suspected of tax evasion. That was when Berlusconi found himself being questioned by a member of Italy's tax police, a captain in the Guardia di Finanza named Massimo Berruti. The Berruti investigation of Berlusconi's company Edilnord ended rather quickly, with no charges being filed. Soon after that, in 1980, Berruti left the tax authority and became a lawyer who began working for Berlusconi's Fininvest. The relationship blossomed, and in the 1990s Berlusconi eventually helped get Berruti elected to the Italian parliament as a Forza Italia candidate.

Berlusconi denies that he bribed Berruti to look the other way back in 1979. He denies any connection whatsoever between Berruti's past as a tax inspector who let him off the hook and his becoming a lawyer for Berlusconi's group. No connection, says an indignant Berlusconi.

"Berruti? He came to make a tax inspection, and he found absolutely zilch, just like hundreds of other tax inspections that I have had in my companies. Nothing. I got to know him and I liked him. He then resigned from the Guardia di Finanza to become a lawyer in Milan, and then he expressed a desire to have a career in politics, and we made him a candidate and he won and he has been a great politician over the years."

The timing of Berruti's resignation from the tax police and his hiring by Berlusconi in the space of less than twelve months has always been considered suspicious by Italian prosecutors, open to interpretation. Now Berlusconi wants to shut the door on any other interpretation.

"All these suspicions are far away from reality," says Berlusconi. "Absolutely false." He glances back at a figure who has appeared in the distance.

From the portico of the villa a face peers out. Berlusconi's live-in girlfriend, Francesca Pascale, is watching her *presidente*. She is following him out of the corner of her eye while chatting with a girlfriend and occasionally throwing a tennis ball out onto the lawn for her white pet poodle, Dudù, to chase after.

Berlusconi pauses for a moment and smiles again. The slightest hint of discomfort crosses his face when the word "Mafia" is mentioned. He does not flinch again, though, maintaining his grinning poker face even when he is asked to explain the strange case of Vittorio Mangano, the Mafia killer whom Berlusconi hired back in the 1970s as groundskeeper right here at the Villa San Martino.

Mangano was a name that would figure in the darkest of the many accusations made against Berlusconi, in this case that he had maintained for many years a relationship with Cosa Nostra, the Sicilian Mafia.

The middle man in this relationship with the Mafia, the Italian courts would rule, was Berlusconi's old college friend and loyal right-hand man, Marcello Dell'Utri. Dell'Utri came from Palermo and had become friends with Berlusconi during their days studying law together in Milan. From the 1970s, he had worked as Berlusconi's personal assistant, and had then graduated to senior positions in Edilnord, Fininvest, and Mediaset before being elected to the parliament as a Forza Italia candidate. Almost no one was closer to Berlusconi than Dell'Utri, except perhaps Fedele Confalonieri, whose friendship went back to high school days.

The accusations of Mafia connections appeared almost as soon as Dell'Utri went into politics with Berlusconi's party. Once the leaks began to appear from the Palermo prosecutor's office as investigations went forward, Berlusconi's critics in the Italian media took it for granted that Dell'Utri was a conduit for Berlusconi and the Mafia. This led to a string of libel cases. But the accusation of Mafia support for political parties was not a shocker for most Italians. Prime Minister Giulio Andreotti had been indicted on the same charges as Dell'Utri, although he got off on a legal technicality.

When Forza Italia did well in elections in Sicily, Italian commentators on the left analyzed how Berlusconi's party seemed to take the place of the party that had previously garnered the most Mafia votes on the island, the Christian Democrats. Dell'Utri would find himself the target of multiple Mafia investigations. He was accused of being the man with the Mafia ties, the man who could fix anything, obtain protection, and even trade political favors in exchange for votes. He denied everything.

Italy's supreme court would ultimately convict Dell'Utri on charges of collusion with the Mafia. The court sentence said that Dell'Utri was the man who in 1974 had engineered a deal between Berlusconi and the Mafia. It was, said the court, "an agreement in which Silvio Berlusconi would pay large sums of money in exchange for protection that was provided to him by the Cosa Nostra of Palermo."

Dell'Utri was first charged with colluding with the Mafia on behalf of Berlusconi in 1996 and was convicted eight years later, in his first trial in 2004. But under Italian law, that was not considered a definitive guilty verdict. He was convicted on appeal again in 2010, some fourteen years after the first indictment. Under Italy's judicial system, this was not considered definitive, either. The final supreme court confirmation that Dell'Utri was indeed guilty of Mafia collusion did not come until 2014.

By the spring of 2014 when Dell'Utri was finally convicted and sentenced to seven years in prison, after eighteen years of trials and appeals, he had disappeared to Beirut for what he would later claim was heart treatment. A warrant was issued for his arrest by Interpol, and Italy asked Lebanon to extradite him. In April 2014, Dell'Utri was arrested by agents of the Lebanese police in a luxury hotel in Beirut, and in June he was sent back to Italy, where he finally began serving his sentence.

For Berlusconi, the most damaging part of Dell'Utri's conviction was the court's description of how Vittorio Mangano had first come to live at Arcore. At the time he was not a convicted Mafia killer; that would come twenty years later, in the 1990s. But Mangano already had a criminal record. He was, as Berlusconi says, a friend of Dell'Utri's from Palermo, and at the time he was managing a small soccer team that Dell'Utri had decided to sponsor, with Berlusconi's money.

It was in 1974, according to the supreme court ruling, and thanks to the good offices of Marcello Dell'Utri, that Berlusconi sat down in an office in downtown Milan and met the godfather of godfathers of the Cosa Nostra, Stefano Bontate, in the presence of Dell'Utri, who made the introductions. Dell'Utri would deny that he had ever met Bontate, the Don Corleone of the 1970s. According to Italy's supreme court ruling, the meeting took place, and it was after Berlusconi met Bontate that Mangano came to stay at Arcore, and not merely to manage the estate and take care of the horses and the stables, but to provide protection and security for the Berlusconi family. Mangano would often take Berlusconi's children to school in the morning, and in time he became a friend of the family and a trusted foreman.

Berlusconi has always denied the meeting with the Mafia godfather. Indignant, he still manages to squeeze out a smile. He insists that he has only had contact with the Mafia once in his life, despite the supreme court's ruling.

"The truth," says Berlusconi, "is that I was the most high-profile entrepreneur on the Italian scene back in the 1970s. The Mafia did do a lot of kidnapping of children from wealthy families in those days. There once was a guest who came to see me here at the villa, a certain Prince Luigi d'Angerio di Sant'Agata, who did narrowly escape a kidnapping attempt. It was just after he left a dinner party here."

Now Berlusconi lowers his voice.

"I began receiving threatening letters at first, which we took to the police," recalls Berlusconi. "There were threats to kidnap my five-year-old son, Pier Silvio. At that point I took my wife and children on a circuitous route through various European countries in order to throw them off the scent, and I settled them in Spain for a few months. I used to go and see them on the weekends, always taking a flight to Frankfurt or London first in order to make sure I wasn't being followed. After a while, I brought the family back to Arcore, and we hired a considerable number of security staff, and I got bulletproof and armored cars. But my wife was still worried and so we decided not to send our children to school anymore, and they had to study here at home, with home schooling by various professors whom we brought to the house here at Arcore.

"My children studied here, at home, until the end of high school," he says with a sigh of regret. "They completely missed out on being able to interact with their peers, which is a vital part of the normal experience of growing up for every boy and girl."

No, says Berlusconi. Mangano was not brought to Arcore by Dell'Utri as part of any protection deal with the Mafia. False. Not true. Even if that is what the supreme court ruling said. He doesn't care. That is not the way he remembers it. So what on earth then could have possessed Berlusconi to hire a man like Mangano, who may not have been a Mafia killer back in the 1970s but who was nonetheless, for the well-informed, a man who was considered close to prominent Mafia families in Sicily?

Now Berlusconi has a slightly irked look on his face. The irritation somehow manages to creep through his smile, like a rash. When he speaks, his voice is matter-of-fact, friendly but flat.

"We did not know this at the time," recalls a grinning Berlusconi. "When Vittorio Mangano was hired, there was nothing to make us think he was tied to Mafia circles. That's the point. When I bought this property we needed someone to manage the place, and we wanted somebody who was good with horses because we had ten or twelve racehorses in the stables. We took out classified ads, but we could not find anybody. Then my personal assistant, my friend Marcello Dell'Utri, remembered a fellow in Palermo who was good with horses. He knew him because this fellow had worked with his soccer team, helping to get kids off the street.

Dell'Utri called him and asked him for help in finding someone. He said, 'Well, if this is Berlusconi's villa, then I will come myself.' That is all there is to the story."

Berlusconi smiles broadly now. He speaks with warmth and affection, and with respect, for his estate manager.

"He came to stay here and he brought his wife and his two children. He even brought his old mother to live here. His kids were the same age as mine." Berlusconi is nostalgic. "He would always bring the children to nursery school, every day. He discharged his responsibilities in an impeccable manner. Then one day he had a bad break, a bankruptcy he had to deal with, and he left Arcore for good. But he remained friends with Marcello Dell'Utri."

Berlusconi is now philosophical.

"He clearly fell under some bad influences and there clearly were these accusations against him. But he always said that the time he spent here was 'the most serene part of my life.' I'll tell you how it all finished up. He was convicted and he developed cancer while he was prison. I have been told that the investigating magistrates would go to see him every week, and every week they would say to him: 'If you talk to us about ties between Berlusconi and the Mafia and Dell'Utri and the Mafia, you can go home this afternoon.'

"He always said to his lawyers that at Arcore he had six of the most peaceful months of his life and he could not make things up about Berlusconi just to get out of prison. And you know when they finally let him out of prison?"

Berlusconi leans forward in his chair. "They let him go home only days before, only just before the day he died."

Berlusconi pronounces these last words with a certain sadness, a mixture of admiration for Mangano and regret that the Mafioso had been harassed by the magistrates even though he was in prison with cancer. Berlusconi sighs. For the courts, Mangano might have been a convicted Mafia killer and drug trafficker. For Berlusconi, he was a loyal friend, to the end.

When the conversation turns to Marcello Dell'Utri, Berlusconi emits a sympathetic laugh, breaks into a big smile, and then turns on the charm.

"He is the most wonderful person you could imagine," says Berlusconi, as if he were speaking of an angel.

He proceeds to reel off Dell'Utri's merits.

"He is highly educated, an expert bibliophile, he knows the *Divine Comedy* by heart. He has a beautiful family with four beautiful children. He was a member of Opus Dei and he is a practicing Catholic. He is much loved and respected by all of his staff. And I am convinced that the only reason he was convicted and put in jail is because he is my friend."

Silvio Berlusconi is still smiling, but he is clearly becoming indignant again. He has defended his friends. He has defended his idea of friendship. He is far more relaxed with the next question. He seems to find it almost quaint that people should still wonder about the origins of his money. For decades, the Italian press, and dozens of prosecutors, have whispered about his early real estate projects being financed by mysterious Swiss capital, money that flowed southward and over the Alps, from the legendary tax haven in Lugano, Switzerland, to nearby Milan. The press has wondered aloud many times: Was this Mafia money? Why Switzerland? Who were Berlusconi's secret backers?

"Yes, we did receive initial financing from some Lugano trust funds because we had investors, like Mr. Rasini, who owned the bank where my father worked, the Banca Rasini, and these investors had their own legitimate deposits in their accounts in Switzerland. They sent their money from Switzerland. But you know..." Berlusconi pauses here and shakes his head with a kind of *tsk-tsk* motion. "You know, there have been so many investigations, and not just by magistrates but by journalists, lots and lots of investigations. And nothing irregular has ever been turned up."

Berlusconi looks up briefly, as if to see if he has made his point, and then resumes his explanation.

"There was nothing wrong with our accounts," insists Berlusconi. "At the time our tax lawyers recommended the creation of

Italian companies that were financed by foreign-based capital. This was done purely for tax reasons, on their advice. So I followed the wishes of my investors, and the tax lawyers, and they sent their capital from nearby Switzerland."

When Berlusconi mentions Rasini, his father's old employer at the Banca Rasini, he pronounces the man's name with reverence. This was his father's boss. Prosecutors in Palermo and Milan have spent years trying to establish that Banca Rasini was a financial link between Berlusconi's businesses and the Mafia. The names of certain big-time Mafia account holders did emerge in investigations in the 1980s and 1990s, but that was after Berlusconi's father had retired.

"Pitiful poppycock," says Berlusconi, spitting out the words dismissively. "Absolute nonsense, put out by my enemies, by those who are jealous of me."

Berlusconi's enemies, who constitute a virtual battalion of judges, prosecutors, and investigative reporters in Italy, might admit that they have not been able to prove a direct tie between the Mafia and Banca Rasini. The investigation of Berlusconi in connection with the Mafia and his father's bank was in fact opened and closed within a year by an ambitious Sicilian judge, who later became a hard-left politician and leading Berlusconi critic.

The same cannot be said about the bribery and corruption case involving another one of Berlusconi's closest friends, his personal lawyer, a co-founder of Forza Italia, an elected member of parliament in Berlusconi's party, and a cabinet member in the first of Berlusconi's governments.

Cesare Previti, a lawyer, was accused of paying off a Rome judge to get him to rule on Berlusconi's behalf in a case involving his fight against rival entrepreneur Carlo De Benedetti for control of the Mondadori publishing empire. The case actually started back in 1995 when a Milanese socialite named Countess Stefania Ariosto, girlfriend of one of Berlusconi's lawyers and also a close friend of Previti, went to the Milan prosecutor's office and started telling them that she had heard Previti talking about bribes being paid to Roman judges to swing the Mondadori case. That led to investigations and indictments and trials over a twelve-year period for Previti. Finally, in 2007, the supreme court convicted Previti for having given a 200,000-euro bribe to a Rome judge, who was himself convicted and sentenced to prison for taking the money.

Berlusconi listens to the litany of bribery and corruption verdicts against his friend, but he does not blanch once. Instead he begins a half laugh, and then flashes a broad smile. There is a bit more of that head motion, from side to side, that seems to say *tsk-tsk*.

"This is the same story as in all of the situations involving the Italian judiciary. It is all false," says a laconic Berlusconi. *Pause.* He sees that he does not need to repeat his thesis about the militant magistrates of Italy's left.

But is he saying that each and every shred of the evidence that was produced in court and used to convict Previti was false or manufactured? All of it?

"I wouldn't know which word to choose," says Berlusconi, sighing. It is here that he appears irritated once again, for a second or two, although he does a mighty job of concealing the emotion. "I don't find this subject distasteful," he observes suddenly, opening his arms out as if to say "I have nothing to hide." "I have no doubts whatsoever about my conduct over the years," he says. And then: "In more than sixty trials that I have been subjected to, they only managed to convict me once. But we can talk about that later.

"I have calculated that in sixty-one cases over more than twenty years there have been more than three thousand court hearings. From the moment I went into politics, back in 1994, I have spent every Saturday, Sunday, and often into Monday morning dealing with lawyers, preparing for court filings and appearances at trials. And I have spent nearly seven hundred million dollars on legal fees over the last twenty years, and believe me, that is a lot of money!"

Seven hundred million dollars does, in fact, sound like a fair amount of money to spend on lawyers. But Berlusconi's own lawyers confirm that between personal court cases and cases involving his companies, Berlusconi really has probably spent that much money over the decades. Nevertheless, throw at him what you like and Berlusconi comes right back at you. Mafia. Bribery. Corruption. How about the case in which Berlusconi was initially convicted of funneling $12 million of funds to old friend Bettino Craxi, the Socialist prime minister whose career ended in disgrace and exile? That trial, involving a complicated offshore network of financial companies, would see Berlusconi found guilty in July 1998 and sentenced to two years and four months in prison. Berlusconi had been found guilty of transferring the funds through his Fininvest group to All Iberian, an offshore company located in Jersey, a tax haven in the Channel Islands (between England and France), and from there to an offshore account in Switzerland controlled by Bettino Craxi, the former prime minister. The guilty sentence was later set aside in 2000, when the seven-and-a-half-year statute of limitations expired.

In this case Berlusconi avoided a definitive conviction thanks to the fact that time had run out on the crime. After he was elected again as prime minister in 2001, Berlusconi managed to get off in several cases thanks to the statute of limitations rather than the merits of the case. All in all, Berlusconi was convicted in a total of seven trials, although only once in a definitive supreme court verdict, but he saw a number of sentences cancelled or he got off because the statute of limitations had run out, for a total of seven times. He was declared not guilty a total of nine times. In another thirty-five cases, the prosecutors' charges were dropped before going to trial. Even today, he still has five cases open.

In Italy's creaking judicial system, one has to travel through a baroque web of appeals court proceedings and extensions and first appeals and second appeals and supreme court rulings that could take a total of between ten and twenty years before any court's sentence was considered definitive and final. So it was not so unusual that defense lawyers would try to string out cases long enough for the statute of limitations to expire. That is what happened in the case of the money transfers to Craxi.

"Ah, that case?" says Berlusconi with a deadpan shrug. "That was just a conviction in the first court case...That kind of conviction is just part of the normal political propaganda against me."

The case of the funds that went from Fininvest to Bettino Craxi, or did not, according to Silvio Berlusconi, is just part of a more complex set of accusations made against Berlusconi in a series of trials that were named after All Iberian, the offshore holding company allegedly used to transfer the money. The man who had helped Berlusconi devise the complex corporate structure of holding companies and offshore bank accounts was a prominent London lawyer named David Mackenzie Mills. He was a corporate lawyer who specialized in work for Italian companies and who was married to a minister in Tony Blair's government, a sociable lady named Tessa Jowell.

To the embarrassment of Blair circles and to polite society in London, Mills was accused of receiving a $600,000 bribe from Berlusconi in order to perjure himself under oath and deny certain aspects of the network of offshore companies he had created. Berlusconi, meanwhile, was himself charged with bribing a witness. Minister of Culture Jowell was an up-and-coming Blair loyalist who was tasked with preparing for the London 2012 Olympics. In 2006, when the All Iberian scandal erupted, she separated from her husband. She claimed that she knew nothing of the $600,000 payment, which she described as a "gift" from Berlusconi. The British press went into overdrive, claiming that Jowell had only left her husband for the sake of appearances and political convenience. Finally, a spokesman for Prime Minister Blair had to issue a statement that Blair still had "full confidence" in the (now separated) wife of David Mills. Six years later, Mrs. Mills finally reunited with her husband, after all of the Italian trial proceedings had come to a close.

In early 2009, a Milan court found David Mills guilty and sentenced him to four and a half years in jail for accepting a bribe from Berlusconi to give false evidence on his behalf in corruption trials in 1997 and 1998. Jowell, still a cabinet minister, said that "although we are separated I have never doubted his innocence." Later in 2009, an appeals court upheld the Mills bribery conviction and he launched an appeal to the supreme court. The statute of limitations ran out early the following year, meaning that under Italian law his guilty verdict was struck from the books. Jowell, who was hoping to run for mayor of London in 2016, then told the press that her husband had been "exonerated" by an Italian court.

As for Berlusconi, who had been indicted alongside Mills, he was no longer a defendant. In 2008, while he was presiding over his fourth government, parliament had passed a law that exempted the prime minister and three other high-ranking Italian government officials from being tried in court as long as the government was in office. A year later the supreme court declared the law unconstitutional but by early 2012 the statute of limitations kicked in for Berlusconi. So did Berlusconi bribe Mr. Mills?

Berlusconi smiles, as though he were presiding over the Oscars. There is laughter in his eyes. He is both giggly and yet passively aggressive.

"This is just one big fairy tale," he says. "In fact, Mills once testified against us in a trial, even though he gave false testimony there. How can anyone think that Fininvest paid a hostile witness? This is absolute nonsense, just like everything else."

Berlusconi is thinking about the British lawyer. He ventures a suggestion, an opinion.

"Maybe this was more damaging to me outside of Italy," he says, "because people don't know the way magistrates in Italy play a political role. But in Italy it didn't really matter. It was of no consequence."

What was of consequence for Berlusconi, and for all of Italy, was a series of laws that his various governments introduced over the decades, a dozen or more, that often seemed tailor-made to suit his personal legal problems. There were laws that decriminalized charges of false accounting. There were reductions of statutes of limitation periods. There was the law that gave the prime minister immunity from prosecution. There were laws that allowed the prime minister and other top officials to avoid court appearances because of their busy schedules and high office. These laws were all known by Berlusconi's critics in Italy as the *ad personam* laws, taking the words from Latin to mean "personalized" or "made-to-measure." Berlusconi's critics would say that the billionaire media mogul was a living conflict of interest, a prime minister whose policies advanced his own business interests, and focused too much on his own legal problems. The critics said he seemed more preoccupied with legislation that would help him escape from justice or protect his media empire than with the big Reagan-style tax cuts and job-creating economic reforms he had promised Italian voters.

How does Silvio Berlusconi account for thirteen such laws over a twenty-year period? How does he explain them? He doesn't. He dismisses them with a singsongy repetition of a single word.

"Nonsense. Nonsense. Complete and utter nonsense."

Berlusconi says this with a big grin on his face. In fact he is trying to contain his laughter. He is defiant, but playful, perhaps because he is now Berlusconi the politician rather than Berlusconi the defendant. He is quite happy to explain why he decriminalized false accounting.

"That was the right thing to do," claims Berlusconi, "because it helped protect Italian businesses from being attacked by any old prosecutor who just felt like having a go at them."

How about the laws that reduced the statute of limitations, allowing him to get off on several occasions?

"It is absurd," he says, "that cases in Italy can go on forever, into infinity, and all because of the complicated procedures of our system."

Berlusconi pauses. He rubs an eyelid, and with his voice rising, half in mocking jest and half in evident irritation, he complains for the first time.

"I don't know if you have noticed, but I am not exactly having a good time here."

He catches himself, though, quickly apologizing.

"I, uh, didn't mean to complain or to accuse you of anything," says Berlusconi. "Really. I was just making a little joke. I just mean I am not having a good time here because this conversation is forcing me to remember all of the things I have had to say and do to defend myself, and for so many years, for such a long time."

Berlusconi is somber now. His joke has fallen flat. There is only one thing left to do. He smiles good-naturedly and apologizes again. He looks fatigued. He has been sitting here for nearly two hours, and his staff are waiting attentively near the teak table in the garden of the Villa San Martino. Francesca Pascale is strolling on the lawn, not far from the portico, playing fetch with Dudù and the newest arrival, a little female white poodle named Dudina. A nervous aide scrambles up to Berlusconi and hands him a plastic cup of mineral water. He takes a sip and then hands back the cup. He seems to crack his neck.

After the litany of cases, trials, hundreds of millions in lawyer fees, the accusations, the indictments, the *ad personam* laws, how can he possibly expect people to think he is completely innocent and just the victim of political persecution? How can he claim that he has never done anything wrong? Surely he can admit to something?

He doesn't mind the question at all. He is unflappable, as always. In fact, he has a playful look. He takes the floor, offering his own distilled version of history, summarizing his decades-long war with the Italian judiciary. How can he claim that he has never done anything wrong?

"The truth," says Berlusconi, "is that all of these trials have their origins in the fact that there is a faction inside the Italian judiciary whose mission is to use the courts and the judiciary as a path to socialism. That means eliminating anyone who stands in the way of the left taking power in Italy. These magistrates went crazy when I decided to go into politics. They have been running wild ever since, and doing everything they can to eliminate me from the political scene. They have tried many times, many times."

A critic might say that Berlusconi believes his own propaganda. But it is equally clear that Berlusconi believes what he is saying.

With that, the billionaire rises, battle-weary but unperturbed. He waves off his staff, takes a quick phone call, and then goes over to greet Pascale before slipping into the villa for a meeting. Waiting for him in the dining room, now a makeshift data room full of Excel spreadsheets, are a dozen advisers, interpreters, lawyers, and investment bankers who have made the trek to Arcore, representing a mysterious Asian buyer for his AC Milan soccer club. In the life of Silvio Berlusconi, today is just another day.

CHAPTER TEN

Eat, Drink, and Kill

I don't want to end up like Saddam Hussein."

Colonel Muammar Gaddafi was sipping tea in the desert and baring his soul to Berlusconi.

The colonel was decked out in his most colorful attire, a bright mustard djellabah. He was hosting Prime Minister Berlusconi at a typically extravagant lunch in a great big air-conditioned tent that was part of a military installation outside the Libyan capital, one of those lavish affairs in the desert that had become a Gaddafi hallmark.

It was a warm winter's day, February 10, 2004, and Berlusconi had just become the first major Western leader to visit Gaddafi since he had come in from the cold.

"When I saw Saddam climbing out of that spider hole," Gaddafi was now telling Berlusconi, "I decided I was not going to be next."

To those within earshot, the Libyan strongman seemed to be in earnest. The Italian premier had only a moment earlier been praising Gaddafi for having recently renounced terrorism, and for having given up his nuclear weapons project the previous December. He had asked the Libyan dictator rather bluntly what had made him change his mind. Here was the answer.

The two leaders were smiling for the cameras, but Berlusconi was not having an easy time with the voluble Libyan leader. Each time Berlusconi apologized for Italy's misdeeds in Libya during its Mussolini-era colonial occupation, the colonel would ask for some kind of reparation. In Gaddafi's outreach to the West, money counted as much as ego.

Berlusconi was milking the moment for everything it was worth. He was lobbying the Libyan leader to agree to a controversial plan to set up receiving centers in North Africa to process migrants and stanch the flood of boat people who kept washing ashore on the coast of Sicily. On behalf of Italy he was offering to build a hospital worth $60 million in Tripoli. But Gaddafi had a higher price in mind. He wanted a modern superhighway to be donated and built by the Italians, a highway that would run for more than a thousand miles, linking the coast road between Egypt and Tunisia. He was trying to persuade Berlusconi to agree to this as proof of Italy's friendship for Libya, and he delivered a long lecture about how Italy could make amends for its colonial past, donate the highway, and then build tourist resorts along the Mediterranean. Berlusconi was balking. The cost of the highway was twenty times more than the hospital he had offered. It was a constant tug of war with Gaddafi, but in Berlusconi he had perhaps found his match. Berlusconi the schmoozer turned on the charm and eventually the deals began to flow. This constant commercial diplomacy between Italy and Libya, like the numerous oil and gas deals that Britain and France would subsequently chase after, was part of the mood music, the backdrop during the transformation of Gaddafi from Public Enemy Number One into friend and ally in the period between 2001 and 2006. Contracts and money would become the currency of reconciliation between Italy and Libya, in a hectic round of rapprochement that followed decades of enmity. The same would be true for Britain and its swashbuckling and pro-Washington premier, Tony Blair, who would make his own visit to Libya a month later.

Gaddafi was sending all the right signals, and he was sending them directly to the three leaders of the Western world who could do the most for him: Bush, Blair, and Berlusconi. Gaddafi's son, Saif al-Islam Gaddafi, and Libyan government officials had spent many months holding secret talks with agents of both the CIA and the British secret service, MI6. Gaddafi had condemned the al-Qaeda attacks on the World Trade Center. In December 2003, Gaddafi had agreed to a deal under which Libya would give up all of its nuclear and weapons of mass destruction programs. The Libyans were being realists. For the West it was a coup, both in propaganda terms and in terms of new business opportunities. Bush and Blair had both announced Gaddafi's capitulation over his nuclear program just before Christmas in 2003, in a triumphant fanfare of nationally televised speeches that were made on the same day. London was in lockstep, as always under Blair, with Washington.

"It was certainly a turning point for Libya," recalls Giovanni Castellaneta, who was seated next to Berlusconi at the luncheon party under Gaddafi's tent on that dusty day back in February 2004. The former diplomatic adviser remembers how frightened and weary the Libyan leader seemed when he spoke about the capture of Saddam in Tikrit, during Operation Red Dawn. Saddam had come out of his hole just eight weeks before, in mid-December 2003.

"Gaddafi really did not want to finish up like Saddam, and that is exactly what he told Berlusconi," recalls the former aide. "They brought us out to this tent in the desert and they served this horrible meat soup dish. It was a mutton dish, with a soupy tomato sauce and a lot of spices. I could barely get it down. Berlusconi was seated there with Gaddafi, being polite. He was trying to build bridges between Italy and Libya, trying to get Gaddafi to become more moderate and reasonable. At that luncheon it became clear to us that Gaddafi wanted to be more cooperative with the West and put the past behind him."

Indeed, thanks to the behind-the-scenes diplomatic efforts of Blair and Berlusconi, Colonel Gaddafi was by 2004 no longer a threat to the West. He was becoming downright cooperative. The

Libyan leader had observed the long arc of history after the end of the Cold War. He had seen the breakup of the Soviet Union. He had watched the Palestinians and Israelis sit down together at the negotiating table. He had observed the spread of Islamic extremism, and he understood the threat it posed to his own survival. It was only reasonable that he would wish to avoid the fate that had befallen Saddam Hussein. So now he was busy signing contracts for U.S. and European oil companies, starting with Italy's ENI and continuing with the Anglo-Dutch company Royal Dutch Shell and America's Exxon-Mobil. He would allow U.S. agents to dismantle and supervise the shipment to the United States of centrifuges and other components of his nuclear weapons program. He would join forces with the intelligence agencies to combat al-Qaeda. He would eventually even shake hands with President Barack Obama.

The man once described by Ronald Reagan as the "Mad Dog of the Middle East" had been turned, tamed, and neutralized. The former revolutionary had decided it was in his best interests to collaborate with the West he had once demonized, if only as an act of self-preservation.

Bush and Blair had cooperated effectively on the Gaddafi talks. Berlusconi had played his own direct role with Gaddafi, given Italy's colonial past, while Blair was a frequent and willing go-between for Bush and Gaddafi. Blair's big move was to open the door to a settlement of what many would say was the Libyan dictator's single worst act of terrorism, the 1988 bombing of a Pan Am jet that exploded over Lockerbie in Scotland and killed 270 people, mostly Americans. British companies would benefit mightily after Blair forgave Gaddafi for Lockerbie. Berlusconi, meanwhile, says he deserves as much credit as Blair for bringing Gaddafi in from the cold.

"I remember telling President Bush that we were domesticating Gaddafi," recalls Berlusconi. "We had educated him, we had charmed him, and we had trapped him. Each of us did our part. I remember working hard to put Italy's colonial past behind us, and I proposed to Gaddafi that we turn over a new leaf, that we forgive our past mistakes. I made a very public apology to Libya and I suggested to Gaddafi that we transform a public holiday called the Day of the Vendetta, that commemorated the victims of Italian colonialism in Libya, into a day of friendship between our countries. That in itself took a lot of time and energy."

While Blair was shuttling back and forth to Tripoli, and Jacques Chirac and then Nicolas Sarkozy were in quick succession making nice with the colonel and peddling contracts for French companies, Berlusconi was busy cultivating the erratic Libyan leader in his own way, using his personal touch, the outsized gestures, the empathetic bonding, the salesman's schmoozing and bonhomie, Berlusconi style.

"The key to getting Gaddafi to be more rational was to become his friend," says a nostalgic Berlusconi. "Whenever I went to visit him in Libya, he always embarrassed me with his largesse, with his presents. He once gave me as a present an entire family of camels, a father, a mother, and a baby camel. He was always very generous with me; we always exchanged gifts, and his gifts looked really expensive. So over the years I was able to establish a really close rapport with Gaddafi and I managed to change some of his attitudes. Not all of them, because he was an unpredictable fellow. But I think we had managed to get him on our side over the years."

After sanctions were lifted and the Bush administration took Libya off its list of states that sponsored terrorism, Big Oil moved back into Libya. Berlusconi made his own big move in the summer of 2008, at another lavish summit with the colonel in Tripoli. He announced plans to pay $5 billion for colonial-era atrocities and damages to Libya over a twenty-year period. In return, the now pragmatic colonel promised Berlusconi he would put a halt to the flow of tens of thousands of immigrants from Libya to Italy. He also promised more Libyan oil. For the next two years the number of migrants coming across the Mediterranean from Libya would drop sharply. It worked.

Doors were opening elsewhere in Europe as well. Soon Gaddafi would be turning up in Brussels as the guest of the European Commission president, José Manuel Barroso. The following year, in June 2009, Gaddafi would make his first-ever state visit to Italy. He insisted, of course, on bringing his massive tent to Rome and it was duly pitched in the sprawling gardens of the Villa Pamphili Doria. The resulting paralysis of traffic in Rome was on a par never before witnessed by Romans, and they had been observing traffic for more than two thousand years. The images of a smiling Gaddafi and a jovial Berlusconi are still clear in the faded official photographs of the time. As he had done before with George W. Bush, and then with his good friend Vladimir Putin, Berlusconi had now struck a very personal chord with Gaddafi. The two men had found in each other a personal chemistry that worked. Both were thoroughly unpredictable. Both believed deeply in their visceral instincts. With Blair and Sarkozy it might have been all about business, about accepting compensation for Libyan-bombed airliners and seeking contracts for British and French companies. With Berlusconi there were also powerful financial interests at play: Libya supplied more than 20 percent of Italy's energy imports. Gaddafi had become a major shareholder in a leading Italian bank, Unicredit, and even a co-owner of the famed Juventus soccer team. Gaddafi had invested billions of dollars in Italian companies. He owned a holding in Italian arms maker Finmeccanica and had even bought into Italy's state energy group, ENI, the same company that had been Libya's biggest oil production partner for more than four decades of Gaddafi's reign. Berlusconi was definitely protecting Italian economic interests, but the key to his relationship with Gaddafi was the personal rapport between the two men. With Berlusconi there was business, to be sure. But there was also heart and soul, and tons of personal charm. Libya's long-serving leader found Berlusconi to be *simpatico.*

Gaddafi's greatest moment was yet to come, and it would be a moment on Italian soil, only a few weeks after the Rome visit. On the evening of July 9, 2009, he would turn up as a guest at the opening dinner of the G-8 summit in the Southern Italian town of L'Aquila. Italy was hosting the G-8 and the colonel was on the guest list.

That night Berlusconi made a huge fuss over the seating arrangements, driving his diplomatic protocol officers crazy and eventually insisting on placing the president of the United States to his right and Gaddafi to his left.

"I wanted them to sit together, or at least nearby so they could meet, so they could talk," says Berlusconi, once again displaying the importance he places on personal chemistry in international politics.

Before the dinner, White House aides had asked Berlusconi's team to please avoid putting the two men together at the table, and to absolutely avoid having Gaddafi anywhere near Obama in the lineup for the official photo of leaders at the summit. As soon as the dinner was over, though, Berlusconi jumped up and physically grabbed the hands of each man, literally dragging them together and forcing them to shake hands and have a conversation. The White House aides cringed. The Italian aides were embarrassed. Still, it was at the summit dinner, thanks to Silvio Berlusconi, that Gaddafi finally got to have his historic handshake with a slightly uncomfortable-looking President Barack Obama. The Libyan dictator, for decades a sociopath and terrorist in the eyes of the American public, had found his own kind of redemption.

Also attending the G-8 summit dinner in L'Aquila that night was the new president of France, a man who at the time was on extremely good terms with Gaddafi.

Nicolas Sarkozy was a hard-driving French politician from the suburbs of Paris who had worked his way up the ranks under the watchful gaze of his mentor, Charles Pasqua, a right-wing politician whose career would be marred by multiple corruption charges. Sarkozy was a Napoleonic figure with a quick wit and a sharp temper, known around the Paris newsroom of the *International Herald Tribune* at the time by the not so affectionate nickname of "Sharky." As a former finance and interior minister under center-right governments, he had made a name for himself as an ebullient politician with a huge ego. He was mercurial. He was unpredictable. He was not afraid of controversy, and he did not seem to care much about protocol. He did care about the high life; he loved hobnobbing with the Paris elite and going on yachts with the rich and famous. As witnesses to his second marriage, he invited the billionaires Bernard Arnault and Martin Bouygues.

Sarkozy's second wife, a political activist named Cécilia Ciganer-Albéniz, had shared his presidential ambitions, and the two had forged a French version of Bill and Hillary Clinton's political marriage. Cécilia Sarkozy served as unpaid adviser when Sarkozy was finance minister, and she headed his private office at the ruling Union for a Popular Movement (UMP) party. They were a political power couple. They were considered by French critics as both pushy and cynical, he more than she. By her own account, even though Cécilia left Sarkozy for another man and moved to New York City in 2005, she returned to Paris to be at Sarkozy's side during his election campaign and victory in May 2007. Five months later, in October 2007, Cécilia dumped him again, and the presidential spokesman at the Elysée Palace announced the couple's separation. Just days later, in November, Sarkozy was spotted at a Paris dinner party romancing a glamorous Italian singer and former model named Carla Bruni. They would marry soon after the New Year.

Cécilia Sarkozy would write in her autobiography that after taking office in 2007 Sarkozy became "agitated" and was prone to "terrible rages" at the presidential palace. She seemed happy for Carla Bruni to deal with the new president's mood swings.

What no one could question was that Sarkozy was an unabashed self-promoter, a man who utterly loved being in the limelight. His critics would say he loved it too much and was not discerning enough about the company he kept. When it came to Muammar Gaddafi, the new French president seemed to have no problems at all. *Au contraire.* Berlusconi and Blair might have been at it for years, but Sarkozy was now impatient to build his own presidential ties with the Libyan dictator. He had known Gaddafi on a personal level for years, having met him during visits to Tripoli as France's interior minister. Now he was *le président,* so it was no surprise that in December 2007, less than six months after taking office as president and while smack in the middle of his new romance with Carla Bruni, Sarkozy invited Gaddafi to Paris and lavished on him all the honors that the French Republic could bestow. The French press did not know which way to turn. On the one hand, here was the bloodthirsty dictator of Libya in a pitched tent across from the Palais de l'Elysée. At the same time all of Paris was talking about the "love affair" with Carla Bruni.

Shaking off the gossipmongers, Sarkozy welcomed Gaddafi with open arms to Paris during what proved a highly controversial and extravagant five-day state visit to France. Gaddafi breezed into town in his Bedouin robes, accompanied by an entourage of four hundred servants, five airplanes, a camel, and thirty female body-guards, and then proceeded to pitch his heated tent on the grounds of the palatial Hôtel de Marigny, just across the street from the Elysée Palace. The French president, meanwhile, was keen to sell a huge array of French goods to Libya, and he ended up announcing $10 billion of new contracts for French companies and an agree-ment to develop "the peaceful use of nuclear energy" in Libya.

When he rolled out the red carpet for Gaddafi, Sarkozy faced a wall of criticism, even from within his own ranks. His own min-ister for human rights said that Gaddafi "must understand that our country is not a doormat on which a leader—whether terrorist or not—can wipe off the blood of his crimes."

As it turned out, Gaddafi bought relatively little from France. Sarkozy kept up his courtship of the Libyan leader for years, though. He considered Gaddafi on a par with Hosni Mubarak of Egypt and other authoritarian leaders in the Arab world who might prove at times a bit politically embarrassing but who could none-theless be relied upon to sign arms deals and oil deals and all sorts of multi-billion-dollar contracts with France.

Throughout this period, French arms makers and energy com-panies such as Dassault and Total were competing for deals in Gad-dafi's Libya with Italian arms makers and energy companies such as Finmeccanica and ENI, respectively. On occasion both the French and the Italians would lose out to Putin's Russia, a favorite of Gaddafi's from the good old days of the Soviet Union.

Everything changed with the advent of the Arab Spring in early 2011. The violence began in Tunisia. Then the Facebook generation kicked in. Social media for the first time became a tool of political revolution, flanking the more traditional method of the demonstrations and violence-scarred protest in Cairo's Tahrir Square. Mubarak would be swept away in a storm of anger and protest. The deserts of the Middle East were suddenly ransacked by a violent wind, by a dust storm of global dimension that came masquerading as the quest for democracy and then morphed into anarchy and fragmentation, into tribal and ethnic war, into failed states and semi-states and rebel militia groups competing with terrorists to overthrow dictators. The Arab Spring, which began with such hope and innocence, would then morph still further, and into its most nefarious and malignant form with the emergence of a medieval cult of caliphate-worshippers as barbaric as anything known to human experience, an army of barbarians somehow more evil than Osama bin Laden himself.

Sarkozy had been slow to react to the Arab Spring. His policy on Tunisia had been inept. He had offered French support to the dictator Zine El Abadine Ben Ali, Tunisia's president, just days before his downfall. Sarkozy's position on Mubarak was ambiguous. He had not been a big fan of the Bush administration's idea of promoting democracy throughout the Middle East. Nor was he a particular fan of Barack Obama, whose own Middle East policy machinery had seemed to have seized up amidst divisions between the gung-ho idealists at the White House and Hillary Clinton's hesitant but changeable vision of U.S. policy. Sarkozy had been slow in making public a clear and coherent position regarding the Arab Spring. His poll numbers were horrendous; his approval rating was just 29 percent at the time. The presidential election of April 2012 was looming and his foreign policy was being harshly criticized. A group of French diplomats published an article in *Le Monde* that called Sarkozy's foreign policy "unprofessional, improvised and impulsive." Nicolas Sarkozy needed a win, badly.

Right after the fall of Mubarak, the French president jumped on the bandwagon. By late February he had become a vocal supporter of the uprisings, including the ones under way in Tunisia and Libya. Suddenly, after trying to sell him on French contracts for the past three years, the president of France was now talking about overthrowing Gaddafi. In the space of a few days at the end of February 2011, Sarkozy had cantankerously lectured a European Union summit on the need for economic sanctions against Libya, made the Libyan uprising his biggest priority, and then on February 25 ceremoniously proclaimed that "Gaddafi must go."

It was now clear that Sarkozy was no longer interested in selling Dassault Rafale or Mirage fighter jets to Gaddafi. He was far more interested in the idea of using them to drop bombs on him.

As the world watched in disbelief, the Arab Spring protests spread quickly across Libya. Gaddafi ordered his security forces to open fire on protesters in Benghazi and the revolt soon escalated into an armed conflict, involving local tribal militias, genuine pro-democracy rebels, and Islamic extremists of varying color and definition. When Gaddafi ordered airstrikes on the rebels, even his defenders like Berlusconi were embarrassed. When he vowed to fight to the last drop of blood and cleanse Libya of the rebels house by house and to kill the protesters "like rats," the tide toward military action in Libya began to turn. Sarkozy began leading calls for the establishment of a no-fly zone in Libya to prevent Gaddafi from bombing his own people.

On March 10, Sarkozy met with the rebel leaders who had formed a National Transitional Council and immediately recognized them as the legitimate government of Libya. The next day, he was out front again at a European summit, joining Britain's new prime minister, David Cameron, to call again for military action and a no-fly zone.

By now Libya had been plunged into full-scale civil war, and Hillary Clinton had begun a week of shuttle diplomacy, flying to Paris for a meeting of G-8 foreign ministers on March 14 and a heart-to-heart with Sarkozy. The French president, emboldened by the fact that the Arab League had also joined calls for a no-fly zone, lobbied Clinton hard. He asked Washington to support a military intervention that would stop Gaddafi's advance toward the rebel stronghold of Benghazi. Hillary Clinton was not convinced. The decade-long trauma of America's wars in Afghanistan and Iraq had momentarily paralyzed U.S. foreign policy. She would soon turn into a hawk, however, ignoring strong objections from the Pentagon and from the CIA, who warned that a military intervention in Libya could turn into a disaster.

In Paris, Mrs. Clinton recalled getting "an earful about military intervention" from a Sarkozy who "loved being at the center of the action" and who seemed to see the chaos in Libya as a "chance to jump into the fray supporting the Arab Spring."

It was a day later, on March 15, that the United Nations Security Council began to examine a resolution that would authorize the no-fly zone and the use of "all necessary means" to protect the civilian population of Libya from an increasingly deranged Colonel Gaddafi. The U.S. secretary of state shuttled off to Cairo to show solidarity with the protesters of Tahrir Square, while finding time to give a light wrist-slap to the ruler of strategically important Gulf emirate of Bahrain, who was also using force to put down protests. Sarkozy continued to growl in Paris, a slightly hesitant David Cameron made the right kind of sympathetic noises from London, while back in Rome Silvio Berlusconi was stewing. He did not want to back a military intervention in Libya. He did not believe there was a workable alternative to maintaining his friend Muammar Gaddafi in power.

On March 17, the UN Security Council approved the no-fly zone and gave Sarkozy and Cameron and even the reluctant Obama administration sufficient political cover to move ahead with plans for a military attack on Gaddafi.

Sarkozy notched up his gung-ho war rhetoric one more time, but this time he got an answer back, from the Gaddafi family.

Gaddafi's son, Saif al-Islam, had already threatened to reveal a "grave secret" if France went ahead with its recognition of the rebel government and pushed for a no-fly zone. In what seemed like wild-eyed desperation, Saif al-Islam claimed that the information could bring down Sarkozy. Now he made good on his threat.

In an interview with Euronews on March 16, Gaddafi's son claimed that Libya had financed Sarkozy's 2007 presidential election campaign and now he wanted his money back.

"Sarkozy," said Saif al-Islam, "must give back the money he took from Libya to finance his electoral campaign. We funded it and we have all the details and are ready to reveal everything. The first thing we want this clown to do is to give the money back to the Libyan people. He was given assistance so that he could help them. But he's disappointed us: Give us back our money. We have all the bank details and documents for the transfer operations and we will make everything public soon."

The "revelation" seemed as surreal as every other aspect of the Libyan nightmare. Sarkozy dispatched his spokesperson to issue a prompt denial, but Saif Gaddafi's televised claims proved the start of a lengthy political and judicial nightmare in France. A former Libyan prime minister backed up Saif's claims. French prosecutors opened a case file. Documents purporting to show the secret agreement were published in the French press. Sarkozy said they were fakes. Sarkozy denied everything, but the allegation would return to haunt him in the middle of his flagging re-election bid in April 2012, when he was accused of taking a cool 50 million euros from the Gaddafi family.

In March 2011 Nicolas Sarkozy wanted the whole world to know that he was bent on bringing down Gaddafi. He would show himself to be a global leader. He would design his moment of French grandeur by hosting a new council of war, an international summit on Libya that would bring everyone together at the Elysée Palace on the afternoon of Saturday, March 19. On the guest list were a dozen world leaders and European officials including German Chancellor Angela Merkel, Britain's Cameron, Silvio Berlusconi, Spain's José Luis Rodríguez Zapatero, Amr Moussa from the Arab League, UN Secretary-General Ban Ki-moon, Qatar's Prime

Minister Sheikh Hamad bin Jassim bin Jaber al-Thani, and Sheikh Abdullah bin Zayed al Nahyan of the United Arab Emirates.

Just before he welcomed his guests, Sarkozy held a private mini-summit with David Cameron and Hillary Clinton. As President Obama had seen fit to proceed with a state visit to Brazil, Clinton was back in Paris representing the United States. In any case, she had changed her mind a couple of days before and was pressing full steam ahead with plans for military intervention in which France and Britain could get out in front. Obama seemed to have abdicated leadership, and some of the wags at CNN were referring to Hillary as "the acting president." The policy of the United States was to provide backing but let others take the lead. The mantra in Washington was "No boots on the ground!" although to European leaders it seemed more like "No visible leadership."

As for Berlusconi, he was definitely having a harder time than had Sarkozy in jettisoning Gaddafi. Berlusconi had a great deal more invested in the Libyan leader than the French president. Berlusconi not only had oil interests to preserve; he had closer knowledge of Libya than Sarkozy and he was convinced it was pure folly to go to war there.

As Berlusconi tells it today, his hand was forced by the president of Italy, a cynical former Communist named Giorgio Napolitano, who had constitutional authority over the armed forces. Berlusconi says Napolitano forced him to provide Italian bases and cooperation for the planned military intervention in Libya.

On the evening of March 17, Berlusconi was at the Rome opera house, attending a performance of *Nabucco*. He was in the company of Napolitano and a sprinkling of senior aides.

"We were at the opera, and the UN Security Council had just approved the no-fly zone resolution," recalls Berlusconi. "I had this discussion about Libya with President Napolitano during an interval at the opera. He had already made up his mind and wanted to support the attack. He had been busy having meetings with the defense minister and pushing the defense committees in the parliament to meet and approve resolutions of support for a military mission. I remember it was a pretty tough discussion with Napoli-tano that evening. He kept insisting that we had to 'stay in line with the others' in Europe. After that meeting, and before even going to the Paris summit, I remember thinking seriously about resigning as prime minister, and I'll tell you why."

Berlusconi leans forward, and as he speaks, his voice grows louder and he begins to bang his fist on the table for emphasis.

"I had become a friend of Gaddafi, and I had enjoyed very close relations with Gaddafi. We had done a lot of things together; we had achieved a lot. We got six thousand Libyan soldiers to stop immigrants from leaving the shores of Africa. I felt that to bring down Gaddafi at this point was both illogical and very dangerous because this was a country ready to explode apart with all of its hundred and five tribes. I felt bound by my friendship with Gaddafi. After all, I had managed to turn him from enemy to friend. So I was absolutely opposed to this attack. I ended up having to go to Paris with my hands tied because of the president of the republic, Giorgio Napolitano, and because of a joint vote by the parliamentary defense committees. I went to Paris, therefore, determined to at least minimize our participation and to offer only the use of our bases but no armed intervention, no bombing by Italy."

Such was the state of Berlusconi's mind at a few minutes past noon on Saturday, March 19, when he got into his bullet-proof metallic silver Audi 8 and headed for the military airport at Ciampino, on the outskirts of Rome. Together with his aides, he boarded the government Airbus and flew to Paris. He was in a very bad mood that day and kept telling his aides the whole thing was a big mistake, that it was a dangerous leap in the dark, that there was no plan for how to keep the country together in a post–Gaddafi Libya.

As soon as they landed, Berlusconi's party headed straight to the Elysée Palace, where he found the other leaders milling around, making small talk, and eating hors d'oeuvres in an antechamber adjoining the Salle des Fêtes on the second floor of the palace.

"The first thing we found out when we arrived at the Elysée," recalled an aide, "was that some leaders had already been briefed by the French, and that there had been a restricted meeting Sarkozy had held with Hillary Clinton and David Cameron. Berlusconi began to realize that everything that was about to happen had been precooked, and that he had been excluded from the process."

As soon as Berlusconi heard this, he marched over to Angela Merkel, who was munching on a biscuit.

"Angela, what is going on here?" Berlusconi asked as the German chancellor recoiled slightly. "This is a farce. We are all called here to Paris, but everything has already been decided."

Merkel, according to those who witnessed the conversation, shrugged and said very little in reply. She was cool to Berlusconi, who now realized there was nothing he could do.

Spain's Prime Minister Luis Zapatero, by contrast, remembers being briefed immediately upon arrival that Saturday afternoon.

"When I arrived at the meeting, Sarkozy's aides had already told my aides that everything was prepared and that the French warplanes were either on their way or were going to be on their way," recalls Zapatero.

While Berlusconi made small talk with the others, Sarkozy had been finishing his little pre-summit summit with Cameron and Clinton. He had told them that French Rafale jets were already headed toward Libya. The British and U.S. sorties would follow later that night, but France was out there already, out in front, ready to strike, even before sitting down for the summit that was supposed to consider coordinated action. Sarkozy had unleashed a squadron of twenty-five aircraft, including interceptors and reconnaissance and others kitted out for air-to-ground strikes. They had orders to strike at tank columns that were making their way from Tripoli to Benghazi along the coastal road.

Clinton has described the look of anger on Berlusconi's face, amid the general consternation among the leaders at Sarkozy's revelation. "When the larger group found out that France had jumped the gun, it caused an uproar," she has recalled.

One European official who was present in that meeting

remembers the Gallic grandeur of the ceremonial meeting chamber, the Salle des Fêtes, and the thirty world leaders and officials seated around the oversize table. He said Sarkozy seemed to be in a hurry.

"Sarkozy started immediately by saying that Gaddafi was nearing Benghazi and that we had to stop him or there would be a massacre," the participant recalled. "Sarkozy then announced that his planes had started their engines. I will never forget how Sarkozy said: 'My planes have started their engines. So I recommend we have a quick meeting.'"

When Sarkozy had finished speaking, they began the traditional "tour de table," the diplomatic ritual in which each world leader around the table would read a brief statement.

"It was a pretty formal meeting," recalls Zapatero. "The presentations were very diplomatically prepared. It was about showing a great coalition with countries of the Arab world. It was about saying that the fall of Gaddafi had started, and that Europe was committed to the Arab Spring. But when the meeting was called, most of the substance had already been prepared."

Zapatero remembers the moment that Hillary Clinton called "an uproar" and he recalls Berlusconi being very angry with Sarkozy.

"Berlusconi was upset," says Zapatero. "In fact Berlusconi was in a difficult position because he condemned Gaddafi's repression of the opposition but he was not in favor of trying to make Gaddafi's regime fall."

As for the uproar, Zapatero says the only person surprised by the vehemence of the clash between Sarkozy and Berlusconi was the U.S. secretary of state. "I wasn't surprised. Both Berlusconi and Sarkozy are very expansive in the way they express themselves. They're vehement, and I was used to seeing that at other European summits. But Hillary wasn't used to European council meetings."

Berlusconi now looked around the room at the Elysée Palace as he took in the news that Sarkozy had already unleashed the first wave of attacks. Everyone else around the table had either spoken in favor of the military intervention or was not really against it. He was isolated.

"Here we are at this crucial summit meeting in Paris, trying to decide what our joint position should be on Libya, and we learn that Sarkozy has already sent his warplanes," says Berlusconi.

Berlusconi is making his hand into a fist, perhaps unconsciously, as he recounts the bitter moment.

Clinton tried to mediate but it was too late. Berlusconi was furious. He told Clinton and the others assembled in Paris that Gaddafi might be a dictator but he was the only one capable of holding the country together. But then he promised that Italy would do its part.

"I was in open disagreement with Sarkozy," Berlusconi recalls, and for once he is not smiling.

Years later Berlusconi would claim that Sarkozy had rushed to recognize the opposition government and had pressed for the campaign against Gaddafi "in order to pursue French commercial interests and because he was jealous of my relationship with Gaddafi and realized he could never compete with me for new oil and gas contracts."

Ask Berlusconi to sum up the legacy of Sarkozy's push to topple Gaddafi and to this day he will still say it was a mistake, that Libya would have had more stability with a strong leader like Gaddafi, that the whole thing was a fiasco that brought about only bloodshed and suffering and paved the way for the emergence of al-Qaeda and ISIS and other terrorist groups across Libya.

Berlusconi is not at all keen to discuss what is perhaps the most controversial allegation ever made about Sarkozy's twisted relationship with Muammar Gaddafi, the claim that when it came time for the Libyan dictator to die, it would be at the hands of a French secret agent with a license to kill. That, at least, was what was later rumored in the French press, that Gaddafi's death was somehow engineered by the French equivalent of the CIA, whose ultimate commander was the French president.

The images of a bloodstained and shaken Muammar Gaddafi

were broadcast to the world on October 20, 2011, from his hometown of Sirte. After being strafed by fighter jets, Gaddafi had been hiding in a culvert when he was hauled out around dawn.

"I don't want to end up like Saddam Hussein," he had told Berlusconi more than seven years earlier.

Amateur video taken that morning shows Gaddafi, dazed and wounded, being dragged off the hood of a car and pulled to the ground by his hair. "Keep him alive! Keep him alive!" someone shouts. Gaddafi then goes out of view and gunshots ring out.

In Paris Sarkozy was jubilant on the day Gaddafi died. Berlusconi was livid. Hillary Clinton's reaction to the news of the death of Gaddafi has been the subject of some controversy over time. She was preparing for a CBS News interview in Kabul that day, when an aide handed her a BlackBerry with the first news that Gaddafi had been killed.

"We came, we saw, he died," she joked to the startled TV reporter, after reading the news flash, throwing her head back in a raucous outburst of laughter.

Sarkozy repeatedly denied the allegations that he ordered the killing of Gaddafi, and soon the issue went away. But in March of 2012, just a few weeks ahead of the presidential election that he would lose to Socialist François Hollande, Sarkozy would again face the claims that he had received secret cash donations from Gaddafi during his first election campaign. Documents were published online and handed over to a French judge. They purported to show what Gaddafi's son Saif alleged, that 50 million euros had been laundered by Libya into the Sarkozy campaign machinery, through bank accounts in Panama and Switzerland. Sarkozy would repeatedly deny the allegations, but they would continue to dog him, and for years to come. For his adversaries in Paris, the ghost of Gaddafi hovers to this day over Nicolas Sarkozy.

Nor was any end in sight to the rancorous relationship between Sarkozy and Berlusconi. The two men were developing a mutual antipathy that bordered on repugnance. Within weeks they clashed again, this time at another European summit, this time on another matter. It happened again and again, and at each and every one of their half-dozen summit meetings throughout 2011, until finally, that autumn, and according to his peers with clear intent, Sarkozy became part of a small band of European officials who would try to drag the White House into a scheme to unseat Berlusconi, to literally knock him out of power.

The story of a French secret agent with personal orders from Sarkozy to kill Gaddafi might be the stuff of conspiracy theorists. But the existence of a plot to bring down Berlusconi, bizarrely enough, turned out to be the real deal, an international intrigue of the old-fashioned kind.

CHAPTER ELEVEN

———

International Intrigue

S arkozy? He was incredibly hostile to me."

Berlusconi is seated on his favorite couch in the living room that adjoins the dining hall of his villa, shaking his head from side to side with evident disgust. He is reconstructing the last few months of his premiership before his resignation in the autumn of 2011. The air in Brussels was thick with recrimination, insults, treachery, and betrayal, all sorts of European political theater amid the tumultuous days of Europe's financial crisis.

"I can never forget what Sarkozy did to me," says a grim-looking Berlusconi. "It was late October and we were just about to begin a Eurozone crisis summit in Brussels when it happened. Sarkozy was leaving one of the anterooms where we were all mingling before the formal beginning of the meeting. And although we may have had our differences, I go over to greet him and I say, 'Ciao, Nicolas!' in my usual friendly way. I offer my hand. He stares at me, and he refuses to shake my hand. Not only that! He physically pushes my arm aside, he actually pushes my arm to one side.

"I think to myself: What an asshole! What arrogance! No one has ever done this to me. Sarkozy is the only person who has ever pushed my hand away and refused to shake it," says a scowling Berlusconi.

"As if that were not enough," he continues, "a few hours later an aide tells me that Sarkozy is going around the summit telling other leaders that he will never shake Berlusconi's hand again. It was crazy. I am not sure if he actually went around and said this to people, but I will never forget that image of myself walking over to him and trying to shake hands and him turning and walking away."

To say that Berlusconi and Sarkozy were not on the best of terms would be something of an understatement. Ever since the uproar in Paris over Sarkozy's premature bombing of Libya, the two men had been at swords drawn.

Six month earlier, in April of 2011, and a month after their rancorous exchange in front of Hillary Clinton, Sarkozy and Berlusconi met again, this time at a bilateral French-Italian summit in Rome. The meeting did not go well. In fact, things were not going well generally for either man. Sarkozy was at an all-time low in French opinion polls. His puffed-up brinksmanship and role as a war leader in Libya was not going down well with the French public. He, like Berlusconi, was also facing various investigations by the judiciary, with magistrates delving into the deeply embarrassing allegation that envelopes stuffed with cash were delivered to Sarkozy campaign officials by emissaries for Liliane Bettencourt, the L'Oréal heiress and France's richest woman. Coming on the heels of the accusations by Gaddafi's son that Libya had financed Sarkozy's 2007 campaign, the Bettencourt affair was proving a vote-loser.

Berlusconi, of course, had his own problems. He had only just recently survived attempts to bring down his government and he was in open conflict with a key political ally, a former neo-Fascist politician who was now the president of the lower house of parliament. Worse, he had recently been put under investigation for allegedly having sex with an underage prostitute. He was facing a global tsunami of derision in the media over the bunga-bunga scandal. The front pages of newspapers from *The New York Times* to *Le Monde* were full of stories about "Ruby the Heart-Stealer" and about alleged harems of women having sex with Berlusconi at

Arcore. The billionaire media mogul was furious. He had recently taken to the airwaves to tell an astonished Italian public: "I have never paid for sex with a woman." It sounded very much like Bill Clinton, Italian style.

Both men were also still upset with each other, still seething over their differences about the war on Gaddafi. Sarkozy had other issues as well. On April 26, the French president stormed into the Rome summit, and according to Italian officials who were present, he almost immediately began attacking Berlusconi, speaking in increasingly loud tones, at one point shouting, ranting about negative articles that had been published about him in the Italian press, particularly a depiction on the cover of one of the magazines owned by Berlusconi of him as Napoleon conquering Libya. Sarkozy was not a man who kept his cool.

Berlusconi was meanwhile complaining to Sarkozy about the thousands of migrants from Libya who were floating across the Mediterranean and washing up on Italy's shores, many of them dead. Sarkozy wanted Berlusconi to strengthen his backing for the allied military action in Libya. He wanted Italian jets to start bombing operations in Libya. Berlusconi still felt the war against Gaddafi was a huge mistake that would only create chaos and instability and strengthen the jihadists in Libya. He ultimately agreed that Italian jets would join the NATO bombings, however, in exchange for Sarkozy's cooperation on the migration crisis.

On another front, Berlusconi wanted Sarkozy's backing for the appointment of a new Italian president of the European Central Bank, and his candidate was the widely respected Mario Draghi. Sarkozy told Berlusconi he would give his support but only on condition that the other Italian board member at the European Central Bank resign first, and make way for a Frenchman. After all, the man Draghi would be replacing as head of Europe's central bank was Jean-Claude Trichet, the very French former governor of the Bank of France. The Italian board member was named Lorenzo Bini Smaghi. Berlusconi promised to get Bini Smaghi to stand down, never dreaming that he would not be able to deliver.

Meanwhile, during the summit, Berlusconi tried to develop a personal rapport with Sarkozy in his trademark fashion, telling Sarkozy an off-color anecdote that brought together the flammable topic of Gaddafi and his own take on the sex scandal allegations being made against him in courts and in the media: the story of the alleged Libyan origins of the term "bunga-bunga." As usual, he was all smiles. Sarkozy, however, appeared embarrassed. His finance minister, a party loyalist named Christine Lagarde, is said to have turned and looked away while Berlusconi told the story.

Two weeks later it became clear that France and Italy had a new problem. Bini Smaghi was refusing to resign. The idea of naming Italy's Mario Draghi to head the European Central Bank was getting rave reviews from everyone in Europe and on Wall Street. The other remaining Italian on the executive board of the central bank, however, the aloof aristocrat from Italy Lorenzo Bini Smaghi, suddenly declared that he had no intention of leaving. The press speculated that he was angling for a consolation prize, perhaps a nice appointment as governor of the Bank of Italy, the post that Draghi was now vacating. With Bini Smaghi holding firm, Sarkozy was furious again with Berlusconi.

Sarkozy dispatched the silver-haired Christine Lagarde into battle. France wanted its seat at the table.

Lagarde went before the press and revealed Berlusconi's promises to solve the Bini Smaghi problem, citing remarks he had made during the Rome summit a couple of weeks before. "On that occasion," said Lagarde, "we made the point about French participation on the board, possibly in place of an Italian. It is not logical for one country to have two seats."

In case anyone had missed the point, Lagarde rubbed it in. "It is logical," she declared, "that one of the two Italians on the board, and not the new president-designate, leaves his post gracefully."

Despite the warning, Berlusconi found himself facing a stubborn Bini Smaghi, who refused to step down until many months later, waiting until after Draghi arrived at the European Central Bank. In his defense, Bini Smaghi claimed he did not resign because he wanted to make a point of principle. "If an Italian board member resigns simply because the Italian prime minister asks him to do so, that would suggest that Italian central bankers are not independent," Bini Smaghi later declared.

Berlusconi remembers things a bit differently.

"Bini Smaghi comes to see me," says Berlusconi. "He has been going around saying that his position is independent and that he cannot be forced to step down. When he comes to my office, he says he will agree to leave the central bank but only if I name him governor of the Bank of Italy. Right then and there I decided not to do it, because it would be a mistake to give in to blackmail. I said to him: 'Do you realize that you are breaking up the friendship of Italy and France? Just calm down and we will find a solution to satisfy you.' No. Bini Smaghi behaved disgracefully," he says, shaking his head again. "As for Sarkozy's reaction to the whole thing, that was excessive, to say the least."

The clash over the central bank nominations was only one of the factors upsetting global financial markets that May. The credit rating of the United States was about to be downgraded for the first time. The French economy was faltering. The Greek debt crisis was worsening and talk abounded of Athens being forced to leave the Eurozone. Italy was another highly indebted country. There was talk of downgrading Italy's debt amid fears that the Greek crisis would spread and could cause a domino effect. The storm clouds were gathering over Europe. A tempest of unprecedented force was about to sweep the world's financial markets.

In Italy, meanwhile, more and more lurid details were emerging from the bunga-bunga investigation. Berlusconi was becoming an object of ridicule not only in the media but in half the chanceries of Europe. He did not help his cause by making sexist jokes about the bunga-bunga during public appearances.

While Berlusconi faced his scandals, Nicolas Sarkozy and Christine Lagarde were facing their own allegations.

On May 11, Lagarde was named by investigating magistrates in Paris in the so-called Tapie affair, a typically French scandal, in that it combined finance and politics. It involved banks like Credit Lyonnais, politicians close to Sarkozy, illicit campaign contributions, and the sale of the Adidas sporting group by Bernard Tapie, a billionaire businessmen and backer of Sarkozy in the 2007 election campaign. The allegation against Lagarde was that as a cabinet minister she had intervened improperly to order a special panel of judges to make a ruling that ended up awarding Tapie a $350 million court settlement.

In Paris, the public prosecutor recommended a full judicial inquiry into Lagarde's role, saying there were "several reasons to be suspicious of the regularity and even the legality" of the settlement, which could constitute "an abuse of authority."

Lagarde denounced the investigation, telling *Le Figaro*: "This is an attempt to smear me." She said she was "as calm as I have always been" over the affair, and added that she had "total government support."

That "total government support" could only mean one thing: Nicolas Sarkozy. A former anti-corruption investigative magistrate claimed that Lagarde had received "instructions" in the Tapie affair directly from the Elysée. Other politicians questioned Sarkozy's friendship with Tapie.

Daniel Cohn-Bendit, the legendary rebel from the 1970s who was now a Green Party member of parliament, told French TV, "What I know is that Lagarde's decision was pushed by Nicolas Sarkozy. It's Sarkozy's responsibility and his friendship with Bernard Tapie that's under discussion here."

By May of 2011, the Lagarde affair was not Sarkozy's only headache. He was focused on trying to recover in the polls ahead of the upcoming presidential elections. Fortunately, France would be hosting the two biggest world summits of the year, the G-8 and the G-20, which were a godsend, a way for him to show his clout as the president, and he intended to make the most of his star turn on the world stage. The G-8 was to be held at the end of May in the stylish French seaside resort of Deauville. Sarkozy also had plans for a sparkling G-20 to be held in glamorous Cannes later that year, in the same *palais* that hosts the annual Cannes Film Festival. He had big plans, visions of grandeur.

After their spats over Libya in March and over the European Central Bank in April, the Deauville summit could have been a moment for reconciliation for the Italian and the French leaders. It was not meant to be. Their differences over Sarkozy's aggressive leadership of the war in Libya remained, as did the festering problem of the French claim to a seat on the board of the European Central Bank. Much of this was hidden from the cameras, which during press conferences tended to see a smiling Berlusconi at Sarkozy's side making pleasantries. Some feelings cannot be hidden, though.

On the opening night of the G-8 summit, the former top model Carla Bruni and her husband, Nicolas Sarkozy, were welcoming their guests to a working dinner at Le Ciro's Barriere, a fashionable restaurant in Deauville. Sarkozy's model-actress-singer wife was now three years into her starring role as first lady of France, even though she was getting more sarcasm than rave reviews from the French public. She certainly seemed to share Sarkozy's love of the limelight, having just made a blitz visit to the Cannes Film Festival for the launch of Woody Allen's new film *Midnight in Paris,* in which the first lady had made a cameo appearance. She was also getting ready to release her latest album, including a love song for Sarkozy that would not exactly enchant the people of France. She was also pregnant. Although she had been coy about announcing that she was with Sarkozy's child, the baby bump was more than apparent under her loose-fitting designer black dress as the elegant first lady stood at Sarkozy's side to welcome dinner guests.

Among the first to arrive at the restaurant was Barack Obama. Sarkozy beamed as Carla Bruni gave the U.S. president a warm kiss on the cheek and then a big hug. David Cameron received a Gallic peck on each cheek, as did Angela Merkel and Dmitry Medvedev, the Russian president. And so it went, with each of the leaders being greeted warmly—all except for Silvio Berlusconi. The images of that evening in Deauville show a polite smile that is plastered on Carla Bruni's face, and an uncomfortable-looking Sarkozy at her side. She shakes hands with Berlusconi, but nothing more. In fact she seems to build an imaginary wall of space around herself, a virtual anti–Berlusconi force field, and as she greets him she maintains her distance from the Italian billionaire prime minister.

Bruni, as it happens, has a long history of hating Silvio Berlusconi. She had been in the Elysée Palace for less than a year when she uttered her first public attack on Berlusconi. It was November 2008, and Barack Obama had just been elected president. Berlusconi had made one of his gaffes, this time quite offensive for Americans because it amounted to a racial slur on Obama. "The new American president," Berlusconi had joked during a news conference in Moscow, "is young, handsome, and always tanned." In the face of a storm of criticism Berlusconi claimed "it was a big compliment" and that he was only being humorous. There is reason to believe that he was being sincere in his explanation; in his own mind he probably thought he was being funny. But no one else found it so.

Bruni, as the first lady of France, was not supposed to make personal attacks on the leaders of other European governments. She cast aside diplomatic niceties, though, and blasted Berlusconi very publicly. "When I hear Silvio Berlusconi joke about the fact that Obama is 'always tanned,' it feels strange to me," she told the French press. Originally from a wealthy Northern Italian family, she added that she was glad to be a French citizen and that she was no longer Italian. The Italians were offended, even those who were against Berlusconi. A former president of Italy announced that he was glad Carla Bruni was no longer an Italian citizen and said that "France should keep her." The Italian press went to town, detailing Bruni's well-known support for an Italian Red Brigades terrorist who for years had been given safe haven by France even though he was wanted on multiple homicide charges back in Italy.

Bruni became the subject of another gaffe by Berlusconi a few months later, at another summit in early 2009, in this case when Berlusconi whispered to Sarkozy that he had "given" him his

Italian-born wife. It was meant to be a joke about Mrs. Sarkozy having been born in Italy, but it was not considered funny. At their press conference Sarkozy appeared to wince visibly. When the French media found out about this gaffe, they crowned Berlusconi "the Oscar winner of vulgarity."

With that kind of history, it was not surprising that Carla Bruni declined to greet Berlusconi with a kiss when he rolled up at the restaurant in Deauville. The French first lady regarded Silvio Berlusconi with obvious distaste, and that was not going to change any time soon. The feeling seems to have been reciprocated.

Berlusconi felt there were other issues as well. "Sarkozy was incredibly hostile to me, for various reasons," he says. "One of them was that he had a real fixation on wealth, a real envy of those with money. He was jealous because I was rich and he was not."

He recalls a meeting with Sarkozy soon after his marriage to Bruni.

"Sarkozy said to me: 'See, Silvio! Now I am a rich man like you!'"

Berlusconi guffaws at the recollection.

Yet back at the Deauville summit of G-8 leaders, Berlusconi was not winning any prizes for diplomacy or elegance and style. For Bruni he was a clown, for Sarkozy he was a rival. For Obama, Berlusconi appeared on this occasion at the G-8 summit to be something of a riddle. The president of the United States was perplexed, even taken aback by Berlusconi's antics.

At the first working session of the summit, with all of the leaders seated around the table and ready to start, and with photographers and cameramen still in the room, Obama looked positively befuddled as Berlusconi whispered some instructions to an Italian TV cameraman and then sidled up to Obama, placed a hand on his shoulder, and said hello. "How are you?" said a polite Obama. "Fine, thanks," said Berlusconi, who then proceeded to ramble on about the prosecutors of Italy to a confused Obama. The president stood up from the table to face Berlusconi, and an interpreter was brought over because Berlusconi was now on a roll. For two minutes, while Angela Merkel and Sarkozy stared, aghast, across the table, Berlusconi complained to Obama about "the dictatorship of left-wing judges" in Italy and explained why he wanted to reform his country's system of justice. Obama listened politely, but across the table Merkel was looking impatient and irritated and Sarkozy was scowling. What was so important that Berlusconi had to violate protocol and stage this mini-bilateral conversation with the American president? Sarkozy finally called the meeting to order and Berlusconi finished his little diatribe.

Sarkozy had the faithful Christine Lagarde at his side. She was still the finance minister of France, but only a day before, with Sarkozy's backing, she had announced her candidacy to take over the leadership of the International Monetary Fund (IMF) in Washington. This followed the resignation of another French politician, Dominique Strauss-Kahn, the oversexed previous head of the IMF who was in prison in New York City. Strauss-Kahn was a Socialist who at the time was Sarkozy's only credible challenger for the presidency of France. He was even running ahead of Sarkozy in opinion polls, but now he had suffered a Shakespearian downfall. Just two weeks before, he had been hauled off a plane at Kennedy Airport that was about to take off for Paris. He was currently in jail, facing attempted rape charges after accosting a chambermaid in his hotel room. The conspiracy theorists would claim that Sarkozy had somehow engineered a honey trap for his political rival, who was known by his initials, DSK. But for the time being that accusation, like the claim that Gaddafi had financed Sarkozy's election campaign, was unproven.

Lagarde, despite her own legal travails in Paris, was considered by the international community to be a spotless replacement for DSK as head of the IMF. She ticked all the boxes. She was a widely respected and polyglot French feminist, a former champion in synchronized swimming, an accomplished lawyer, a breaker of glass ceilings who felt as comfortable in the salons of Georgetown and Park Avenue as at her Paris home. She had worked and lived in the United States and was as user-friendly as any IMF chief that

Washington could hope for. She was even on good terms with the U.S. secretary of state, Hillary Clinton, and she appeared to be a charming and distinguished guest during her frequent softball interviews with CNN's Christiane Amanpour.

In terms of talent and experience, Lagarde proved a good replacement for DSK. In France her appointment was a big political win for Sarkozy. His Socialist rival, DSK, was knocked out of the picture, and his right hand and former finance minister was now the head of the IMF. With France also in the chair as the revolving president of the G-8 and the G-20 all year long, Sarkozy was feeling good; perhaps he could realize his true potential and become the real leader of Europe. As Hillary Clinton would note, he craved being "the man at the center of the action." It was clear to everyone who met him that year that Sarkozy wanted to be the man who would single-handedly stave off the market speculators, keep his own triple-A credit rating for France, solve the Greek debt crisis, save the euro, lead the war on Gaddafi, advance the Arab Spring, and then get himself re-elected in 2012. According to one former European prime minister who saw him more than a dozen times during the year, Sarkozy was "drunk with ambition and power and this vision of himself as the absolute star of the show." For much of the year, said the former prime minister, Sarkozy was on overdrive: "He was overpowering, he was bullying, and he was commandeering."

By June, the Eurozone crisis was threatening the stability of Europe's financial system. It was considered a risk for the global economy. The White House was worried about a collapse of the euro, the European single currency. A new $150 billion rescue package was being prepared for Greece by the Europeans and the IMF. The Portuguese had just agreed to a $100 billion package. The Irish had received a similar bailout. The *Financial Times* popularized a new term, "PIGS," to describe the most highly indebted crisis countries that were attracting market speculation, and it soon became PIIGS: Portugal, Ireland, Italy, Greece, and Spain were all at risk. At the end of June, at another European summit, Berlusconi and Sarkozy would meet and have yet another unpleasant exchange, since Berlusconi was still unable to deliver on his promise to get Bini Smaghi to resign from the European Central Bank. The Europeans managed to formally name Draghi as the new head of the bank anyway. Meanwhile, in Washington, at the IMF, Lagarde's nomination as the new managing director was also approved. Sarkozy immediately pronounced it "a victory for France."

The IMF that Lagarde inherited from DSK was now preaching the gospel of austerity to the crisis-stricken Europeans. That June, Greece was told to impose new austerity measures or risk not getting any more of its rescue loan. Speculators began speaking of contagion risk, and so they started dumping Italian bonds, among other things. This caused the yields to jump and with them the cost of borrowing for Berlusconi's government.

Berlusconi was facing a rancorous coalition and a weakened government that was riven with internal feuding. He and his finance minister were barely on speaking terms. The opposition was pounding him on a daily basis. He was also facing more and more allegations in the bunga-bunga scandal. But he remained the sitting prime minister, the legitimately elected head of government. Weakened, but still in charge.

At this point, in the middle of 2011, it was too early to speak of an international intrigue to unseat him. That came later, after the summer. But there is no doubt that powerful forces on the home front were already paving the way for him to be replaced. It was during that fateful month of June 2011 that a series of events were set in motion in Rome and Milan that would change the course of Italian history, and stretch the country's constitution near to the breaking point. Italy's president, Giorgio Napolitano, would initiate secret contacts with the man he would later name to replace Berlusconi as prime minister, a mild-mannered academic and former European commissioner named Mario Monti.

Monti was everyone's definition of a technocrat. An ambitious economist who had worked his way up from the provincial

University of Turin to become head of the prestigious Bocconi University business school in Milan, Monti was at first an arriviste in Milanese society. The social part of being a member of the establishment seemed to hold enormous appeal for Monti, and for his equally ambitious wife. Soon he had garnered directorships on prestigious corporate and bank boards like Fiat and Banca Commerciale Italiana. In 1994, Berlusconi would name him to the European Commission, where as competition commissioner he became known as "Super Mario" and as the man who took on Microsoft and made Bill Gates pay a $600 million fine for monopolistic practices in Europe.

By 2011 Monti was back at Bocconi University, this time as president of the business school. It was then that President Napolitano first contacted him to ask if he would be available and willing to take over, if needed, from Berlusconi. For Monti this was thrilling stuff. He went around confiding his secret to his most important friends, including the former Olivetti boss and Berlusconi archenemy Carlo De Benedetti and former prime minister Romano Prodi, who had been Berlusconi's greatest political rival. Both men say they were asked for advice by Monti that summer. Both men say they told Monti what he apparently wanted to hear, which was that if the president of the republic was offering him the job of prime minister, he had no choice but to accept, and the sooner the better.

Monti himself would not talk about the whole thing for a long time, but when he finally did, it produced an uproar in the Italian parliament and even calls for the impeachment of President Napolitano. The octogenarian former Communist was accused of abusing the Italian Constitution, which allowed him to name a new prime minister only once a government had fallen or lost its majority in parliament, but said nothing about the idea of secretly offering the job to an unelected citizen while Berlusconi was still the legitimate head of a democratically elected government.

At the time, Berlusconi and the Italian public knew nothing of all of this. Nor did Berlusconi know that Napolitano had also been working with the chief executive of Italy's leading bank on a full-fledged economic policy plan for a post-Berlusconi government. For a period of several months Corrado Passera, a former McKinsey consultant who was running the Banca Intesa group in Milan, worked through four drafts of the document, which contained wide-ranging "shock therapy" for the Italian economy.

Monti eventually admitted to the secret meetings. He confirmed that he had been contacted by Napolitano in June 2011 and sounded out for the job. He also confirmed that he knew all about the Passera document and had discussed the draft economic plan with Napolitano that year. None of this was known to Berlusconi, nor to the wider world, during that torrid summer of 2011. What was known was that the financial markets were losing faith in Italy's ability to withstand the euro crisis and they feared the contagion effect of the Greek crisis, which had begun roiling markets around the world.

At the end of July, after the Greek bailout was agreed upon at another European crisis summit, it emerged that Deutsche Bank had slashed its holdings of Italian bonds by 88 percent, a reduction from 8 billion euros to less than 1 billion euros. To many, it looked like a no-confidence vote in the Berlusconi government. In fact, the big German bank was shedding its risk to all of the PIIGS countries, to Ireland and to the heavily indebted Southern European countries of the Eurozone.

By early August, the tempest in the financial markets was raging. The spreads on Italian bonds skyrocketed as hedge funds and other speculators began looking at Italy's two-trillion-euro debt and seeing an opportunity to go short, that is, to speculate against the Italian debt. Even everyday newspaper readers suddenly learned about this new measure of risk for Italy and Spain and Greece, the difference between the interest paid on German treasury bonds and everyone else's. In June of 2011, Italy was paying 1.5 percent above the German rate, or a spread of 150 points. By early August, Italy's spread had jumped to more than 500 points (5 percent), ringing alarm bells across the Eurozone.

The European Central Bank, or ECB, began buying Italian and Spanish treasury bonds in an attempt to stop the sell-off of these bonds and show that these countries would not be cut off from financial markets. It was at this point that the ECB began to use its bond-buying power as a weapon aimed at Berlusconi's government.

During this market chaos, Napolitano continued his secret talks with Monti, broadening the conversation to include possible economic policies, such as those proposed by the banker Corrado Passera in the secret document he and Monti had reviewed. Then, on August 5, Berlusconi faced another humiliation. The ECB chief, Jean-Claude Trichet, sent confidential letters to Berlusconi in Italy and to Spanish Prime Minister José Luis Rodriguez Zapatero. The letter to Berlusconi was co-signed by Mario Draghi, still the governor of the Bank of Italy but already designated as the next ECB chief. The letter was tough, calling for a lengthy list of economic policies and reforms that Italy was supposed to implement immediately. Most of these were nearly verbatim restatements of policies that Berlusconi had already announced, leading him to suspect that the secret authors of the letter were his political rivals in Rome. He suspected his own finance minister, Giulio Tremonti, and later told friends he thought the idea of the letter had been orchestrated by Napolitano himself.

The demands being made on Berlusconi included achieving a balanced budget within twenty-four months, a feat that nobody in their right mind believed possible.

The letter was unusually harsh in tone. It even set a deadline of the end of September for Berlusconi to get new economic laws passed by parliament. Trichet and Draghi ended the letter with a menacing sentence: "We trust that the government will take all the appropriate actions."

Although the letter did not say so explicitly, it was clear that the ECB was telling Berlusconi to toe the line if he wanted help from the European Central Bank in buying Italian bonds.

In Madrid, Prime Minister Zapatero kept quiet about the letter and kept his head down; he did not even reveal it until years later. In Rome, the letter was leaked to the press in less than twenty-four hours.

Berlusconi has called that letter the beginning of a coup against his government. It certainly was a clear case of the current and future heads of the ECB essentially dictating a detailed economic policy agenda to Italy's prime minister. The message was clear: Do as we say, or the European Central Bank will stop buying Italian treasury bonds and your borrowing costs will soar. That was the nature of the beast as the Eurozone crisis exploded upon a continent that was magnificently unprepared. Stock markets were plunging and the Eurozone was in chaos. Europe's leaders did not seem to sense the urgency, despite the market panic. Calls for a big rescue fund fell on deaf ears in penny-pinching Berlin. Angela Merkel was the biggest hawk and was firmly against the idea of increasing Europe's emergency facility. Sarkozy was trying to persuade her to use European Central Bank funds to fight what was becoming a full-fledged Eurozone sovereign debt crisis. But she would not hear of it. The White House chimed in, worried that Europe was not doing enough. The problem was that the Europeans thought they had enough money to deal with the crisis in Greece, but it kept getting worse. They had endless meetings, but the only message coming through was Merkel's sermon on austerity. Partial solutions were found for Greece, but the fact remained that Greece was essentially bankrupt, and Europe did not want to make it official and write off hundreds of billions of dollars of Greek debt. Merkel wanted to protect German banks, which were big creditors of Greece, and save the euro, and also teach Greece a lesson. There might have been enough money in the European kitty to finance rescues for Greece, and for smaller countries like Portugal and Ireland, but there was no safety net if something went wrong in Italy or Spain. Merkel's intransigence and Sarkozy's confused make-it-up-as-you-go policy had effectively paralyzed the Eurozone, and in the middle of a financial crisis. It was all a taste of things to come, an early indicator that Europe's single currency, the euro, did not work so well for the weaker economies of Southern Europe.

While the euro crisis was worsening that summer, the president of the European Commission, a jovial former Portuguese prime minister named José Manuel Barroso, worried in public that Europe's leaders were failing to prevent the sovereign debt crisis from spreading. That statement did not prove helpful, but it was a sign of the frustration of many in Europe at Merkel's tough austerity line. Sarkozy, who had plenty of problems with his own failing economy, was happy to partner with Merkel whenever he could. He was, after all, co-star of this partnership. Merkel's defense of austerity, and her stern, teacher-like stance on Greece, would actually worsen the euro crisis in the end and condemn Europe to years of uncertainty and later deep political divisions over the festering problem of Greece.

On August 16, Merkel joined Sarkozy in Paris for another euro crisis meeting. This time it was just the two of them, for a two-hour conversation at the Elysée Palace. The world's financial markets held their breath, hoping that Merkel and Sarkozy might finally agree that a bigger bailout fund was needed to save the Eurozone. But it was not to be.

Merkel had a Prussian-like belief in strict discipline, and she refused to consider increasing the size of the bailout fund. Traders reacted with exasperation, and markets fell again as Merkel and Sarkozy came out of their huddle. They spoke of their "absolute will to defend the euro," yet refused to back the shattered currency with sufficient financial resources.

Europe's failure of leadership in the face of the storm could not have been clearer.

Instead of taking concrete actions, Merkel and Sarkozy laid out ambitious plans for closer integration of the Eurozone countries, and proposed a new economic government for Europe. Again, they preached the need for austerity measures and warned that straying from Eurozone rules and fiscal targets would no longer be tolerated. They preached tough love. Perhaps their most audacious move was to demand that each of the seventeen Eurozone countries adopt a balanced budget amendment to their constitution, and quickly. This, they announced, would be part of a new "golden rule" that would bring Europe closer together.

Berlusconi struggled to bring forward austerity measures and promised to follow the golden rule. His coalition government was ornery and fractious. Across Rome, meanwhile, at the Quirinale Palace, President Napolitano continued his secret talks with Monti and Passera.

By the middle of September, and in record time, both Italy and Spain had passed balanced budget amendments to their constitutions, although the precise Italian wording, in the best Italian tradition, left some room for interpretation.

Berlusconi now faced massive protests in the streets of Rome over the austerity measures. The situation in Greece was deteriorating and Italian bonds were under attack again. By the middle of the month, when Italy saw its credit rating downgraded, the speculators struck again. The IMF announced that the world economy had entered "a dangerous new phase" of sharply lower growth. The perceived weakness in Europe's response to the crisis was a key factor in the continuing market turmoil.

Merkel and Sarkozy were seen to be dragging their feet, unable to take any bold action.

The chief economist of the IMF, Olivier Blanchard, sounded increasingly desperate in his public statements. "There is a wide perception that policymakers are one step behind the action. Europe must get its act together," said Blanchard.

Timothy Geithner, the U.S. secretary of the treasury, soon added his voice to those calling on Merkel and Sarkozy to act quickly and to show that they actually had a strategy for dealing with the euro crisis. He called on the Europeans to create a "firewall" of rescue funds and warned they should not wait "until the crisis gets more severe." The White House soon let it be known that President Obama was in favor of a firewall, too. Merkel did not want to listen.

Far from steering Europe through the storm, Merkel seemed to have crashed onto the rocks of her belief in austerity and discipline. Sarkozy, on the other hand, was still trying to prove his leadership, or at least the co-leadership of Europe. He had his differences with Merkel, and he hated the fact that she almost always won the argument. Sarkozy could not stand being the junior partner to Merkel, but he was at least happy to bask in the limelight. For Sarkozy it was important to be in the frame. It was all about being present for the cameras, standing next to Germany's chancellor. From her perspective, the pragmatic and straight-talking German leader might have found Sarkozy occasionally irritating, given his frequent attempts to steal the show, but at least she could do business with the man.

The same could not be said about her relations with Silvio Berlusconi.

"I think all my troubles with Merkel began with the publication of that supposed quotation of mine, the one where I was accused of calling Merkel an unfuckable lard-ass."

Silvio Berlusconi displays little emotion as he analyzes what went wrong in his dealings with the German chancellor during the euro crisis that autumn. While Merkel and Sarkozy were racing around European capitals like Batman and Robin, an Italian newspaper published what it claimed was a wiretapped conversation between Berlusconi and a man who was under investigation for procuring prostitutes for Berlusconi's bunga-bunga parties. That was when Berlusconi was said to have used the indelicate description of Merkel. The German press was swift to respond, with *Der Spiegel* calling Berlusconi "vulgar and boorish."

Berlusconi immediately denied everything, but the damage had already been done. Merkel would have one less Christmas card to send that year.

"We had other differences, but we normally got on fine," recalls a smiling Berlusconi. "I think the one thing that really made her angry was that quote. But I never said it. It was a complete fabrication by an Italian newspaper, by someone who wanted to damage me and create conflict between me and Angela."

The infamous quote may or may not have been a fabrication, but it triggered an avalanche of laughter and derision from the rest of Europe. Berlusconi had said so many outrageous things over the years that this time even other world leaders believed it to be true. He would later tell friends about an episode just weeks after the alleged Merkel wiretap made the rounds. It occurred during a visit to Russia in early October to celebrate Vladimir Putin's birthday. Already at Putin's side was former German chancellor Gerhard Schroeder, a glass in hand. "Silviooooo!" he cried out to the approaching Berlusconi, who yelled back at Schroeder, "I never said it!" To which Schroeder is said to have replied, "You did great. It's totally true."

Today Berlusconi recognizes the damage that was done.

"I think that she was very upset with me," says Berlusconi. "She was really offended."

Merkel was not very happy with Berlusconi. That was patently clear from her body language and her rhetoric. She and Sarkozy were under extreme pressure to find a solution for the euro crisis, though, which by the end of October was entering its most dangerous phase. European officials were now openly voicing their fear that Italy could follow Greece with its own debt crisis. Italy's two-trillion-dollar debt mountain was suddenly the focus of ruthless market speculation, and it became a stick that was used by Sarkozy and Merkel to beat Berlusconi.

On October 23, at a European summit in Brussels, they subjected him to another humiliation. Ahead of the summit Merkel gave a speech in Germany in which she singled out Italy for its debt burden, and said that investors weren't wrong to demand higher yields on debt from Prime Minister Berlusconi's government. For the financial markets, that kind of rhetoric was like pouring gasoline on the flames. Sarkozy also kept up the pressure, demanding to know why Berlusconi had not forced Lorenzo Bini Smaghi to resign and make way for a French member of the board of the European Central Bank. "What should I do, should I kill him?" Berlusconi reported telling Sarkozy in reply.

Both Merkel and Sarkozy by now saw Berlusconi as a liability for the entire Eurozone. On that long Sunday in Brussels, they sat him down for a brutal lecture, described by those present as a harangue. They told him to forge ahead with economic reforms and do something about the Italian debt. They told him to return to another crisis summit on Wednesday with a letter setting out his plans to cut spending and make reforms. They laced into Berlusconi, but the fractious summit ended without any broader agreement on how to solve the growing debt crisis and restore market confidence. Once again the markets voted with their feet. Once again there were complaints from Washington that Europe was failing to come up with a convincing plan that could stop the crisis.

Berlusconi remembers being severely admonished by Merkel and Sarkozy on October 23 in Brussels; he remembers being lectured. And he remembers saying that day at his own press conference that "nobody in the European Union has the right to nominate himself commissioner and give lessons to other governments." The leaders of France and Germany were not done humiliating him, though, and this time on live TV.

That afternoon, after telling Berlusconi to put his house in order, Sarkozy and Merkel held a joint news conference that would trash and ridicule Berlusconi before the entire world. A French reporter asked Merkel and Sarkozy if they felt reassured by Berlusconi that he would really implement the economic reforms that he had promised. The reply was an embarrassed silence. Sarkozy turned to catch Merkel's gaze and their eyes met in a knowing smile that expanded into a wicked smirk. The chancellor then allowed herself a tiny titter of laughter and the French president tilted his head from side to side in a knowing way. When the news conference ended and the leaders had left the stage, Merkel turned to Sarkozy and was overheard giving a wry assessment. "We've never been so efficient with just a silent movie," said the chancellor of Germany.

For Berlusconi, that smirk was devastating. He was now the official laughingstock of European leaders, publicly humiliated by Sarkozy and Merkel, and all this in an embarrassing video that would be played over and over again.

Berlusconi says the summit in Brussels was like a bad dream.

"That smirk at the press conference happened on the same day that Sarkozy refused to shake my hand. He was really angry with me," recalls Berlusconi, leaning forward to confide another memory. "After Merkel had finished that press conference, we saw each other again, that evening, and she actually came up to me and apologized. 'I am sorry,' she said, 'I guess that after this you won't want to speak with me anymore.' I told her not to worry. I tried to be good-natured. I said: 'Look. I am still speaking with you, right here.' And that was that. I remember this clearly."

Despite all of this, Berlusconi looks wistful as he conjures up a very different memory of his times with Merkel.

"I always gave a lot of presents to Merkel," he says. "Every time I went to Germany I would bring her necklaces and bracelets that cost me fifteen or twenty thousand euros each. I couldn't bring her cheap stuff. I paid for it all for myself, all the gifts, out of my own pocket. She always accepted all of my gifts, and very happily."

Regardless, Berlusconi knows Merkel was in touch with President Giorgio Napolitano during those fateful days of late October 2011. "Napolitano telephoned Merkel with a certain regularity," he says, with a slight grimace at the Italian president's name.

In fact Berlusconi was not the only person who suspected that Angela Merkel might have been conspiring against him in some way.

"Merkel and Napolitano spoke frequently that autumn but I do not know the details of their conversations," said José Manuel Barroso, who as president of the European Commission back in 2011 sat in on each and every one of the European summit meetings.

According to *The Wall Street Journal*, Merkel placed a particularly important call to Napolitano on the night of October 20. She was worried about the Eurozone crisis, and about Berlusconi's ability to manage the Italian economy and deliver on promised reforms. Napolitano gave his reassurances to Merkel on behalf of

Italy, and the German chancellor thanked the Italian president in advance for doing what he could to promote reform. Napolitano's team would deny that he and Merkel had discussed replacing Berlusconi, but they did not deny having the conversation.

While Berlusconi's world was slowly disintegrating, and he shuttled from one European summit to another, taking his licks like a punch-drunk boxer, fears were growing in Washington that the euro crisis could lead to an even bigger economic shock and a potential European depression that could harm U.S. exports and damage the entire world economy—and all of this on the eve of 2012, the year in which Barack Obama needed to get himself re-elected.

CHAPTER TWELVE

———

Obama Steps In

T he Obama administration had been watching the European crisis as it unfolded for many months now, and many in the White House and treasury department were horrified by what they saw. Tim Geithner, as treasury secretary, had been the most vocal exponent of a firewall of one or two trillion dollars that Europe could put up to protect itself and its single currency. He was in close contact throughout the autumn of 2011 with IMF chief Lagarde, with the European Commission, with his finance ministry counterparts in major European capitals, and with most of the European leaders. Merkel herself was never said to be particularly fond of Geithner; she disapproved of his advocacy of using the European Central Bank to print money and of European governments making huge contributions to an emergency bailout fund to create a strong enough firewall to protect the European economy.

Merkel's lack of fondness for Geithner wouldn't prevent something very odd from happening in that autumn of 2011, something that seemed more the stuff of thrillers than of boring U.S.–Europe political or economic relations. It was a particularly provocative proposition that was put to Geithner and the White House by France and Germany. It all started just before the G-20 summit that was due to take place in early November in Cannes.

As Geithner would later tell the team that helped him prepare his memoirs, "There's a G-20 meeting in France that Sarkozy hosts, which was a really incredibly interesting, fascinating thing for us and for the president.

"The Europeans actually approach us softly, indirectly before the thing saying: 'We basically want you to join us in forcing Berlusconi out.' They wanted us to basically say that we wouldn't support IMF money or any further escalation for Italy if they needed it, if Berlusconi was prime minister. It was cool, interesting. I said no," said Geithner.

"I thought what Sarkozy and Merkel were doing was basically right, which is: this wasn't going to work. Germany, the German public, were not going to support a bigger financial firewall, more money for Europe, if Berlusconi was presiding over that country. He was at that point in the midst of one of his trials for sex with minors and things like that."

For Geithner, the scheme to oust Berlusconi may have even had merit at first glance, but it raised all sorts of flags. It might have appeared like a fascinating European scheme to Geithner as an American, but it was also a bona fide international intrigue aimed at bringing about regime change in Italy. It was also a plan that would mean subverting the role of the IMF, using it like a political tool in order to unseat Berlusconi. Geithner proceeded to inform Obama.

As Geithner would later recount in his memoir, "We told the president about this surprising invitation, but as helpful as it would have been to have better leadership in Europe, we couldn't get involved in a scheme like that. 'We can't have his blood on our hands,' I said."

"The Europeans had had enough with Berlusconi," said a U.S. official who was part of the U.S. delegation to Cannes. "They were trying to design this system where he was no longer head of state. So they were playing around with lots of ideas. Could they force him to take a rescue loan from the IMF? Could they force him into any IMF program?"

The logic was that once Berlusconi was forced to accept an IMF rescue loan or any kind of IMF loan, he would have no more political credibility and he would have to resign.

Other Washington officials confirmed the scheme, on condition they not be identified by name. A former White House official who had worked closely with Geithner said the scheme to oust Berlusconi was discussed "at the most senior levels." "Merkel could not stand Berlusconi," the official said. "Yes, they had this crazy scheme. The president wasn't going to be involved. That was fine for European internecine politics."

As for the idea of a so-called precautionary IMF program being imposed on Berlusconi, this Obama administration official did not mince words: "Sarkozy and Merkel didn't want a precautionary program. They wanted to get rid of Berlusconi."

Of course, the Americans weren't the only ones aware of what was afoot. Former European Commission president José Manuel Barroso recalled in an interview, "For me it was clear that Sarkozy wanted blood. He wanted the scalp of Italy."

Inside Lagarde's IMF, there were senior officials who would later confide that it was well understood that Berlusconi would not survive politically if he signed an IMF program. "I don't think there was anything subtle about it," said one person close to the IMF. "You can call it a plot or whatever. But I think people felt that Berlusconi had lost all credibility, internally and externally, and therefore the only thing that would provide credibility would be an IMF program, and you didn't have to be a Nobel laureate to imagine that would be a deal breaker. His European partners would have been perfectly happy for him to be vaporized."

This was the backdrop to one of the most dramatic global summits in recent history, the meeting of the Group of 20 leaders in Cannes on November 3 and 4, 2011.

On the morning of November 2, Sarkozy woke up in Paris to read panicked headlines splashed across the front pages of the French press. "The euro in peril!" screamed one headline. "A clap of thunder from Greece" read another. The reference was to an episode that had sent Sarkozy and Merkel into spasms of anger: Just a few days earlier, they had finished months of tortuous negotiations to come up with another solution for the Greek debt crisis, a whopping $200 billion bailout package this time. Now Prime Minister George Papandreou had pulled the rug out from under their feet by making a surprise announcement of plans to put the entire rescue package to a popular vote in a nationwide referendum. If the Greeks voted against the rescue plan and the tough austerity plan that came with it, then Greece would come tumbling out of the euro in a catastrophe that was being nicknamed a "Grexit." That, in turn, could lead to financial disaster, deep recession across Europe, and a major threat to the world economy.

The frazzled Greek premier was summoned to Cannes for a dinner that night with Merkel and Sarkozy. It would turn into a showdown at the OK Corral. The German and French leaders arrived in Cannes for a preparatory meeting at five-thirty that afternoon. Merkel wanted clarity and Sarkozy wanted the Greek problem fixed before the start of his G-20 summit the next day. Lagarde, Barroso, and other European officials joined Merkel and Sarkozy for the session, as did a representative of the European Central Bank.

"They were extremely angry with Papandreou because he had announced the referendum without any kind of consultation," recalls Barroso. "The idea was that we had to be firm with him and make clear that there would not be a penny more for Greece before this referendum."

Both Sarkozy and Merkel were furious about the referendum. The German chancellor felt that if there was going to be a referendum, it should be about Greece being in or out of the euro. She was turning hawkish. By the end of that long day she would say so in public.

That evening, as various participants recall, Sarkozy was more aggressive than usual. He arrived at the meeting room in the Palais des Festivals, the same building that is normally used to host the Cannes Film Festival. The modern conference center is an ugly building of glass and steel and concrete, a piece of bad French 1970s modernist architecture plunked on the famous Boulevard de la Croisette. Outside, a cold drizzle was falling.

Choosing Cannes as the location had been one of Sarkozy's attempts at elegance and grandeur. But it was an odd location for a G-20 summit, a venue far more accustomed to seeing Nicole Kidman or George Clooney smiling on the red carpet for the paparazzi.

Still, by eight-thirty on the evening of November 2, Sarkozy had finished a formal meeting with Hu Jintao, the Chinese president, and had gone to rejoin Merkel and the others. Rather embarrassingly for him, the Chinese were at the same time letting it be known that they had declined European requests for investments from Beijing in the new European rescue fund. The Chinese were not going to help bail out Europe. That was Europe's problem.

Barroso was the first to enter the room, together with the European Commission team. Papandreou cut a lonely figure as he trudged into the building, a folder under one arm. Lagarde, as usual, was elegant and sober.

The table was set for dinner, but nobody ate much that night. Seated in front of crystal glasses, with the finest French porcelain laid out before them, Merkel and Sarkozy glared at the two men seated on the opposite side of the table, the Greek premier and his finance minister, Evangelos Venizelos.

Sarkozy did not wait. He laced into Papandreou while Merkel looked on approvingly. According to participants in the room, he was literally ranting and raving. One observer would call his performance "the full Sarkozy."

"In all my years I have never witnessed behavior so undiplomatic," Venizelos later recalled. "Sarkozy was extremely irritated. Nobody could speak because he was talking continuously. Merkel was calmer but her message was clear: Either you cancel the referendum or you hold one, immediately, that asks: 'yes or no to the euro.'"

"It was a very tense meeting, with President Sarkozy putting a lot of pressure on Papandreou," recalls Barroso. "Basically he was telling him that 'You have betrayed us but we want to help you.' So your referendum has to be yes or no to stay in the euro.

"Merkel said that if Greece leaves Europe, then we will have to respect it. Greece can come back in the future, for instance in ten years."

Papandreou was now in a corner. The taboo of a Greek exit from the Eurozone had been broken. The Greek premier dug in his heels over the referendum, but there was a feeling that time was running out.

What Papandreou and the others did not know was that the president of the European Commission had already been on the phone to the Greek opposition leader earlier in the day, talking about how to stop a referendum and maybe form a national unity government. Now, as Sarkozy and Merkel glared across the table, backed up in their argumentation by occasional outbursts and reprimands from Lagarde, the Greek prime minister looked like he was on the verge of a physical collapse. The air was still. Faces were grim. It was then that Barroso went over to Venizelos and whispered something to the Greek finance minister, something that Papandreou did not hear.

"I told him we had to stop this referendum, that they could end up with Greece out of the euro," recalls Barroso.

Late that night, after the Greek prime minister and his deputy had landed back in Athens, at four forty-five in the morning, Venizelos released a terse statement, rejecting the idea of a referendum, and publicly contradicting his own prime minister. Within days Papandreou would be gone. The name of his replacement, Lucas Papademos, a technocrat former official of the European Central Bank, was meanwhile already being discussed by Barroso and his advisers at Cannes.

While Merkel and Sarkozy had been beating up the Greeks in Cannes that Wednesday evening, in Rome a weakened Silvio Berlusconi was facing his own disaster. His unruly center-right coalition seemed to be falling apart and he was struggling through an emergency cabinet meeting that evening, unable to get approval for the economic reforms he wanted to present the next day at the G-20 summit. Berlusconi had hoped to arrive in Cannes with a law in hand that he could announce to calm the markets and reassure Merkel and Sarkozy. But he failed to get his own cabinet to approve the package, mainly because of disagreements with his finance minister, Giulio Tremonti, who by now, like his counterpart in Athens, had turned on his boss. Tremonti had become a rebel minister, a potential rival, or even a plausible replacement.

On the morning of November 3, Berlusconi and Tremonti boarded the prime minister's Airbus for the short flight from Rome to the South of France. Now, for the first time, Berlusconi began to hear details about Sarkozy's bust-up with Papandreou the night before. But he had his own problems. His failure to push through the package and his fights with Tremonti were damaging his credibility in the eyes of financial markets, and in the eyes of Sarkozy and Merkel. It did not help matters that on the eve of Cannes the European media was still brimming with tales of Berlusconi's bunga-bunga parties, and salacious photos of South American models, members of an alleged prostitution ring, a virtual harem of more than thirty women that Berlusconi was said to have set up, housed, and financially maintained, were circulating in the press and on social media.

Berlusconi, arriving in Cannes, was perceived to be a battered man.

"I saw a very weakened Berlusconi," recalls Barroso. "He was completely demotivated."

"His image was terrible," said a senior European official who was present in Cannes. "He was refusing to make any structural reforms. And on top of that there were all the scandals surrounding his own person. I would say that he struck me as being very old and tired during those days in Cannes. He did not have the energy, nor the credibility, nor the trust of all the others."

One of his own top aides in Rome described the seventy-five-year-old Berlusconi as "tired and stressed" upon arrival at the G-20 summit.

The stress would only build. Berlusconi was caught off guard when other prime ministers began asking him embarrassing questions. "There in Cannes some friends of mine, from different countries, came up to me and asked me if I had decided to resign, because they were all hearing that within a week there would be a new Monti government installed," recalls Berlusconi, adding, "I had a sense that something was up."

Among those also hearing the Monti rumor was Spanish Prime Minister José Luis Zapatero, who had been invited to a special meeting that morning, even though Spain was not part of the G-20. Sarkozy had called a meeting before the official start of the summit in order to specifically focus on Italy and Spain, and Zapatero arrived with some trepidation.

"When I arrived in Cannes the situation was unstable, very unstable," recalls Zapatero. "We in Spain had already undertaken reforms, we were better at controlling our deficit, more efficiently, and it was more credible. At Cannes the idea that predominated was that Italy was not credible. The idea that the reforms that Berlusconi promises to make he doesn't make, he doesn't reduce the deficit. That's the idea that prevailed. And that's what I saw during the crisis, all of the time. When the markets got bad, there was a country that had to pay. And at that moment, that country was Italy."

Zapatero heard of the rumor of Monti replacing Berlusconi from the moment he landed in Cannes that morning, but his biggest surprise came from Angela Merkel. She greeted the Spanish premier by asking him if he would be willing to accept a precautionary IMF line of credit, a form of financial aid for Spain in the form of a $50 billion loan that could be drawn down from the IMF. She quickly added that Italy, of course, would also get money; it would get $85 billion from the IMF. It was clear to Zapatero that Merkel had a plan, but he did not want any part in it. So Zapatero politely declined, saying Spain did not need any precautionary IMF money.

"At that time," Zapatero recalls, "Spain didn't have any

problems—of course we had problems, but fewer problems. But when she asked me that, I remembered what my aides had said to me about Mario Monti. When Merkel talked about the line of aid for Spain and Italy, I realized that she was really focusing on Italy. That's the conclusion I reached, because when I said no to Angela Merkel, she didn't insist. And that is why I immediately thought that they were actually focusing on Italy, and that's exactly what I saw in the meetings that day."

At ten-thirty that morning of November 3, Sarkozy called to order the special pre-summit meeting of France, Germany, Italy, Spain, the IMF, and European officials. Seated in an anodyne conference room in the Palais des Festivals, Berlusconi found himself staring across the table at Merkel and Sarkozy, at the dynamic duo that had dispatched George Papandreou to his political grave just hours before.

Sarkozy had started his day an hour before, welcoming Barack Obama to the conference center and smiling for the photographers. Then, after saying that the United States wanted to help Europe solve the euro crisis, Obama went to the elegant Carlton Hotel for a one-on-one meeting with Angela Merkel. She, in turn, sent her trusted finance minister, Wolfgang Schäuble, to join Sarkozy and the others who were facing Berlusconi over at the conference center. Schäuble was wheelchair bound and feisty. The German minister had survived an assassination attempt many years before, and he was known across Europe as the most hawkish of hawks, the man who was perfectly willing to see Greece exit the euro and who believed in the Holy Grail of austerity with a religious-like fervor.

Schäuble was now seated next to Sarkozy, not far from the steely-eyed Christine Lagarde, with Berlusconi directly across the table.

Sarkozy went immediately into overdrive.

"There was huge pressure from Sarkozy, and with the active support of Schäuble," recalls Barroso. "What he said to Berlusconi was: 'Italy must ask for a precautionary credit line from the IMF. If not, then there will be a tragedy, because the markets will be furious. We need immediately for Italy to act.' And Berlusconi said: 'No, the economic situation in Italy is good. There is no Italian problem. We already sent a letter to the Euro summit of October with the list of measures we will take, as recommended by the Commission.' But Schäuble insisted again. He said they should take the measures or they would face a catastrophe."

Barroso recalls what Nicolas Sarkozy did next. "In his very urgent and pushy style he almost shouted out at Berlusconi: 'Silvio! The G-20 will start in two hours. Can you please ask for a loan from the IMF? If not, it will be a disaster!' He was very emotional, he was overdramatizing the issue."

Berlusconi, exhausted and battered after the onslaught, tried to cling to what shreds of dignity he had left. He repeated that Italy had already agreed with the European Commission on a detailed series of reforms to be implemented. He promised to get his cabinet to approve everything rapidly. He even said he was willing to work with the IMF on joint monitoring of the European Commission program, but there was no way he was going to ask for an $80 billion loan that would look like a rescue. That would have spooked the markets and meant Italy giving up its sovereignty.

"When they offered me the IMF loan, I was very firm in telling them I had no idea what they were talking about, that we did not need it and so I said, 'No thanks!'" recalls Berlusconi. "It would have led to the colonization of Italy and the imposition on a sovereign country of the troika of creditors [the IMF, the European Central Bank, and the European Commission] like in Greece. I guess I was pretty firm in my reply."

Sarkozy would not give up.

"Sarkozy was pushing Berlusconi in a very dramatic way, because when Sarkozy pushes, he's not pushing, he's bullying!" said Barroso. By contrast, since all the attention seemed to be focused on Italy, Spain's prime minister was doing his best to keep his head down. "Zapatero," said Barroso, "did not open his mouth. Not once, not a single word."

As Sarkozy made his case, he frequently turned in the direction of Christine Lagarde, who had arrived in Cannes saying, "Italy has no credibility." Lagarde, according to Barroso's recollection, was devastating in her assessment, right there in front of Silvio Berlusconi.

"Christine Lagarde was very tough. She said nobody believes in Italy," recalls Barroso. Instead, Lagarde proceeded to extol the virtues of Italy requesting a precautionary pre-bailout loan from the IMF, claiming this would help calm the markets.

Barroso remembers that he and the European Council president, Herman Van Rompuy, both warned at the November third morning meeting that an IMF plan for Italy that was worth only $80 billion could trigger the opposite reaction to the one they desired, namely, it could trigger alarm bells in financial markets instead of reassuring them. Since Italy had debts of nearly two trillion dollars, an emergency facility of just $80 billion would seem like peanuts, said Barroso.

Zapatero, who had sat there in silence, mesmerized by the drama unfolding before his eyes, was relieved that the group's attention had turned away from Spain. He had coffee later that day with Italy's finance minister, Giulio Tremonti, and talked about the pressure that was being applied to Berlusconi by the French and Germans to take an IMF loan.

"Tremonti said, 'I know better ways of committing suicide than asking the IMF for help.' He must have repeated that phrase twenty times on that day, with Italian humor. He was an intelligent character, with finesse."

After that morning meeting, the attention of the summit swung back to the Greek crisis, and to a general fear of what the markets would say about the summit. Sarkozy's fixation on financial markets and the media may have been excessive, but it was not unusual among the most powerful leaders of the world.

"The image for the public is always of these leaders who decide everything. But when you're on the inside, you see how it really happens," says a thoughtful Zapatero, reflecting on the bunker mentality that prevailed inside the Palais des Festivals in Cannes on that day, and in general about the behavior of prime ministers and presidents at the pinnacle of world power. "Yes, leaders decide," explains the former Spanish premier, "but they're always looking at what the *Financial Times* will say and what the markets will do. That's how things really are. Politics is an extension of life. You would think that governments have special powers, but in this global world that is not so true. So political leaders, market leaders, and the top officials, all they do is read the *Financial Times*. The problem with the *Financial Times* is it's like the Bible. Like the Bible, it's a great book, but it admits only one interpretation."

That evening, with the pressure on Berlusconi still mounting and the euro crisis still raging, a high-level meeting was convened after the official G-20 dinner. Barroso would later call the evening "a crash course in European politics for Barack Obama."

Crammed into a small conference room were the same players from the morning, Sarkozy, Lagarde, and Schäuble, but this time Merkel was in attendance. Barroso and Van Rompuy were in the room, as was Mario Draghi, making his first appearance as head of the European Central Bank. Also around the table were Zapatero and his finance minister and of course Berlusconi and Tremonti. But this time, as Sarkozy prepared for another round of crisis talks, the Europeans were joined by the president of the United States.

"With Barack Obama in the chair, everyone was listening," recalled one of the Europeans who was present in the room.

Obama, accompanied by Timothy Geithner, wanted to talk about how to stop the chaos in financial markets. The U.S. president, reflecting what Geithner had been advising, wanted to face down the speculators in the financial markets by creating a big enough firewall to protect the Europeans from a debt crisis or a threat to the world financial system. To build the firewall, he was asking Germany to make gigantic financial contributions, which visibly upset Merkel. Sarkozy liked the idea of the firewall, but he was still fixated on the idea of coming away from the summit with an IMF package for Italy, with at least one tangible result.

The meeting opened around nine-forty p.m., and went on

until nearly eleven p.m. What transpired in that room would not ultimately solve the Eurozone crisis, but it was undoubtedly the moment of truth during the acutest phase of the entire crisis.

"Obama started the meeting saying that we needed a solution for Italy and a European firewall; these were his two issues," Barroso recalls. He adds that both Obama and Sarkozy pressed Merkel hard to agree to come up with new financial resources for a trillion-dollar-plus firewall.

Both Barroso and Zapatero also watched the prolonged attack on Berlusconi by Sarkozy, and then by Lagarde, with Merkel nodding her approval.

"It was an offensive—by sea, air, and land," says Zapatero, now reliving the dinner that he swears he will never forget. "I remember the expressions on people's faces, and them saying: 'Italy doesn't have credibility, you haven't undertaken any reforms'—and they would all repeat this to Berlusconi.

"Obama," recalls Zapatero, "was always the most polite. He's very polite and elegant."

Obama did not start the meeting as the referee. He sort of grew into the role. The way three former prime ministers tell it, Obama was initially open to the idea of an IMF loan for Italy. But he changed his mind over the course of that meeting.

"President Sarkozy considers this is a very good idea," Obama said at first, without pushing too hard.

Berlusconi recalls telling the assembled forces of Obama, Merkel, and Sarkozy again that Italy did not need an IMF loan and would not agree to one.

"Italy is a rich country," Berlusconi argued. "We can handle high interest rates, if need be, for a year."

Obama tried a different tack, saying: "We need to break the cycle to give confidence to the markets."

Berlusconi stood firm, though, with the support of almost nobody except Barroso.

"When I started to see the huge pressure being put on the Italians during that meeting," recalls Barroso, "for me it was clear that

Sarkozy just wanted an event. Nicolas had great qualities, he was strong-willed and so on. But he is a guy who gets obsessed. He just wanted the Cannes summit to say 'Okay! We have solved the euro crisis because Italy is now under the IMF program.' So I said to Silvio: 'Don't give up, stand your ground.'"

"Tremonti and Berlusconi were showing a lot of resistance," recalls Zapatero. "It was impressive, since they had been under attack for hours."

It was at this stage, with Berlusconi refusing to budge, that Lagarde let loose with her own tirade. It was less emotional than Sarkozy's attack, but in some ways more lethal.

Zapatero recalls, "Lagarde was very harsh with Italy and Spain. And that's why I haven't forgotten. She was very harsh, but in an unfair and unjustified way. It was surprising to see that the IMF would play this role, a supporting role to the position of large powers without really having its own opinion."

A former top aide to Berlusconi was more direct. "I was in the room at Cannes and I can tell you that Christine Lagarde was behaving like a ventriloquist's dummy, and Sarkozy was pulling the strings. She was speaking like a trained parrot."

Zapatero readily concurs with the rather colorful Italian characterization. "Yes, yes, yes," he repeats. Zapatero's recollection of that critical evening at the Cannes summit is compelling. He says that in his opinion Lagarde's IMF behaved "more like a political arm" of certain governments than as the leader of an international organization. "Yes," he says, "that is how it seemed."

Zapatero was not the only one in the room who came away with the impression that Lagarde was in lockstep with Sarkozy when it came to Italy. She was the perfect straight man in Sarkozy's overblown political cabaret. He would begin a harangue and then turn to Lagarde. She was always prepared, always rational and steady, ready and willing to press home the case for an IMF loan.

Christine Lagarde's unusual chemistry with Nicolas Sarkozy should not have surprised anyone at the Cannes summit. The fact that for the past four or five months she had been the IMF chief could not change her history: She had spent the past decade as a loyal political aide and ally of Nicolas Sarkozy. Politically, the two were joined at the hip.

Somewhat embarrassingly for Lagarde, during a police raid of her Paris flat some eighteen months later, a rather personal letter came to light and was published in newspapers around the world. The letter, addressed to Sarkozy and signed by Christine Lagarde, was discovered in connection with the investigation of the Adidas mogul Bernard Tapie. Now the world's press was going to town with her letter to Sarkozy, in which Lagarde swore eternal allegiance to Sarkozy and wrote these telling words: "I'm at your side to serve you...Use me during the time that suits you best and fits your action and your casting. If you decide to use me, I need you as my guide and my supporter: without your guidance I might be ineffective, without your support I might not be credible." The letter's sign-off was cringe-worthy: "With my immense admiration, Christine L."

Back at Cannes, however, the meeting was now entering its most dramatic moments. Sarkozy was rounding on Berlusconi one last time, when Obama turned to Barroso and asked him what he thought of the idea of an IMF loan package for Italy.

"Obama saw my body language," says Barroso. "I was very negative about an IMF loan. I said the commission would monitor the Italian measures but the solution must be European. I said that in no way could the IMF replace the European Commission's role. This was a European matter. And frankly, I said that eighty billion dollars was peanuts compared to what we were doing with the other countries. It was less than we had given to Greece. If the news got out that Italy was getting an eighty-billion-dollar rescue loan from the IMF, then that would be a disaster."

Berlusconi was nodding his head in agreement. Sarkozy was quietly fuming. Merkel was staring. Lagarde kept her poker face. Obama stepped in again among the squabbling Europeans.

"I understand that Italy can accept the monitoring by the IMF, but not the full program," said Obama, now the official arbiter.

Then he said he agreed with Berlusconi about the IMF loan plan being a bad idea. "I think Silvio is right," he said.

That was the end of it. Italy would accept a form of monitoring but no loan from the IMF. Sarkozy did not get his scalp. He and Obama could still press Merkel on the idea of a firewall, so now the voluble French president was turning to the German chancellor. They pitched her hard, arguing the merits of a huge financial shield that would protect Europe and the world economy.

Merkel tried to explain that she was not against the idea, but that under German law she simply could not order around the Bundesbank, Germany's powerful central bank. Obama and Sarkozy insisted, arguing that she could find a way. Berlusconi by now was sitting back and breathing a sigh of relief. Zapatero kept quiet.

It was then that Merkel, perhaps exhausted by the previous twenty-four hours of nonstop stress, perhaps because she did not want to be blamed by history for failing to do her fair share to save Europe, broke down in tears.

"There was a moment at the end of the evening," recalls Zapatero, "when we saw Merkel was very affected, with tears in her eyes. She didn't want it to be thought that Germany wasn't willing to help, or that Germany didn't want to pay. She talked about what had happened in history. Everybody was quiet. I remember looking at my minister of economy. It was a very intense moment. The whole history of the twentieth century was concentrated right there into a few seconds. And in my opinion that sort of changed the atmosphere, curiously. And this is important," concludes Zapatero.

Berlusconi, battered and bruised, could nonetheless straggle back to Rome as the man who had said no to Merkel and Sarkozy's plan for an IMF program, though most of the summiteers saw him as a man who was not so much defiant as on his last legs. Down in Rome, adversaries armed with long knives awaited his return. That the president of Italy, Giorgio Napolitano, had a Plan B in mind had become "quite clear" to Barroso just a few hours before the dramatic evening session with Obama.

"That day, during the summit, I received a phone call from Napolitano," recalls Barroso. "I did not take notes, and nobody was listening to the conversation, but what I remember is that he said to me very formally: 'Mister President, I want to assure you on behalf of Italy that there will be no problems and the government will respect all the economic reforms and policy commitments made in the letter sent to you by Prime Minister Berlusconi.' I understood clearly that he was speaking here as if he was already thinking of the solution beyond Berlusconi. That was quite clear for me, quite clear."

Barroso understood that Napolitano was about to force Berlusconi to resign, or at least that he was poised to take some form of action.

The Cannes summit ended the next day without much success. It was just another example of Europe's inability to take clear and bold action. The markets roared their disapproval and Italy's interest costs on its debt shot through the roof again. By the time Berlusconi got back to Rome, his fate had been sealed. He had fought off the IMF loan, but then he had also revealed at a press conference that this was the advice of the IMF. That just made things worse with the financial markets.

The international intrigue to oust Berlusconi had apparently failed, having been stopped on the beach at Cannes by Berlusconi's stubborn refusal to accept an IMF program. Or had it? For some observers, the actions of Sarkozy, Lagarde, and Merkel in Cannes pretty much knocked Berlusconi out, and Napolitano applied the coup de grâce. He had been preparing his stand-in, Mario Monti, since the previous summer.

Tim Geithner, in his private musings to a team of collaborators for his memoirs, saw the outcome as the successful completion of the scheme to bring down Berlusconi. When asked by one of his team if Merkel and Sarkozy had succeeded in getting rid of Berlusconi, Geithner said yes they had.

"They ultimately did it," said Geithner, "but they did it pretty deftly, actually. We sat around a table late at night, basically trying to induce the Italians to earn back some credibility... The debate we were having by then was whether they would agree to having the IMF, in effect not lend them money but... come in sort of like an auditor in some sense, and validate, and give a public assessment of whether they are actually doing those things. And you know, for any country the IMF is often the kiss of death, so most countries don't like to have that unless they really hit the wall, and Berlusconi was still playing for more time."

When the Cannes summit ended, Berlusconi had avoided the kiss of death of an IMF loan, but he ended up with a lethal bear hug from Lagarde and the IMF anyway; that happened when he agreed as a compromise that the IMF could come every three months to Rome to monitor Italy's progress.

The international humiliation of Berlusconi at Cannes was now actively contributing to his downfall, creating ammunition for his enemies in Rome. The diplomatic counselors to President Napolitano had eyes and ears at Cannes. Back in the land of Machiavelli, the president's scheme to replace Berlusconi with Mario Monti was about to enter its final stage. Giorgio Napolitano was moving quickly.

On November 9, just five days after the Cannes summit, Napolitano named Monti a senator-for-life so as to get him a seat in parliament. Then Berlusconi was told to come and see Napolitano on November 12 at the presidential palace in Rome. Napolitano offered a variety of reasons why Berlusconi should resign, and the billionaire premier finally buckled. It is said that Napolitano told Berlusconi that he believed he no longer had a reliable parliamentary majority. Berlusconi himself says that Napolitano put him under enormous pressure to resign. Normally he would put up more of a fight, but not this time. The president then hurried through the formality of holding political consultations, and within less than twenty-four hours he had appointed Monti as the new prime minister of Italy.

"Call me naïve if you like," says Berlusconi, "but when I went to see the president that day, I did not realize that the naming of

Monti was all part of a long-standing plan to bring down my government, a scheme that had been developed under the direction of
Napolitano."

For Berlusconi things would only get worse after leaving office
at the end of 2011. And within twenty months he would be facing
his Waterloo, at least in terms of his war in the courts. On August
1, 2013, on a hot summer day in Rome, the supreme court would
deliver Berlusconi's first definitive criminal conviction, a guilty
verdict and four-year prison sentence that could not be undone. Or
at least so it seemed.

CHAPTER THIRTEEN

Guilty

Silvio Berlusconi was sweating. He had already changed his shirt twice today. Yes, it was partly due to the weather. It was a sweltering summer day in Rome, the first day of August of 2013.

More than twenty months had passed since Berlusconi's humiliation at Cannes and his replacement as prime minister by Mario Monti amid the international intrigue involving Merkel, Sarkozy, and Napolitano. For Berlusconi things had gone from bad to worse, especially on the legal front.

Inside the Palazzo Grazioli, Berlusconi's Roman headquarters, it was hot, muggy, and humid. The air-conditioning was not working too well, but that was not surprising in a seventeenth-century palace with thick stone walls and eighteen-foot-high ceilings. The mood inside was funereal. A vigil of sorts was under way; it was a painful period of waiting, for a sentence, for a ruling. Aides were scurrying in and out of Berlusconi's office on the second floor of the imposing baroque palace just a stone's throw from Rome's fabled Piazza Venezia. Liveried manservants were busy carrying small silver trays with servings of espresso and mineral water for each of the many guests. Berlusconi was hunkered down inside the ornate chamber, receiving a virtual parade of visits from political delegations and top aides and advisers and lawyers and friends and family.

Berlusconi had been there for days, barricaded inside his presidential-style office, the one with the gilded consoles that featured his memorabilia and photographs of himself with his friends Bush and Putin and walls that were covered in golden damask silk. He sat there receiving his guests, one after the other. His staff was in a state of high agitation, fearing the worst, but Berlusconi looked melancholic and pensive, uneasily still. If he was nervous about the verdict, he was doing his best to hide it.

On this first day of August in 2013, a Thursday, however, something changed. He might have seemed strangely calm to those around him, but today Silvio Berlusconi was on the edge as never before. Today his whole life was on the line.

Today was the day that the supreme court would hand down its final verdict in a long-running tax fraud case. Everyone in Italy expected the supreme court to uphold two lower court convictions and that would make Berlusconi officially, in the eyes of the law, a convicted criminal with a prison sentence, guilty of tax fraud and barred from elective office. This was it. This was his last stand, the last stop, the make-or-break moment for Berlusconi. For twenty years he had always escaped final conviction, but this time things were looking dicey.

A crowd of supporters began milling about in the street below in front of the palace. Some of them were hoisting placards and wearing Berlusconi buttons in a show of solidarity. A phalanx of camera crews, working for CNN, Fox, and the BBC as well as the local Italian channels, was lined up outside, kept at bay by machine-gun-toting carabinieri and by policemen who had transformed this busy thoroughfare in downtown Rome into a high-security red zone, with traffic blocked off at the Piazza Venezia.

Marina Berlusconi arrived at the Palazzo Grazioli just before three o'clock that afternoon, having flown down from Milan, where she was running the family-owned Mondadori publishing group. She was effectively the heir apparent to Berlusconi, being his eldest child and the daughter from his first marriage. She went straight to her father's office, and found him sitting there with his lawyer of many years, Niccolò Ghedini.

Francesca Pascale, Berlusconi's Neapolitan girlfriend, had decided to cope with the stress by venturing out of the palace for some retail therapy, or at least to walk her dog. Each time she emerged, she put on a veritable fashion show for the camera crews gathered outside. The former showgirl was seen gliding in and out of the palace several times that day, in the morning clad in cool, pale pastel shades of yellow, with matching Ferragamo ballet slippers and oversize Fendi sunglasses, and in the afternoon in a powder blue outfit, each time carrying Dudù, her cuddly white poodle, in her arms.

Upstairs it was like a war room. Berlusconi's political lieutenants were trying to figure out what the damage would be if he received a guilty verdict. The issue was threatening to tear apart Berlusconi's party and to bring down the government. There was no Plan B for Berlusconi. There was no succession plan. He had a sidekick in the party, a former Christian Democrat from Sicily named Angelino Alfano, who was his number two, but the man lacked charisma. As the debate raged about who might lead his party into the next election if Berlusconi were to receive a prison sentence, the name of Marina Berlusconi was invoked by several party loyalists.

"The alternative to Berlusconi," tweeted the party stalwarts, "is Berlusconi."

This was the atmosphere that Berlusconi's daughter Marina walked into when she arrived that afternoon. By four p.m., Berlusconi's chief political adviser, a long-serving lobbyist and Fininvest vice president named Gianni Letta, had left the Palazzo Grazioli. As he left the meeting, Letta was sporting a deep frown, and then a look of resignation at what was about to happen. Berlusconi's right-hand man at Mediaset, Fedele Confalonieri, and his son Pier Silvio were still up at the TV network's headquarters on the outskirts of Milan, following it all from a distance.

For more than an hour, Berlusconi sat alone in his office with his daughter Marina. They spoke first about the two alternative scenarios that were possible that day, either an acquittal or a conviction. Berlusconi was meanwhile working on a statement. He was writing it all out in longhand, with good old-fashioned pen and paper. When Marina realized that Berlusconi was drafting the text of a video message that he would broadcast on his channels in case of conviction, she begged her father to drop it, to leave it alone. Berlusconi kept on writing.

According to those who were in the room with him that afternoon, he looked like a man who was resigned to the worst, yet serene. His family members and aides remembered he had displayed the same kind of almost surreal calm just a few weeks before, in mid-June, when a Milan court had handed down a guilty verdict in his bunga-bunga trial. He had prepared a video message on the day of that conviction as well, swearing to the Italians that he was not guilty of having had sex with an underage prostitute.

Shortly after five p.m., Marina watched her father finish writing the statement. The supreme court sentence had still not been announced; that was more than two hours away. Berlusconi called in his top image maker, a television veteran named Roberto Gasparotti. As he had on many other occasions, Gasparotti recalls having to scramble to set up the lighting, get the cameras in position, and watch the makeup lady finish patting down Berlusconi's forehead. Berlusconi was miked up, in his chair, behind the desk, the flags of Italy and Forza Italia behind him, as on sober occasions. It was the full Berlusconi presidential address setup, with Berlusconi looking directly into the camera.

Berlusconi finished taping the nine-minute address and retreated from his office to a nearby living room in the company of his daughter. On the grand "Noble Floor" of the Palazzo Grazioli, which served as both his political headquarters and his Rome residence, was a living room with a sixty-inch LCD TV screen, a circle of beige couches, a liquor cabinet brimming with rare whiskies and cognacs, a gilded Napoleon Troix console with marble pedestals, golden tapestry wall coverings, more memorabilia, and in one corner of the room, as though set up for year-round Christmas, a large Swarovski crystal Christmas tree. On this occasion it was not turned on.

At seven-forty that evening, father and daughter sat on the living room couch, staring at the screen. Live on national television, the supreme court judges rose to read the verdict. For the Italians this was a moment of historic proportions. Berlusconi's political staff and lawyers gathered in an adjoining room to watch the verdict. After nearly twenty years of court proceedings, Berlusconi's fate was decreed in just one minute and fifty-six seconds by the chief justice. Berlusconi remembers these as the worst two minutes in his life. Across Rome, jubilant anti-Berlusconi crowds took to the streets to cheer the court sentence, popping open bottles of Champagne and rejoicing in this, the first definitive and binding guilty verdict ever handed to the billionaire former premier.

Pier Silvio and Confalonieri left their Milan office, headed to the civil aviation zone at Linate Airport, and boarded the Mediaset private jet for the short flight to Rome. By now other family members were turning up at the Palazzo Grazioli, including two of his children from his second wife, Barbara and Luigi. So was another lengthy line of pilgrims from Berlusconi's party, ministers, members of parliament, and assorted party hacks and strategists. They had come to pay homage and Berlusconi kept receiving them long after midnight. The guilty verdict was about to unleash a political tsunami from which Berlusconi would find it hard to recover. It marked a seminal turning point in Berlusconi's political career, and would lead to his being expelled from the senate and declared ineligible for public office. The full horror of his situation was just beginning to sink in. The nervous faces of Berlusconi's army of party supplicants and opportunists said it all as they came and went, followed incessantly by the paparazzi and TV crews outside.

Early the following morning, after less than four hours of sleep, Berlusconi awoke to the news that a couple of embarrassed carabinieri in full uniform were waiting in the living room. They apologized to Berlusconi, but they had come to confiscate his passport. This was a detail of the conviction, while he was awaiting sentencing. While his enemies celebrated across Italy, Berlusconi felt humiliated. Yes, this was true disgrace.

Guilty. Silvio Berlusconi had finally been convicted of a crime. The man who had dominated Italian politics since 1994 had been declared a criminal, and by the highest court in the land.

How did Berlusconi feel when he heard that guilty verdict? What kind of emotion did he experience in that moment?

"More than an emotion, I experienced a kind of incredulity that the judges had managed to stack the cards against me. That verdict is a disgrace for the Italian judicial system. It is a deep wound, an injury inflicted not just on me but on the entire judiciary."

Now Berlusconi pauses ever so slightly and looks down for a moment. When he looks up again, his face betrays the slightest twitch. His left leg starts bobbing nervously up and down beneath the table. When he speaks again, his voice is low and carries the slightest tinge of conspiracy.

"I know," says a tremulous Berlusconi, "that one of the justices who handed down the verdict now regrets his decision. In fact, he has said that this was not really a panel of judges but a firing squad, with its guns trained on Berlusconi as the political adversary. One of the judges who ruled has said this."

He ends up insisting on one very simple point, and he bangs it home with increasing irritation.

"The law under which I was convicted says that in order to be convicted of this crime, you need to have personally signed the tax return. You need to have had signing power over the company's accounts, meaning you had to be either a company executive or a board member. I never signed a single account at Mediaset. I am the owner of a financial holding company that controls sixty percent of another financial holding which in turn owns thirty-four percent of Mediaset. I never signed anything at Mediaset," says a defiant Berlusconi.

It is true that when the fraud took place, in 2001 and 2002 according to the court sentence, Berlusconi was prime minister, fending off attacks from his political rivals who were accusing him of having a massive conflict of interest. While he had resigned his Mediaset positions back in 1994, he had never put the media empire into a blind trust. So most of his political opponents, and numerous magistrates, tended to operate not so much on documented evidence of the crime but on the thesis that he could not have *not* known what was going on at Mediaset, having his best friend running it and his children as top executives in his business. Confalonieri, who *did* have signing power at Mediaset as the company's president, had been acquitted. Yet Berlusconi, who insisted again that as prime minister he had never signed the tax returns at Mediaset, had been charged with fraud and convicted. How on earth could that be, Berlusconi demands, his voice now rising to full-throated tenor.

As far as the supreme court judges were concerned, Berlusconi's argument held no water because he was "the brains" behind the entire operation. He was the architect, the court claimed, of the fraud. Berlusconi's lawyers lodged an appeal with the European Court of Human Rights in Strasbourg, France, hoping to overturn Italian law and allow Berlusconi to continue to be eligible as a political candidate, and in the turbulent months that followed Berlusconi would cling to this hope of final redemption like a drowning swimmer.

"What I want," says a dreamy Berlusconi, as though he is speaking to some higher power, "is a full and complete declaration of innocence from a court that is truly above suspicion, the European Court of Human Rights."

While his critics would later smirk at Berlusconi's European court petition, it was the only way he could hope to have his ban on holding public office reversed. That was the big problem he was now facing. How could he lead a political party if he was about to be expelled from the senate and banned from running in elections for the next six years? By now Berlusconi was nearly seventy-seven years old, and six years seemed like a very long time.

The truth is that by the summer of 2013, after the supreme court ruling, Berlusconi was facing the risk of political extinction. He called the verdict a "judicial coup" and went on passionate rages against the magistrates of the left, in public and in private. It was futile. His personal and political problems were beginning to converge in a way that would threaten everything he had built. To Berlusconi, it looked as though it might all come tumbling down. He complained to friends about his "personal liberty" being taken away. He complained that if he were expelled from parliament he would lose his immunity from arrest, and he feared that some activist judge would put out a warrant for his arrest. "They can do it. They can come and get me," he assured friends. "They will not be satisfied until they see me behind bars."

Berlusconi was now fearful and suffering from bouts of depression. He was feeling constantly humiliated—the court ruling also meant that he would be stripped of his Italian knighthood, for service to industry, which he had collected back in 1977, in the heyday of his career as a real estate developer. He was proud of that honorific and the nickname-loving Italian press had long called him the "Cav" in print. That was short for "Il Cavaliere," the Italian expression for "The Knight." Now the newspapers made fun of him, calling him the "Ex-Cav."

Berlusconi had plenty of other worries that summer, especially on the political front. If he were taken out of circulation for a year of house arrest and banned as a candidate for the center-right, how would he keep his party together? In the twenty-one months since he had resigned as prime minister, Italy had been bumping along the bottom, ravaged by a deep recession and high unemployment, and now it looked like the government that President Napolitano had installed to take the place of Berlusconi was on its last legs.

Mario Monti, the mild-mannered economist whom Napolitano had groomed for the job, had proven a disappointment. His appointment had helped to stabilize the economy for a while, and he had pushed through important pension reforms, but Monti soon ran out of steam, and fresh elections were held in February 2013.

With Berlusconi still free to campaign, his center-right coalition came a close second to the center-left Democrats. It was as close to a tie as Italy had ever seen. Berlusconi managed to win 29.4 percent of the national vote, with the Democrat-led coalition coming first with 29.8 percent. A new third party, unbelievably headed by a former stand-up comedian with a talent for social media, had managed a huge protest vote, a 25 percent share that made it the third-largest party in the country. This was itself an earthquake in Italian politics. Then, under an Italian election law that would soon be declared unconstitutional, the Democrat-led coalition was given a 150-seat bonus in the lower house. The problem was that they were still a few votes short in the senate. Meanwhile, President Napolitano's term in office was expiring, and he was about to turn eighty-eight years of age. It was all pure Fellini.

The result of the February 2013 election and the haggling over a successor to Napolitano wreaked such havoc that Italy actually went without a new government for two full months. At the end Napolitano was asked to serve a second term as president, but only on his terms. The president then insisted on forming a Grand Coalition of left and right, practically all the parties except for the followers of the comedian. Berlusconi gave his support to the new government, and so at the time of his guilty verdict in August 2013 he was the leader of a center-right coalition that had five cabinet seats and whose votes were crucial to keep the government afloat. Unfortunately, the government was again in the hands of a political lightweight, a prime minister who, as things would have it, also happened to be the nephew of Berlusconi's chief political fixer, Gianni Letta.

Prime Minister Enrico Letta, also known as "Letta Junior," was already floundering when Berlusconi received his guilty verdict that summer. As soon as Berlusconi was convicted, his government teetered further. Would Berlusconi pull the plug on the coalition government as revenge for his conviction? Did he now hope that President Napolitano might give him a pardon?

The octogenarian former Communist put his foot down right

away. The government would continue, he declared, and Berlusconi's legal problems were his own business. Case closed.

That autumn, when it looked like things could not get any worse for Berlusconi, they did. Another supreme court ruling was handed down, another verdict against him. Another old problem come home to roost. This time it was a civil suit that had been making its way through Italian courts for more than twenty years. This was a court ruling that nearly brought Berlusconi's empire to its knees. The family company, Fininvest, had to pay a whopping $700 million in damages to his archrival Carlo De Benedetti, on the basis that Fininvest had illicitly gained control of the Mondadori publishing house back in 1991 by bribing a judge to swing a key decision. Berlusconi had been acquitted in the criminal bribery case years ago, but the civil lawsuit brought against him resulted in a sting of huge dimensions. The payment drained Berlusconi's company of nearly all of its cash at the time, adding serious financial worries to his legal and political troubles.

The decision came in the middle of September, on the same day that Berlusconi was preparing to relaunch his Forza Italia party, having decided he would reinvent himself politically by shelving his existing center-right coalition, which he had called the Freedom People Coalition, and going back to basics. His old party was in serious disarray. The issue was Berlusconi's looming expulsion from the Italian senate, and his future as a political leader. The prime minister, Enrico Letta, was standing firm, saying that he would not allow Berlusconi's legal travails to dictate the longevity of his struggling coalition government. President Napolitano was chiming in, letting it be known in no uncertain terms that he would not countenance any new elections and calling upon Berlusconi to be responsible, which was a way of telling Berlusconi not to bring down the government as a protest against his guilty verdict. Berlusconi was meanwhile wondering aloud whether there was still a chance he might win a pardon from Napolitano, and hesitated about causing the government to collapse.

All through September, Berlusconi shuttled between Arcore

and the Palazzo Grazioli in Rome, Francesca Pascale in tow, trying to hold things together but facing a wall of opposition, especially in his own party. The so-called hawks in his party wanted him to pull out of the government and force elections. The doves wanted to keep supporting the government and they were resigned to seeing Berlusconi being kicked out of the senate. These rebels against Berlusconi included his number two man, Deputy Prime Minister Angelino Alfano, who was quite happy in his job as deputy prime minister and did not want to bring down the government at all.

At the end of September, as Berlusconi's expulsion order passed through a key senate committee, the billionaire finally showed his anger. He ordered his five ministers in the cabinet to resign, and that included Alfano. The ministers hemmed and hawed, and for a moment it seemed they would stand up to Berlusconi. They did hand in their resignations, potentially opening up a government crisis. Berlusconi now seemed bent on bringing down the government, but actually he had lost control of Alfano and the other cabinet ministers—all of whom loved their jobs and perks—plus nearly thirty members of parliament. So the resignations were taken back in a matter of days and the rebels remained part of the government. By November, when the full senate vote on Berlusconi's expulsion was just days away, Berlusconi held a celebration to relaunch his beloved Forza Italia. On the same day Alfano and the other doves left Berlusconi for good. They formed a new micro-party that immediately pledged its continuing allegiance to the center-left government of Prime Minister Letta, in return for keeping five cabinet posts.

The betrayal had come quickly, and by this point Berlusconi was not surprised. Weeks before, he had told friends that Alfano was a traitor, that he was an ungrateful prodigal son, that he would end up as a political failure if he left the party that had given him everything. By the time he was voted out of the Italian senate in late November 2013, Berlusconi had already lost one-third of his party in parliament. He had decided to vote against the government, and for the first time in years his party was back on the opposition benches. He was out of parliament and out of power.

He was also facing yet another indictment, this time for allegedly paying millions of dollars in bribes to a senator from Naples to buy his vote in parliament as part of a scheme to bring down a center-left government at the end of 2006. Berlusconi naturally denied everything, even after the senator in question admitted receiving the money. Berlusconi was increasingly bitter. Things were not going his way, not at all.

On the day that Berlusconi was voted out of the senate in Rome, a lesser known politician was sitting in the Palazzo della Signoria in Florence, giving an interview. The youthful mayor of Florence, the thirty-nine-year-old Matteo Renzi, was extolling the economic policies of Bill Clinton and Tony Blair and explaining why he was running to become party leader of the Democratic Party in Italy. He was making all the right noises, pledging modernizing reforms and articulating a vision of a post-Berlusconi Italy that he wanted to build. Renzi was known as the most ambitious man in Italy. He was also becoming the most popular politician. A few days later, Renzi would win the primaries in his own party and try to whip the lethargic Premier Enrico Letta into shape and re-energize the government, which was floundering again. Renzi was a Tuscan, which in Italian terms means that he is stubborn, has a strong character and quite a tongue. For a while, though, Renzi emitted only reassuring noises to the hapless Letta, reassuring him of his support and promising party unity. This was the state of affairs at the beginning of 2014, with Renzi as party leader and Letta as prime minister. If Letta was the symbol of everything that was old and archaic about Italy's Old Left, then Renzi was the future.

The hard-charging and social media–savvy Renzi came onto the national scene like a hurricane. One of his first acts after taking over the center-left was to hold a most unusual powwow with Silvio Berlusconi, inviting the archenemy to visit the headquarters of the Democratic Party. When Berlusconi's Audi A8 powered through the narrow cobblestoned alleyways of Rome and pulled up on January 18 in front of Renzi's party office, jaws dropped.

What was Renzi up to? Why would he deign to meet with Berlusconi? And how could this be Silvio Berlusconi, walking into the headquarters of a party that for twenty years had advocated his annihilation? The answer was not complicated. For months now, Berlusconi had been languishing in disgrace and embarrassment, and being invited by Renzi to this meeting was like a political rehabilitation. What emerged from their ninety-minute conversation would, for the first time in a long time, give Berlusconi fresh hope. He had met a politician who seemed willing to do business. He had met a pro-business politician from the center-left, which was quite a novelty in Italy, a man with as much empathy as he had himself, a charmer, a schmoozer, a good fellow. What Renzi was offering may have rekindled Berlusconi's hopes of a presidential pardon. He was offering him a seat back at the table, a piece of the action, a bipartisan pact on key reforms.

On January 18, 2014, Renzi and Berlusconi agreed to cooperate in parliament on a set of constitutional reforms and a new election law to replace the existing and by now unconstitutional law that was still on the books. The deal became known as the "Pact of Nazareno," a reference to the Democratic Party's offices on Largo Nazareno in Rome. Nothing in the recent past had cheered Berlusconi as much as his meeting with Renzi, who had faced the cameras afterward and spoken of a "profound harmony" of views with Berlusconi. What was strange was how much Berlusconi seemed to genuinely like Renzi. In fact, the Italian press had already started commenting on the odd couple, noting that the thirty-nine-year-old left-of-center politician seemed to be the most natural heir to Berlusconi that anyone had ever seen.

"Renzi is certainly a new protagonist on the scene," Berlusconi would say a few days after the meeting. "He is trying to reform and modernize the Democratic Party, and he has announced with a bit of courage and a bit of arrogance that he is going to get rid of the Old Guard of his party. And he is actually doing it. So I hope he continues going in the same direction."

It was a pretty big pat on the back for the man who was supposed to be on the opposite side of the political spectrum. Renzi had charmed Berlusconi, at least momentarily. There would be plenty of time later on for Berlusconi to claim that he had been cheated and misled by Renzi. For now, he was back in the game, even back in meetings at the presidential palace, once again a player. For Berlusconi, being able to reclaim a semblance of dignity mattered, no matter how many of his enemies were beginning to write him off as a political has-been. So, throwing caution to the wind, Berlusconi embraced the new alliance-friendship with Renzi and throughout the year the two men met on eight separate occasions and had numerous phone conversations. Their aides met dozens of times, preparing the way, sorting out disagreements, renegotiating pieces of the deal. A number of Berlusconi's remaining supporters were beginning to question his strategy. What was the point of doing a deal with Renzi to vote together on certain reforms if they were supposed to be in the opposition? Berlusconi brushed aside the complaints by saying he was doing the responsible thing by cooperating on such important reforms. According to those who were with him in that spring of 2014, in his heart of hearts he was still hoping for a pardon.

The result of Berlusconi's support for Renzi's reforms was about to prove disastrous; it would in fact boomerang in electoral terms. He was still barred from participating in any election. Forza Italia's numbers were crumbling in the polls, and Berlusconi's remaining party loyalists were worried they were about to take a beating in upcoming European parliamentary elections.

It was on April 15, 2014, amid this general sense of decay and despair, that Berlusconi was finally informed when he would begin serving his sentence. The supreme court had sentenced him to four years in prison, of which three were annulled, thanks to a partial amnesty that had been proclaimed in order to deal with Italy's overcrowded prisons. The remaining twelve months, a Milan tribunal now decided, would be served doing community service at a Catholic-run old-age home on the outskirts of Milan, the Fondazione Sacra Famiglia. There, every Friday morning, the former prime minister was to work in the section dedicated to caring for people with dementia and Alzheimer's disease.

The sentence was not among the most onerous, but Berlusconi's world continued to implode. Next up on the docket would be the sentence of an appeals court on his bunga-bunga conviction for abuse of office and sex with an underage prostitute. Meanwhile, he had been indicted in Naples on charges of buying votes in the Italian parliament, and he was being questioned by more magistrates. Still other magistrates were developing new charges to file in connection with allegations that he had paid millions of dollars of hush money to some of the girls from the bunga-bunga nights in exchange for perjured testimony. To make matters worse, the results of the European elections that spring would soon trigger an open rebellion inside the newly re-established Forza Italia.

For Berlusconi, that guilty verdict was more than just a defeat for a man who was always used to winning. For Silvio Berlusconi it was the beginning of the end.

CHAPTER FOURTEEN

———

Endgame

The lights are dimmed low in the living room of Berlusconi's mansion in Arcore, as though the great big villa were somehow in mourning. The effect of the half-light is to create sinister-looking shadows on either side of the marble fireplace and to exaggerate the already gloomy mood of this tenebrous night in the Milan countryside. A stern figure in a wrinkled white shirt presents himself at the doorway. He is bearing a silver tray containing assorted bottles of mineral water, both sparkling and still. It is Berlusconi's faithful old butler, Giuseppe, a slightly haggard figure with a cynical and knowing "I've seen it all" smile on his face. The *maggiordomo* of the Villa San Martino explains in an apologetic whisper that this is the way that the boss likes the lights, turned down low. He pours the sparkling water into a crystal glass and silently withdraws.

From the adjacent dining room come the sounds of raised voices. A heated discussion appears to be under way. Berlusconi's full-throated tenor is unmistakable, as are the voices of some of his closest aides, a Neapolitan newcomer named Mariarosaria Rossi and Deborah Bergamini, a seasoned spokesperson whom Berlusconi had originally hired from Bloomberg Television. The door opens and Giovanni Toti, Berlusconi's latest protégé, emerges. He looks a bit dazed. The former talk show host from Mediaset has just agreed to Berlusconi's request that he run for governor as a Forza Italia candidate in upcoming state elections.

It is a Friday evening and Berlusconi is talking electoral politics with members of his inner circle, a tiny coterie that the Italian press derides as "the Magic Circle." The key member of this circle is his girlfriend, Francesca Pascale, and she and the so-called Magic Circle have mesmerized the aging Berlusconi and isolated him from the world, doing irreparable damage to both the man and Forza Italia with their inexperience, bad judgment, and personal ambitions, or so the story goes. The story is only half true. Pascale is not, however, sitting in on this particular strategy meeting. She is upstairs in the family residence, preparing her toilette. Tonight she will be in designer beige, eschewing her normal in-house attire of track suits or denim jackets. Dinner will be served shortly and Berlusconi's meeting is running late.

There is something eerie about the Villa San Martino on this evening of March 27, 2015. It may be the dimness, or the way the big villa sits in the shadows, or perhaps it is the darkness of the mood. Perhaps it is because today is the anniversary of Berlusconi's first election victory in 1994, a day more than two decades ago that transformed him from controversial billionaire media mogul into a controversial billionaire prime minister. In 1994, he changed the face of Italian politics with a slick campaign that conquered the hearts and minds of millions of Italian voters. Twenty-one years later, his party seems to be imploding, struggling for its very survival. A number of Berlusconi's top lieutenants are turning their backs on him, some are demanding primaries to elect a successor to Berlusconi, and others are arguing that they are being barred access to Berlusconi by the Magic Circle and Pascale; still others are saying that Berlusconi has damaged his own party by refusing to consider a plan for succession. All of this has cast a pall over the Villa San Martino. The air is thick with dejection, even despair.

An aide to Berlusconi confides that at lunch today the boss spoke for the first time about throwing in the towel. Sure, the Ruby conviction was finally canceled by the courts just a few weeks ago. Yes, Berlusconi had been fully acquitted, and this time on criminal charges of underage prostitution and abuse of office as prime minister. He should have been feeling elated. He was not. Instead he was telling his family and friends that he expected the magistrates to come after him again, this time with an indictment for witness tampering in the Ruby case. A number of wiretapped phone conversations among the alleged harem of girls that Berlusconi maintained in an apartment block are finding their way into the press. That evening Berlusconi bemoans the "media campaign against me by the magistrates, with the publication of all sorts of embarrassing telephone wiretaps and other confidential materials that are being leaked every day." He is not happy at all.

On this March twenty-seventh evening, Berlusconi looks like a man in a funk. He is worried about his legal travails, he is worried about his businesses, he is worried about the mounting losses from his ownership of the AC Milan soccer club, and he is worried about his political future. He is especially alarmed by the desperate state of finances at his Forza Italia party. The party's debts amount to more than $130 million, he tells a visitor, and a new law on campaign contributions prohibits individual contributions of more than a hundred thousand euros. "I will have to pay it off myself, the entire accumulated debt," he says with a grimace. Even worse, his own party is still reeling from nearly a year of internal rebellions and mutinies. Many of his loyalists are upset that he has appointed a political nobody from Naples, Mariarosaria Rossi, as the party treasurer. Rossi is a Forza Italia senator but her greatest credential so far appears to be that she is Pascale's friend and sidekick. The Italian press paints a dark picture, in which Rossi and Pascale are the villains of the piece, manipulating a doddering Berlusconi amid the fading glory of the now slightly spooky Villa San Martino. It rings true for many. For a long time now, Berlusconi has been isolated at the villa in Arcore, spending the better part of a year with a strict curfew and tight restrictions on his movements while he serves his sentence and performs community service. He has been invisible on television and on the political scene. His party's numbers are plummeting in every poll. Politically, he seems to be in freefall. Inside the big old villa is a man who is furious at what has beset him, a man who has been boiling in anger and frustration that he has had his movements restricted, that he cannot say what he really thinks in public for fear of the magistrates, that he is unable to travel around Italy, a man who is impatient for a return to the stage and aghast at the way his numbers are dropping.

During his period of community service, and until early 2015, the most significant damage that Berlusconi suffered in political terms was not, however, a result of bad advice from the Magic Circle. Rather it was the ascendancy of Matteo Renzi as Italy's new prime minister. With a Twitter-generation coolness and a Bill Clinton pro-growth economic policy, Renzi had taken over as prime minister the year before, in 2014. He was proving to be a cool free-market liberal with a social conscience, a conservative Democrat in American terms. While Berlusconi did community service and watched his fractious party from a distance, Renzi was busy driving a truck through Italy's center-left Democratic Party, killing off his adversaries on the extreme left and infuriating them with his pro-business and jobs reform policies. Yet, this being Italian politics, one of the main reasons why Renzi was able to push through his reforms was thanks to the Nazareno Pact he made with Berlusconi.

In exchange for providing Berlusconi a seat at the table as the leader of the parliamentary opposition, as an equal, and the political credibility and standing that came along with it, Berlusconi had pledged Forza Italia's senate votes to Renzi on key reforms. With those votes, Renzi could threaten the left-wingers in his own party and ram through reform legislation even if the liberals voted against him. It was an effective threat, and for a while it worked. Many of the dissidents fell into line, Berlusconi's opposition forces voted for the reforms, and everybody benefited.

For Berlusconi the dialogue with the new premier was like a political life support system. Berlusconi felt rehabilitated by Renzi, who just happened to be pushing through some of the same labor market and economic reforms that Berlusconi himself had tried and failed to achieve over the past twenty years.

Renzi had found it useful to keep Berlusconi alive politically by engaging him in the bipartisan constitutional reforms. As Renzi moved to the center, though, he began a kind of triangulation, Italian style. He was stealing Berlusconi's political clothing just like Bill Clinton had once stolen the policies of moderate Republicans. Even worse, from Berlusconi's point of view, Renzi was as able and telegenic a communicator as the Master himself in the days of old. Renzi was using the new media of Facebook and Twitter to get his message across, while taking a leaf out of the old Berlusconi playbook when it came to messaging and sloganeering. Renzi's pro-business and moderate economic policies were attracting Berlusconi supporters, and pieces of Berlusconi's traditional electorate soon began to fall away. Berlusconi's party, as he began serving community service, took a beating in elections for the European parliament in the spring of 2014. His vote collapsed to just 16.8 percent, a historic low. Renzi had managed to hold on to the left while eating into Berlusconi's electoral base.

Although he tended to minimize the problem, Berlusconi was watching, apparently helpless, as key members of his party left him, one after the other. He was under fierce attack from many in his own party for the alliance he had made with Renzi. Even to Berlusconi's inner circle it was painfully clear that his bipartisan support for Renzi had confused Forza Italia voters and cost him votes. On the eve of another round of elections in spring 2015, the race for governorships in key swing states, Berlusconi's electoral base was trending still lower, at around 10 percent.

"The big problem," said an exhausted aide that evening at the Villa San Martino, "is not the internal feuding in Forza Italia. It is Renzi. He is appealing to our moderate electoral base and he is stealing our supporters."

Just after seven-thirty that evening, Berlusconi sat down to dinner, with Rossi and Pascale to his right, and Deborah Bergamini across the table. He had complained earlier in the day of how he felt betrayed by the new premier, who at first had seemed so promising. Now he spoke in even more plaintive tones.

"Renzi seemed so *simpatico* at first, but he is not *simpatico* at all. He just wants power."

Silvio Berlusconi is evidently hurt.

Pascale has ordered her standard large green salad in a big bowl. This evening she allows herself a glass of red wine. Berlusconi is glaring at a bowl of broth, complaining about the crash diet he is on. He plans to make some public appearances now that his sentence is finally over, and he wants to get in shape. In some ways Berlusconi's diets go with his mood swings. He can drop a few pounds rather quickly, only to put it all back on in a binge of comfort food.

Now Berlusconi decides to ignore his soup and launches instead into an impromptu spiel about how his new archenemy, Renzi, is destroying Italy.

"The situation in Italy is getting worse every day because of the way Renzi is appropriating power. After he has finished all these reforms, he will control the senate. He will control his party. In fact, he will have the entire country in the palm of his hand. The only hope…"

Berlusconi drifts off for a minute, samples the soup, and continues.

"The only hope is if I can somehow get back on the playing field myself. Just think about it: I have been pretty much invisible to the Italians, I have not been on TV much, and I have been gone from the scene for nearly a year."

Berlusconi pauses again. The Magic Circle listens intently.

"I think I can only make a comeback when it is perfectly clear to everyone that I am innocent. I was an innocent man and they convicted me anyway. They threw me out of the senate. They made me politically ineligible. They pushed me off the political stage. They attacked my personal wealth; I had to pay out seven hundred million dollars to Carlo De Benedetti. They thought they could bankrupt me but they failed. I found the money and I paid De Benedetti without even needing to go to the banks."

Berlusconi pauses for a spoonful of broth and a sip of mineral water. There is no wine for Berlusconi on diet days.

"So what does all of this mean?" Berlusconi finally asks, rhetorically. "It means that it is impossible to mount an operation like we did back in 1994, where we brought together the entire spectrum of the center-right. What we should be doing in Italy now is creating a Republican Party just like the one in the United States, a big container, a big tent for moderates and conservatives that goes beyond Forza Italia."

Berlusconi has ditched the soup now and is talking a stream. His inner circle is still listening intently as he speaks with rising passion.

"The only way forward for us is to transform Forza Italia into the Republican Party, using the American example, the example of the greatest democracy in the world. We already have Democrats here in Italy, with Renzi. Now what we need is Republicans. In order to fight the Democrats in Italy, we will need a Republican Party."

Rossi nods her head in agreement. She and Francesca jump into the conversation. They urge Berlusconi to be strong, to be tough, not to give up, and to move ahead even if the situation seems difficult. He smiles but with a trace of bitterness.

Berlusconi does not blink when he is asked what he really wants to do. Does he really want to continue in politics, at the age of nearly eighty, and beyond, or wouldn't it make more sense to just pack it in and enjoy life? After all, he always complains that he works so much and never gets to visit his sumptuous villas in Antigua or in the Caymans or in Sardinia. Berlusconi puts down his soup spoon with a precise movement and fixes his interlocutor with a penetrating stare.

"Actually, I was speaking about that subject earlier today, at lunch right here in this room, with all of them," he says gravely, gesturing to the members of the Magic Circle.

"I was speaking about the future. I am totally distraught by the fact that it seems impossible, as things stand today, to rebuild a really effective center-right opposition to Renzi. We can only achieve this with my return, with my resurrection, as an innocent man who can then stand up and speak to that silent majority of Italians who are disgusted by politics and who are half of the population, those who don't even vote anymore.

"For all of this to happen I would need an acquittal from the European Court of Human Rights in Strasbourg," he continues. "They can overrule the Italian supreme court at the European level. There are sixteen separate items in my appeal so the European court has to just decide on any one of them and I will be free to continue in politics and be a candidate again."

He explains patiently the mechanics of how the European court ruling would trigger an obligatory Italian court ruling in which he would regain his eligibility to stand for office as a candidate. He is clearly placing his hopes on this last appeal as his final chance at redemption.

"I really don't want to throw in the towel," says Berlusconi, now wearily scrounging around for a piece of bread to stave off his hunger.

By the end of dinner, it is clear that Berlusconi is asking himself the big questions. He is turning over his options in his own mind and in this conversation with his inner circle. At times he is ebullient, cheerful, and enthusiastic. He also has darker moments.

"He has his ups and downs," admits his old friend Fedele Confalonieri. "But I don't see him giving it all up. His main enjoyment in life is his work and he has always been like that. I know he talks a lot about a lot of things, but I don't think that Silvio will ever really leave politics. Frankly, I don't think he can afford to."

Confalonieri is one of a small group of Berlusconi's closest friends and advisers who think he has made a serious mistake in not sticking close to Renzi. The truth is that any media mogul, whether his name is Rupert Murdoch or Silvio Berlusconi, has to cultivate good relations with government regulators and, at their level, with the leaders of governments where their businesses operate. For twenty years Berlusconi has been accused of being a one-man walking conflict of interest because of his media power. His critics say that he only entered politics in the first place in order to protect his business interests. But his business interests have been taking a battering lately, starting with the nearly $700 million he has paid out to his rival Carlo De Benedetti.

By the spring of 2015, Berlusconi may have been uncertain about his political future but he was certainly looking after his billions. His net worth was still somewhere north of $8 billion, but he was determined to replenish the coffers and his group had been busy selling off a variety of assets.

The Berlusconi family holding company, Fininvest, had started at the end of 2013 by first disposing of shares in its Mediolanum financial services for $350 million. In April 2014, Mediaset brought in $400 million of fresh cash by selling shares in its broadcasting towers subsidiary. In the summer of 2014, Mediaset brought in another $400 million by selling a stake in its pay-TV platform in Spain. At the end of 2014 came the sale of Berlusconi's shares in a multiplex cinema chain in Italy, for $45 million cash. In February 2015, Berlusconi's Fininvest raised a further $430 million by selling a 7 percent stake of its shares in Mediaset. That lowered Berlusconi's stake in Mediaset to just 34 percent, but it was still worth $2 billion. Add up all his other holdings and Berlusconi's empire in 2015 was still worth $8 billion or more. He was not exactly broke. In fact Mediaset was busy spending another billion dollars, financed by bank loans, in order to buy the 2015–2018 television broadcast rights to the European Champions League and Italian Serie A soccer games. The soccer rights were being bought for Berlusconi's new Italian pay-TV platform, a service called Mediaset Premium. Berlusconi had a problem, however. His pay-TV service had only two million subscribers while the leader of Italian pay-TV, Rupert Murdoch's Sky Italia, had five million subscribers. It was the first time Berlusconi had been challenged on his home turf in television.

Murdoch and Berlusconi had always been friendly rivals, and

as far back as the 1990s they had had talks about finding a way to join forces, or buy into each other's businesses. Now both men were facing the same threat of new and aggressive competition in the fast-changing media world. They were worried about the power of Netflix, the digital disrupter that had already laid waste to large swaths of America's pay-TV market and was now marching across Europe. Both men had something else in common. It was called mortality.

So it was not surprising that on April 27, 2015, just before lunchtime on a drizzly Monday, Rupert Murdoch's car pulled up and parked in the gravel courtyard in front of the big villa at Arcore.

Berlusconi was agonizing over his role in Italian politics and how best to protect and relaunch his business empire. He was trying to plan for the future of his children. For months he had been thinking about what part of his business to keep, what part to sell, and what kind of new and strategic alliances might be needed if he were to keep his media empire going in the changing digital environment.

The eighty-four-year-old Murdoch had also been busy reorganizing his global empire, pooling all his European television assets into one company and bringing his son Lachlan into the business. Certainly if he could buy Berlusconi's pay-TV assets in Italy or at least get his hands on the soccer rights, that would help Murdoch to consolidate his position in the European market.

Now the two media tycoons, one a full-fledged octogenarian and the other on the cusp of eighty, were meeting at Arcore for one of Berlusconi's extended lunches. Murdoch had brought his son Lachlan, and Berlusconi's son Pier Silvio was at his father's side. Confalonieri had not been invited. This was a meeting of just fathers and sons, except for the presence of the man who had brought them all together, a Tunisian-born media executive named Tarak Ben Ammar.

"It really was an occasion for Silvio Berlusconi and Rupert Murdoch to spend some time together," recalls Ben Ammar, who has been a top adviser to Murdoch for as long as he has been a business partner to Berlusconi. It was Ben Ammar who helped put together the multi-billion-dollar media holdings of Saudi Arabia's Prince Alwaleed bin Talal. It was Ben Ammar who had helped the Saudi prince take key equity stakes in both Berlusconi's Mediaset and Murdoch's News Corp.

If anyone could bring the two moguls together for a meeting of the minds it was Ben Ammar, a serious mover and shaker who seemed to spend most of his time with billionaire media moguls. Already a film producer, Ben Ammar had gone into business with Berlusconi in launching a successful commercial TV network in North Africa called Nessma. As part of his asset disposals, Berlusconi had also sold back to Ben Ammar an equity stake in Ben Ammar's Paris-based company, Quinta Communications. Ben Ammar was making films with Luc Besson and was a key adviser to Vincent Bolloré, yet another flamboyant billionaire media mogul, who controlled Vivendi and Canal Plus, the monopoly pay-TV platform in France. Bolloré had also bought a key stake in Telecom Italia, and had put Ben Ammar on the Telecom board to represent him. Ben Ammar had also just joined the board of Vivendi and the group was sitting on tens of billions of dollars of cash. There was also talk of an alliance or share deal between Vivendi and Berlusconi's Mediaset. At the end of the day, the two biggest pay-TV players in Europe were Murdoch and Bolloré, and Berlusconi's Italian pay-TV assets could represent an attractive target for both of them. For Vivendi, gobbling all of Mediaset might someday appear attractive. It would only cost five or six billion euros.

Now a relaxed Murdoch and a smiling Berlusconi join their sons and sit down to lunch along with Ben Ammar. They are trying to figure out if there is a way to work together, and in particular how they can best counter the threat from digital online content, from Netflix and others. Berlusconi will speak later that day of the importance of allowing the two sons to bond, and seemed to like the idea of his son Pier Silvio, who is forty-six, developing business deals alongside Lachlan Murdoch, who has just turned forty-three.

"The future belongs to our sons, so it is right they should spend more time together," says Berlusconi to a visitor an hour after the Murdochs leave Arcore.

"Having their sons present was an important part of the lunch," explains Ben Ammar.

The long lunch at Arcore did not yield any immediate results, mainly because Murdoch wanted to be the majority shareholder of any combined pay-TV operation, an idea that did not sit well with Berlusconi. The two media tycoons would later face an investigation by Italian tax inspectors, who were probing suspicions of market-rigging between Sky and Mediaset over the sharing of the expensive broadcast rights for Serie A soccer matches.

Soccer was very much on Berlusconi's mind throughout the spring and summer of 2015. His beloved AC Milan was performing miserably, and Berlusconi had for all intents and purposes fired the hapless coach of the team, Filippo Inzaghi. He had humiliated Inzaghi in public by saying that he and the coach had "divergent views." That was enough of a clue in soccer-crazed Italy. The press was now full of speculation that Berlusconi was about to fire Inzaghi, and about whom he would hire. On top of this, a day after Murdoch left Berlusconi's estate at Arcore, another billionaire tycoon was seen being driven through the iron gates of the villa at Arcore. The Italian journalists and camera crews camped outside could see that the new guest was Asian. The word was that Berlusconi was about to sell the legendary soccer club. The asking price was rumored to be more than a billion dollars.

"Objectively speaking, this team is very expensive to maintain. It really costs a lot," says Berlusconi.

It is another cloudy late April day at Arcore, three days after the Murdoch visit. Berlusconi is back on the couch, the one he likes in the family living room. He is sitting there in his jet-black shirt and blazer, in front of the 1970s-style beige telephone on the coffee table, alongside a legal pad and pen and a glass of mineral water. Berlusconi is nibbling reluctantly from a plateful of low-calorie fresh apple slices. In the dining room next door and in other meeting rooms of the huge house, more than a dozen Milanese lawyers and investment bankers and accountants and interpreters are speaking in hushed tones. Berlusconi takes no notice. He is talking soccer.

"The story is fairly simple. I have put a lot of money into Milan. The way to win at soccer is with money, with talent and with luck. I have been president of Milan for twenty-nine years, and today we are one of the world's most trophied teams in history. Great! But it also costs a lot of money to maintain a soccer team these days. So today Europe's clubs are opening up their capital to investors from Russia, from Qatar, from oil-rich countries, from China, from Indonesia, from Asia. It simply costs too much for a family like mine to own a team on our own because the competition is really fierce and the prices are crazy. The top players cost fifty million euros and more. The prices for top players like [Cristiano] Ronaldo or [Lionel] Messi have skyrocketed to absurd and completely ridiculous levels. So it is not sustainable. Just take the last three years as an example. My family, through our holding company Fininvest, put in sixty-two million euros three years ago, and seventy million two years ago, and one hundred and two million euros last year. It is too much! So we have to find alternative solutions, and where do we find them? In the oil markets, in Asia, in the emerging economies. So when we let it be known that the majority of Milan could be up for sale, we began to receive a variety of offers. One of them came from a young financier from Thailand named Mr. Bee Taechaubol, and he came to visit me here yesterday."

Berlusconi reels off the details of the proposal from the Thai businessman, whose name he pronounces as "Meester Bee."

"Actually, his proposal is quite interesting. First he would make a large cash payment up front to show that he is serious and then, since Milan is such a valuable brand, we are talking about maybe quoting the club on the Hong Kong or Singapore stock markets, and even opening a brand merchandising operation in China and across ten Asian nations. That is a market of 242 million fans of

Milan, and we can expand into restaurants, perfumes, soft drinks, and we make this a really profitable business. I would stay on as president, and we would have a big budget to buy new players, so I would have a lot of fun. And the fans would also have a lot of fun, that much I can promise. So ideally I am looking for someone who can help me to share the costs of keeping Milan going, with the best players. But that does not mean I would go away. Not at all," Berlusconi explains.

A few weeks later Berlusconi made his deal with Mr. Bee. The Asian consortium of investors promised to put up 480 million euros for 48 percent of AC Milan. Berlusconi maintained majority control. The fans of Milan cheered. They were happy. So was an enthusiastic Berlusconi.

"The Milan brand is worth a lot, and when we quote AC Milan on the stock exchange in Asia, probably in 2016, it should achieve a great market valuation and become a company which earns a lot of money. I will put up one hundred fifty million euros myself to buy new players, and the Asians will put in five hundred million. But I will keep control. Then we can float a part of the company on the stock market, maybe twenty-five percent, and that would raise another billion. We could maybe get a stock market value of four billion euros for Milan, and I would have done quite well, eh? At that point we can start to have some serious fun, when we have raised a billion. Then we will become the most unbeatable team on the planet. On par with Real Madrid."

Berlusconi goes on, dreaming of a future in which he is the beaming president of AC Milan, fulfilling his boyhood dreams and now making plans to open a new office for the fabled soccer club in Shanghai. He gets carried away as he analyzes the deal and the attractiveness of the fast-growing economies of Asia.

The plan to exploit Milan's value across Asia is a shrewd move, and Berlusconi becomes animated and emotional when he speaks of his beloved soccer club. Finally, after a fair amount of prodding, he explains why he had to replace Inzaghi as coach of AC Milan, and there are no surprises. He explains that he has hired a new coach, a veteran from Serbia named Sinisa Mihajlovic, who is the best man to help lead the team back to greatness. "He has a strong personality but also a great humanity and this comes from being the father of six children. He has always had good relations with the players in all the teams he has coached, and he told me that he had always nurtured the dream, in his head and in his heart, of one day becoming the coach of Milan. I think he will be fantastic," says Berlusconi.

As for the future of his family's holding in Mediaset, the Italian media empire, he is pretty clear. Berlusconi is determined to see control of the company remain in the hands of his family, at least for the near term.

"We will keep Mediaset," he says quietly. "That is important, whether I remain in politics or not."

Keeping control of Mediaset, which in the summer of 2015 was still the core asset in Berlusconi's empire, may have been at the heart of the billionaire's business strategy. Yet when it came to his political strategy and his own political future, he was hesitant, reluctant to commit himself, even in his own biography.

Work in progress.

Berlusconi had been sending out mixed signals since May 2015, when he was campaigning in what turned out to be a reasonably successful result. His assistant, Giovanni Toti, was elected as governor of the state of Liguria, and he managed to share in another victory in the Veneto region, but in both cases this was only because of his alliance with the xenophobic Northern League party. Berlusconi found himself dependent on an Italian equivalent of Tea Party militants who were trending at around the same level as Berlusconi's party, around 14 percent. The fact is that Berlusconi, as he endlessly repeated to the Magic Circle, had managed to improve Forza Italia's showing by getting out on the stump and campaigning. But he did make some embarrassing mistakes, at one point turning up at the wrong rally, in the company of his Magic Circle, and cheering on a candidate who turned out to be from the wrong party, and on another occasion appearing to announce his withdrawal from active politics. He was beginning to show his age.

"I am really out of politics," he said at one point. "I am just someone who has a great sense of responsibility toward his country."

His opponents seized upon the remark as proof that his political career was over. He clearly had an exit strategy, they said, and it involved staying in politics just long enough to protect his business interests.

Berlusconi quickly explained that what he had really meant is that he had been thrown out of the senate and declared ineligible to run for office, and that he was now looking to reinvent himself one last time as a founding father of a new political movement, the Republican Party for Italy that he had begun talking about incessantly. At the age of nearly eighty, and banned from public office until 2019, Berlusconi had one more plan up his sleeve, or at least a vision of what he wanted his political legacy to be.

He called it a "crusade" in which he wanted to persuade the disparate smaller parties of the center-right to come together, or at least cooperate, as a united center-right political alliance that could regain a majority vote in Italy's next elections in 2018. Nonetheless, the signals seemed mixed. Was Berlusconi retiring or still in the game? He employed soccer terminology to explain himself, saying he would be like a coach on the sidelines of a game, giving advice in the future, but that he would himself not be the future leader. When asked who his heir would be, Berlusconi said he did not know. There was no natural successor at this point, or so it seemed. Berlusconi's ranks had been depleted by all the defections.

In some ways Berlusconi was growing weary of the game of politics, especially when it appeared that there was no way to stage a flashy comeback. "I have never enjoyed politics. I am not a professional politician. I am an entrepreneur," Berlusconi would tell his friends over and over again. He would complain about "the professional full-time politicians who are parasites and who have used me" and he would complain about their lack of loyalty. He would shrug off the stream of defections from Forza Italia, the old friends and trusted allies who were now walking away from him and diminishing his own party's numbers dramatically in parliament. The only thing he could hope for now was to withdraw gracefully as an elder statesman or at least as a political power broker who has a say in naming the future leader of Italy's right. But he was not quite ready to throw in the towel.

The truth of the matter, for those who knew him through the summer of 2015, was that Berlusconi didn't really want to give up the limelight, and he wanted above all to leave on his own terms. Throughout his life, as a boy who had been evacuated from Milan during the Allied bombings, and as a ruthless billionaire mogul who took no prisoners, Berlusconi had always been determined to win, and to win big. So it was not surprising that when a guest asked him when he thought he might leave the scene he remained in silence, but scribbled some words, out of habit, on the white notepad before him. He crumpled up the page afterward and took it with him, but the imprint of his pen had been strong enough to trace out the lines of just one sentence that remained impressed upon the page below: *I will leave when I have had another victory.*

The story of Berlusconi's life is not an easy story to tell. Not as easy as it might seem to be, given his extraordinary adventures in politics, soccer, television, and real estate, or the way he became Italy's richest billionaire, or given the demonology surrounding his relations with women, or the huge number of indictments and trials he has faced over the years, with more still to come.

Berlusconi is still a larger-than-life presence on the Italian scene, even as his political importance is waning. In no other Western country has one national leader so dominated a country's life or stamped his own personality and tastes on its culture for a period of more than twenty years. His influence over Italy, starting with the moment in the 1980s when he filled the airwaves with American-style hedonism and introduced yuppie consumerism to Italy, cannot be overstated.

Berlusconi remains a controversial and polarizing figure, in Italy and around the world. To many he is a buffoon, a convicted criminal, a womanizer, a shady billionaire who used political connections to bootstrap his media empire into the stratosphere and then faced his ultimate destiny with the supreme court sentence that finally declared him guilty. To many he is the devil incarnate.

There is, however, more to the story than the press clippings may imply.

As he told the story of his life, in his own words, in more than thirty days and in over a hundred hours of meetings and videotaped interviews and endless conversations, in the garden, in his study, in the dining room, or in his favorite living room at the villa in Arcore, a fuller picture of the man began to emerge. He appeared moody at times, lamenting his struggles with the magistrates on almost every occasion. Yet he also seemed to be struggling with his own destiny, still restless for one more victory. Berlusconi had never fully recovered after the supreme court sentence of August 2013. His psyche had taken a huge beating and there were times when the former prime minister felt the weight of the court's verdict, and you could tell that he felt humiliated and disgraced. Yet he refused to give up entirely, even as he faced up to his own mortality. He was no longer the Berlusconi of his younger years, but he still had his charisma. He remained a consummate schmoozer, a showman, a joke-teller, a charmer, a mischief maker, and above all a man not quite ready to leave the stage or give up his role as the star in the story of his own life.

"They can do many things to me," he told a friend on one occasion, "but they can't get me to resign from being myself."

His years as Italy's prime minister were part of a lengthy period of decline in the country's history, and he never managed to achieve his dream of a Reagan-style, free-market revolution. Nor has he ever managed to shake off the charge, which he denies, that he engineered a dozen pieces of legislation to help himself in pending court cases over the years.

On the European stage, Berlusconi was undoubtedly a protagonist and a witness to history during the two decades that followed the collapse of the Berlin Wall. However controversial he might have become after the bunga-bunga trials, he had moved among the giants, Kohl, Mitterrand, Chirac, and Merkel, and at a time of epochal change in Europe. He dealt with three U.S. presidents, Bill Clinton, George W. Bush, and Barack Obama. His friendship with George W. Bush definitely allowed Italy to punch above its weight in foreign policy. In Iraq and Afghanistan and for several years, Berlusconi was the second-closest ally the Bush administration had in Europe after Tony Blair. His effusive declarations of friendship for Vladimir Putin appear to be sincere, but they mask the real and important role Berlusconi played on occasion as a discreet back channel between Washington and Moscow. Berlusconi's fights with Nicolas Sarkozy are legendary, but when it comes to the decision to send in the bombers and overthrow Gaddafi at the beginning of the Arab Spring, Berlusconi seems to have been on the right side of history and it was Sarkozy who got it wrong. The evidence can be seen today in the ruins of a fragmented and ISIS-filled Libya, another failed state that is overrun by terrorists.

Berlusconi's take on the historic euro crisis also turned out to be right. Although he was humiliated at the G-20 summit in Cannes, his stubborn opposition to Sarkozy's plan to send the IMF into Italy with a rescue loan turned out to be the right decision for Italy and for the Eurozone. Even Obama said so. By opposing Christine Lagarde and the IMF so stubbornly, Berlusconi did not forestall his own downfall, but that was because the campaign by Sarkozy and Merkel to wear him down had been running in tandem for several months alongside President Giorgio Napolitano's lengthy preparations to groom a replacement for Berlusconi. As Tim Geithner told his staff: "They ultimately did it, and they did it pretty deftly."

There is little doubt that the indiscretions in Berlusconi's personal life, and a constant stream of leaks from the Milan prosecutor's office over a five-year period, hastened his downfall. He got off in a number of cases because the statute of limitations expired. This happened again in 2015 in the case of the alleged bribes to buy a member of parliament. Berlusconi was convicted in July

2015 and sentenced to a three-year jail sentence, but the statute of limitations would run out and the sentence would be annulled just a few months later, before it could be heard on appeal. It mattered to Berlusconi that in March 2015 he had finally been acquitted by the supreme court on charges of paying for sex with an under-age prostitute. But the leaking of embarrassing telephone wiretap transcripts in which alleged escorts spoke of extracting payments from Berlusconi continued throughout the summer of 2015. For the Italian public, reading leaked transcripts of wiretapped phone calls in a Berlusconi sex-related investigation has become a national sport.

Berlusconi's ravenous appetite for beautiful women, just like his passion for AC Milan, has not exactly been a secret over the years. In fact, in many ways, Berlusconi is an open book. The question is why millions and millions of Italians kept re-electing him as prime minister if he was such a controversial billionaire tycoon. The answer is that for twenty years Berlusconi held the aspirations, the passions, and the dreams of the Italians in the palm of his hand, and for better or worse he reshaped much of Italy in his own image. His influence over the nation and over generations of young Italians who grew up knowing only Berlusconi would be hard to overstate. No other political leader has so completely dominated the country for such a long period, shaping and reshaping the nation in political, cultural, and social terms. No one had done it, arguably, since the days of Mussolini.

Berlusconi managed to become both the most hated and the most beloved man in Italy over a period of two decades. For his critics this was due to his monopoly control of television and his abuse of media power. It may have also been because in many ways he was the most empathetic and media-savvy prime minister that Italy had ever seen, but also the most typical Italian ever to rise to the post of premier. Berlusconi is and has always been the archetypal Italian, the schmoozer, the salesman, the charmer, the teller of jokes, and the natural-born seducer. He has each and every one of the foibles and weaknesses of the typical Italian, but with a healthy dose of timing and flair and genius for innovation. Deep down Berlusconi embodies both the best and the worst character traits of all Italians, and his electoral success owes much to the fact that he is the personification of an Italian dream, a mirror image of what many Italians want and dream about, a reflection of the very voters who elected him.

On another hazy Monday morning in the summer of 2015, Berlusconi is at home in Arcore. He seems sentimental, musing about his life with friends in the room next to the family chapel. It may be the proximity of the chapel, with the ashes of his mother and his father still resting on the mantelpiece, or it may be that Berlusconi is thinking about the regular Monday family luncheon at Arcore that he is about to attend in the dining room. His daughter Marina is already waiting in the living room along with Fedele Confalonieri and a trio of veteran managers from Fininvest, the men in gray suits who are handling the financial deal for AC Milan. But Berlusconi hangs back; he is talking about his future, and he has one more thing he wants to share. "I told my kids and my family," he now confides, "that after I am gone they can sell everything. They can sell the villas and the companies and the shareholdings and whatever they want. But there are just two things I told them not to sell. One is a share stake of AC Milan and the other is this house, this place here in Arcore."

He pauses. "You know," he says, "I am nearly eighty years old and I am beginning to feel my age."

With that, Berlusconi exits the room, heading out to the portico. He glances up at the cloudy sky and strolls along the crunching gravel that separates the portico of the villa from the garden and the rest of this 180-acre property. There is a flurry as aides scurry forth from the big house and Giuseppe the butler emerges to indicate that the guests are already in the family dining room. Today the Villa San Martino seems vibrant and alive with activity. Silvio Berlusconi strides into the dining room and embraces his daughter Marina. At the end of the table Confalonieri looks up from his plate and shouts out a friendly salute. The gray-haired

financial men from Fininvest take their place across from Berlusconi, who now has Confalonieri on his right and Marina on his
left, and at the other end of the table, a thin and lanky, bespectacled Nicolo Ghedini, his long-suffering top lawyer, takes his own
appointed place in silence. Marina is having a green salad in a big
bowl. Her father is staring grimly at some boiled vegetables on his
small plate. Diet food.

Confalonieri devours his pasta with relish; it is a kind of car-
bonara sauce over delicate taglini. He immediately pronounces it a
success. The red wine served at this family luncheon is an exquisite
Lambrusco. The men from Fininvest eat in silence, glancing up
from time to time when Berlusconi speaks. Even in the autumn of
his years, he is most definitely the boss and most definitely in command. They speak of AC Milan at first, with Berlusconi complaining that he and the team vice president, Adriano Galliani, thought
they had lined up the first two big hires, two great players who
would help Milan's return to greatness. "But as soon as they hear
it is Milan that is buying, the price goes even higher," grumbles
Berlusconi. Confalonieri nods in agreement. The three men from
Fininvest share the moment. Ghedini finishes his pasta.

Midway through the Monday lunch, Pier Silvio appears and
takes a seat near to his sister Marina.

Throughout the extended luncheon a waiter occasionally
brings in printed dispatches from news agencies, with updates on
Italian politics or world events. Berlusconi sets them down in front
of his plate, ignores the vegetables, and reads from them. The latest
opinion poll is now placed before him and he remarks on how he is
sure that the center-right parties can catch up with Renzi in time
to beat him at the next election in 2018, if only he can unite them.
He is strategizing, bouncing ideas off the family.

There is brief mention of Berlusconi's legal travails. A few days
after the lunch, Milan prosecutors would recommend to the state
attorney that Berlusconi be indicted on charges of having paid
bribes to thirty-four people, most of them the girls who attended
the bunga-bunga parties and whom Berlusconi had housed in

apartments in his own Milano Due residential complex. The accusation was that Berlusconi had given them millions of dollars' worth of gifts and had paid for their housing and had arranged for huge wads of cash to be delivered to them to keep them from talking at the trial in which he was accused of having had sex with Ruby the Heart-Stealer, the allegedly underage prostitute. The supreme court had acquitted Berlusconi of that charge on the grounds that he could not have known the exact age of Ruby at the time, and the courts had been unable to prove they had ever had sex. The Milan prosecutors persisted, upping the ante, and now they were claiming that Berlusconi had bribed dozens of girls to commit perjury on his behalf. Berlusconi's reply was to admit that he had paid the girls but to claim it was "an act of generosity" and not a payment for any ulterior motives. He had spoken about it with passion a few weeks before.

"All of my guests, even those who had only been here for one dinner on just one occasion, ended up seeing their names in the newspapers. From that moment on, their names were linked to this trial and if you go on the Internet they are all described, all of them and just as the prosecutors wanted, as Berlusconi's escorts," said Berlusconi. "Their lives have been ruined. They cannot raise a family. They cannot find a serious boyfriend. They cannot find a job. Even my own directors and producers at Mediaset refuse to hire them. They cannot find a place to live because they have no income and no way to guarantee they will pay the rent. I have always said that I don't feel guilty about anything, but I do feel responsible for what happened to these girls because their lives were ruined after coming to my dinner parties and by an unfair trial that in any case resulted in my being acquitted of all charges. That is why I helped them, I continue to help them, and I will do so in future until they can start afresh. But at these dinner parties there was no sex, and even if there had been sex it would not have been a crime."

Back at the luncheon table, Berlusconi is talking about one of his favorite movies, in which the bad guy is a Communist mayor of a small town. "Last night I saw the 1950s film, one of my favorites, *Don Camillo*," says Berlusconi. Pier Silvio joins in and soon everyone around the table is talking about vintage films. The Monday family business luncheon proceeds on a lighter note. Confalonieri is talking about music, and about the good old days in high school and college when he used to accompany Silvio on the piano. He is asked if he would be willing to perform again, just him on the piano and Silvio as the crooner. Would he be willing to do a Sinatra song with Berlusconi singing, like they used to do back in the 1950s? Confalonieri says sure, why not, and he turns to his lifelong friend: "Silvio? Would you sing with me?"

Berlusconi's face lights up with a smile. He nods his agreement to Confalonieri's request.

The two old friends then decide which song they will perform. As Confalonieri would put it, there could be no other choice. The song that Silvio Berlusconi would sing in their upcoming duet had to be his favorite song by Frank Sinatra. It had to be "My Way."

For a moment, Silvio Berlusconi has the appearance of a man who is not burdened by the slightest shred of regret about his life. He is in the sanctity of his own inner world, in the microcosm of his own custom-made universe. If history is to judge him properly, it must take note that here was a larger-than-life figure who did not play by the rules of normal society. He ruled a nation, and built an empire, and he did much of it thanks to his own wit. Although a flawed character, Berlusconi is perhaps the most influential shaper of modern Italy since the Second World War, for better and for worse.

ACKNOWLEDGMENTS

From the moment that Silvio Berlusconi agreed to tell his life story, to answer any and all questions I put to him, and to provide unfettered access to his personal archives, it was clear that this would be an ambitious project. From start to finish, the project took eighteen months and involved a team of editorial staff, researchers, and fact-checkers interacting with publishers and with an experienced television production staff.

The person who coordinated and supervised the team and deserves my greatest thanks is the immensely talented Emanuela Minnai. This book would not have been possible without her dedication to excellence in journalism and writing. Emanuela manages to combine the skill sets of literary agent, head of research, translation supervisor, sounding board, and psychotherapist, and most of all she does not seem to mind being disturbed ten to fifteen times a day. We first worked together in the late 1980s on my biography of Gianni Agnelli, the playboy turned industrialist who owned Fiat. My last book on Italy was possible thanks to her. The same is true of *Berlusconi*. Thank you, Emanuela.

Among key team members, special thanks go to Massimo Birattari, whose meticulous fact-checking and research were always timely. Birattari, who has translated Mordecai Richler, Paul Auster, and Vikram Seth, is a world-class bookman. Véronique Bernardini and Antongiulio Panizzi led a superb production team, as they have in past television projects.

I also want to thank my agent Caroline Michel and Rachel Mills and Tessa David at PFD in London.

I would also like to thank Deborah Bergamini, a former Bloomberg journalist who has been serving as Berlusconi's spokesperson and who is also an elected member of parliament. Her assistance in keeping everything on track over an extended period of time was vital. Thanks also go to Fedele Confalonieri, Berlusconi's oldest friend and a great raconteur, and to members of Berlusconi's family, his son Pier Silvio and daughter Marina in particular, for their willingness to answer numerous questions in repeated conversations.

In Moscow, I would like to thank Dmitry Peskov, spokesman for President Vladimir Putin, and his team for helping to organize an enjoyable and interesting interview with President Putin.

At Hachette Books in New York my thanks go to Mauro DiPreta, a wonderful publisher and a great editor, and to Ashley Yancey, Michelle Aielli, Betsy Hulsebosch, and Christopher Lin.

At Rizzoli in Italy my thanks go to Massimo Turchetta, who first challenged me to see if I could get Berlusconi to agree to cooperate, and who formed a partnership between Rizzoli and Hachette as anchor publishers that made this project possible.

Back in his heyday Silvio Berlusconi used to test-market his ideas for television and politics with his closest friends and family, a kind of focus group that helped him order his thoughts. My focus group consisted of the patient friends and family members who read early drafts of individual chapters and offered me their feedback, which was precious. Among those I wish to thank are Vivian Oppenheim, Jamie Harpel, Jonathan Ehrlich, Anita Friedman, Charles Friedman, Ion Marin, Eckart Sager, and Lionel Barber.

My biggest thanks go to the person this book is dedicated to, my extremely understanding and unflappable Tuscan wife. *Grazie, Gabriella!*

INDEX